KEN & EM

KEN & EM

A biography of
Kenneth Branagh and Emma Thompson

by

Ian Shuttleworth

St. Martin's Press
New York

Library of Congress Cataloging-in-Publication Data

Shuttleworth, Ian
Ken & Em : a biography of Kenneth Branagh and Emma
Thompson / Ian Shuttleworth.
p.   cm.
"A Thomas Dunne book."
ISBN 0-312-13531-9
1. Branagh, Kenneth.   2. Thompson, Emma.   3. Actors—
Great Britain—Biography.   I. Title.
PN2598.B684S5   1995
792'.028'092241—dc20   95-4899
[B]   CIP

First published in Great Britain by Headline Book
Publishing

First U.S. Edition: September 1995
10   9   8   7   6   5   4   3   2   1

Contents

Acknowledgements

I am indebted to the friends and colleagues of Kenneth Branagh and Emma Thompson who agreed to be interviewed, to my own colleagues in the press and broadcast media who aided my research, and to those friends who offered contributions, advice and support during the writing of this book.

Particular thanks are due to the following: BBC Northern Ireland; the *Belfast Telegraph* archive; the *Daily Mail*; the *Financial Times*; the *Irish Times*; the *Sunday Express*; Cambridge Footlights archive and its archivist Dr Harry Porter; Paul Dempsey; Dr Jean Gooder of Newnham College, Cambridge; John Hazelton; Dr Peter Holland; Frank Hopkinson of *My Guy* magazine (successor to *Oh Boy!*); Malcolm McKay; Oliver Morton; Richard Nash; Quintin Oliver at the Northern Ireland Council for Voluntary Action; Siôn Probert; Progress Theatre and Chris Bertrand; Alex Renton at the *Evening Standard*; Nick Waring; Leslie Gardner, my agent at Artellus, and Roger Houghton, my editor at Headline, for keeping the project on the rails; Gaie Sebold for her invaluable research work and Louise Chantal for her equally invaluable help and support.

KEN & EM

Introduction

Heirs Apparent

One of the upmarket English Sunday newspapers included in its New Year 'silly season' list of predictions for 1994, amongst all the global prophecies, 'Kenneth Branagh and Emma Thompson to separate.' This may have been an early, discreet reference to the rumour that Branagh had become involved with the female lead of his film *Mary Shelley's Frankenstein*, Helena Bonham Carter. What it indisputably demonstrated was that, in the absence of any royal marriages left to hit the rocks, Branagh and Thompson are the next best thing: a high-profile, golden showbiz couple with more class than the usual suspects regularly rounded up by the tabloids, but still instantly recognisable enough to be news to everyone. And, like the Prince and Princess of Wales, friends and colleagues are sometimes more protective of them than are the couple themselves.

Branagh himself professes, for instance, to be above all mystified by the appearance of this book: 'I can't understand,' he told a colleague, 'why anyone would be interested in writing a book about two minor celebs.' A curious reaction from someone who wrote his own autobiography at the age of twenty-eight and has an agreement to provide a second volume in a few years' time. 'I think ambition is a healthy thing,' he has said, and he has certainly taken a corresponding approach to his life and career. In ninety-nine cases out of a hundred, his astounding and genuine charm enables him to strike the deals that he wants, but on occasion his determination can be overbearing. 'However inspiring he is,' said a colleague, 'he drives himself like a steamroller over you.'

Still only in their middle thirties, Branagh and Thompson have achieved an astonishing professional and personal prominence which is much more than simply the product of a media hungry for 'celebs' to consume. Between them they can boast a cabinetful of stage and screen awards including an Oscar, a seat on the board of the British Film Institute and even the friendship of the Prince of Wales (who agreed to become patron of Branagh's now dormant Renaissance film and theatre companies, and – it has been suggested – was inspired in part by Ken's performance in the Royal Shakespeare Company's stage production of *Henry V* when he named his second son Harry). However persistently they may be derided as gushing, insincere theatre caricatures – 'luvvies', as the British press would have it – even the derision keeps their names in the public eye. The cliché is that they're the Laurence Olivier and Vivien Leigh of our times – minus the bisexuality and nymphomania. It's a comparison which bores them, and not without reason.

However, Branagh in particular seemed to spend a lot of time in the first phases of his career paralleling Olivier: the snottiness of youth; the sometimes ill-judged early flirtation with Hollywood (his first American film *Dead Again* was critically vilified in Britain but did solid box-office business on both sides of the Atlantic); the establishment of his own company rather than submit to being processed by the machinery of a larger set-up, and, of course, the film of *Henry V*. One colleague, asked during the 1980s what he thought Ken would do next, replied, 'It depends on what chapter of Olivier's biography he's up to now.'

Now, a man for whom even Robert De Niro is prepared to spend hours in prosthetic make-up as Frankenstein's monster, Branagh has no need to labour the comparisons; however, they won't go away. One of several film projects which he is rumoured to have in development is a version of *Hamlet*, the lead role in which, at the age of thirty-three, he has already played three times on stage and once on radio. However, in an August 1994 public interview at London's National Film Theatre, he played down any notion of future Shakespeare films: 'I would like to make a film of *Hamlet*, but that's a pathetic thing to do. Is the world waiting for another *Hamlet*? I don't think so.' Moreover, the examination of his more recent film career and relationship to the British film industry, which is dealt with in Chapter 9, suggests that Olivier may no longer be the most apposite acting peer with whom to compare Branagh.

Apart from a clutch of productions for Branagh's Renaissance company in the late 1980s, Thompson has not been seen on stage since the West End production of *Me and My Girl* that furnished her with her first theatrical break in 1985. Music and comedy were her first strengths: she appeared in the Cambridge Footlights revue which also introduced Tony Slattery, Stephen Fry and her ex-boyfriend Hugh Laurie, and her appearances in the Granada TV series *Alfresco* garnered an early clutch of enthusiastic reviews. Casting her in the female lead role of the BBC drama series *Fortunes of War* was not a predictable decision. Her husband was played by a young actor, rising too slowly for his own liking, who was trying to drum up money and interest for a theatrical enterprise of his own. Somewhere amid all those location shoots and all that hustling, Branagh and Thompson metamorphosed into Ken and Em.

Although they tried initially to keep their relationship out of the public eye, they could not succeed for long, and subsequently attempted instead to make a virtue of necessity. For a while they were ostentatiously a couple: he *danced* on her disastrous solo television series; she acted in all his feature films until *Frankenstein* and has even written the screenplay for what seems now set to be his next big-screen project. They have nothing but praise and admiration for each other, and for virtually all their colleagues.

In the past few years, however, each has emerged from this phase of coupledom to become recognised as leading an independent individual career. Branagh returned all too fleetingly to the stage with what could be the definitive Hamlet of his generation and is now increasingly looking to Hollywood for both financial backing and screen talent for his films. Thompson, in turn, in a 1994 award speech, credited two people with 'keeping me off the street' – Branagh came second to director James Ivory, with whom she worked on *The Remains of the Day* and in her Oscar-winning role in *Howards End*. She is, say many, a better screen actor than Branagh, who now looks more likely to become a 'player' in the film world as a director and producer who also acts, whilst Thompson moves ineluctably towards the front rank of cinema stardom.

Naturally, there is continuous speculation about the cracks beneath this too-good-to-be-true veneer. The Helena Bonham Carter rumour is only the latest in a series of mutterings about Branagh's predilections which have flown around many of his enterprises. Off-the-record stories abound, to the extent that one wonders whether the image of Kenneth Branagh the Don Juan has become the theatrical equivalent of an 'urban myth'. Many claim that friends of friends have proof of one rumour or another, but no one ever seems to have witnessed such events him- or herself. Branagh has repeatedly asserted that his private life should be precisely that, and even went to the extent in his autobiography of either not mentioning romantic partners or cloaking them in pseudonyms, a move made without consulting the people in question, and which irked at least one former partner.

An unauthorised biography cannot ignore such rumour and secrecy, but nor should it attach undue weight to them. Without speculating as to the truth or otherwise of any particular set of whispers, the fact that they exist in such number is in itself significant. It speaks of the couple's status both within the industry and as public figures; it reflects the amount of media attention paid to them and their relationship with those media; and, regardless of whether hard evidence exists, the circulation of such rumours attests that their subjects live lives of a kind which can conceivably support stories of that nature.

As a biographer, I am not trying to have my cake and eat it in this respect; books like this are always to a certain extent exercises in tightrope-walking, the more so when, as here, one's subjects are reluctant to be examined. Throughout *Ken & Em* I have tried to draw general inferences from information already on the record or given to me in first-hand interviews, together with my own direct experience of Branagh's and Thompson's respective backgrounds and my knowledge of the worlds in which they work. The tabloid approach of, so to speak, going through dustbins in a battered trilby and stained trenchcoat is unnecessary as well as degrading to all concerned. The story to be told is rich and fascinating enough as it is.

The following account broadly follows the chronology of events, but on occasion it has been necessary to depart from a strict time-line: connections jump forwards and backwards in time, and sideways from person to person; character traits persist through the years, and may demand to be dealt with by adducing several examples at once. I have endeavoured, rather than simply chronicling my subjects' lives, to build up character portraits. As Kenneth Branagh and Emma Thompson stand on the verge of front-rank prominence before an international audience, now is the time to take stock of how they have reached this position, of where they go from here, and of who they are.

Ian Shuttleworth
London, September 1994

1

To Dougal a Daughter

The family into which Emma Thompson was born – on 15 April 1959 at St Mary's Hospital, Paddington, in west London – has always been closely knit. Emma has lived all her life in the same road in West Hampstead, and even today her mother lives a few yards up and across the street and her actress younger sister Sophie a few minutes' walk away. 'We've been looked after,' said Emma in an interview. 'It's probably been a sheltered sort of life, you can't deny it.' In 1990, she and Ken were on the verge of buying a larger house in the more prosperous district of Hampstead itself, but late in the day changed their minds and elected to remain in the unflashy semi-detached house in the only home neighbourhood she knows, literally a stone's throw from the Thompson family house.

Her mother, Phyllida Law, was a respected actress whose career was boosted in the late 1980s and early 1990s by a number of parts in her daughter's television series and her son-in-law's films. Her father, Eric Thompson, first struck lucky as the stage director of the early hit comedies of Alan Ayckbourn (who in recent years has moved to the top of the league table of the most frequently performed playwrights in Britain, eclipsing even Shakespeare); however, he is now remembered most fondly for creating one of the prime British cultural institutions of the 1960s.

Having persuaded the BBC to acquire a French series of

five-minute animations, Thompson *père* replaced the political satire of the original dialogue with the kind of English surrealism that burgeoned in the middle of that decade and reached full flower with *Monty Python's Flying Circus. The Magic Roundabout* was screened as a children's programme immediately before the BBC's early-evening news bulletins, but rapidly attained a broader cult status, particularly on the nascent psychedelic scene. Dylan the lethargic folk-singing rabbit, Ermintrude the frightfully camp cow, and the other inhabitants of the bizarre garden in which the series was set became massively popular with flower children and real children alike. The series has been repeated every few years since the original broadcasts (the rights are now owned by Channel 4), and parents are now able to argue with their children over the relative merits of the 1990s revisions (with updated references but remaining faithful to the characters which Thompson devised) and the 'original' version.

Emma has said that, as far as she was concerned, Eric's character bore a close resemblance to that of Dougal, the cynical dog of the show, whose endearing grouchiness defined his relationship with Florence, one of the few human characters. 'Dad taught us the importance of laughter. He had the knack of being witty about the things that hurt.' No doubt he was amiably scathing about Emma and her friends' pretence, in front of him, to prefer the rival French series *Hector's House*, which alternated with *The Magic Roundabout* in the 5.40 p.m. slot on BBC1. As an example of Eric's unorthodox humour, she offered the fact that he 'always talked about *Romeo and Juliet* as if it were a comedy. So we learned to look at things askance – and not take them too seriously.'

This wry vision seemed to permeate most aspects of family life. There was little 'not in front of the children' hypocrisy in the Thompson household: their parents would even walk around the house naked (a revelation which Emma's friends found disgusting when she told them). 'When we were children we were treated as grown-ups,' Emma recalled, 'respected as adults who just hadn't lived as long. I've rarely seen a more

That's the way it all should happen
In the fairy-tale state you're in;
Have you got your pen and notebook ready?
Sign right here and we'll begin...

Van Morrison
'Saint Dominic's Preview'

successful marriage, without anybody trying to sacrifice any part of their personality, which quite often happens and mostly happens to the woman. They weren't rich. Mum worked but she was always there when we got home from school, talked to us about the day. Then there were the golden years when Dad did the Ayckbourn plays, when we had holidays in America and we used to get taken off to department stores and told we could choose anything we wanted. All I can remember picking is two absolutely terrible corduroy dresses.'

She also remembers family holidays in Argyllshire, at Ardentinny, where Loch Long meets the Firth of Clyde, and where the Law and Thompson families bought a stone cottage shortly after Emma was born. 'The entire family – my mother, my brother and us – scraped together the princely sum of £1,000,' recalled Phyllida Law. Ardentinny neighbour Mary Murton remembered Emma and Sophie playing with her own sons Gerry (who died of leukaemia when Emma was fourteen) and Paul. 'They were all lovely, innocent, glorious children who went on their ponies, swam together in the loch, picnicked, just playing for hours.' (In 1989, Emma would play a part closely based on Mary Murton in her son Paul's fifty-minute film *Tin Fish*.) Phyllida Law still spends much of her time in Ardentinny, and other family members are frequently grateful for such a refuge from metropolitan pressures. Ken and Emma have been known to spend evenings in the cottage literally sitting by the fire, reading Dickens aloud ('Oh God!' offered an embarrassed Emma by way of confirmation).

West Hampstead, Emma's lifelong home patch of London, is a comfortable district in the north-west of the city, but without the rarefied and rather snobbish aura that surrounds Hampstead proper further up the hill on the eastern side of the main Finchley Road. The mere presence of the 'H word' in describing a property's situation adds a few thousand pounds to its value – hence the largely euphemistic term 'South Hampstead' for the district around the Swiss Cottage junction and the early twentieth-century expansion of genteel housing westward towards the less salubrious areas of Kilburn and Cricklewood.

West Hampstead's leafy streets of Edwardian and 1920s semi-detached houses originally offered the cachet of a fashionable location without the social and financial strictures which hindered admission to the true 'NW3 set' in the neighbouring postal district.

From such origins, the area has acquired a distinct character of its own. The pebble-dashed houses around the grounds of the Hampstead Cricket Club (including the house where Emma Thompson and Kenneth Branagh themselves now live) give way to Edwardian apartment buildings towards the hub of the district on West End Lane, and in the 1980s it came to be inhabited by greater numbers of media types and young urban professionals. The shops, pubs and restaurants of the neighbourhood give it a character with much of the 'funkiness' which accompanied yuppie culture, but without the slavish fashion-consciousness that led to so many jokes about the stereotype. Yes, the Branaghs today buy some of their home furnishings from modish Scandinavian superstore Ikea; yes, they separate their recyclable rubbish into labelled sacks containing paper, glass and so forth; yes, Ken prefers to drink in the area's 'real ale' pub... but the only extraordinary thing about such a lifestyle is that it is not in the least extraordinary.

Similarly, Emma's upbringing just a few yards up the street was neither resolutely bourgeois nor the stuff of theatre-dynasty cliché. Although she has spoken of having had a sheltered early life, this testifies to the warmth and together-ness of her family rather than any strain of isolation or protectiveness. Middle-class districts such as West Hampstead seldom possess any real sense of community; the focus of life in such areas, if there is to be one at all, must generally be the family unit. The Thompsons were an exceptionally focused family in the best senses of the term, and Emma was an ordinary middle-class girl.

Looking back on her childhood, she sometimes seems to feel that she was almost *too* ordinary. She never rebelled against her parents because there was never any need to rebel. Twenty years later she mused in the *Daily Mail*, 'I don't know whether

I would have liked myself as a child. I always feel I was deeply punchable, overweight, with a plait. I went to the state primary down the road and suffered at school; I was unfortunate in having a posh accent, I was simply disliked. Then I changed my voice, learned how to swear and it was all right.' The most telling aspect of this recollection is not the reference to self-reinvention – most children go through such a process to a greater or lesser extent (although few to the degree or for the reasons that would drive Kenneth Branagh to give himself such a comprehensive overhaul when his family moved to England). The allusion to her weight touches on a point which has cropped up on a number of occasions in Emma's self-criticism. She has frequently seemed unable to conceive of herself as – for want of a better term – a sex object because she thinks herself too 'meaty', and any sexual elements in her screen roles have been deliberately shot through with a defensive strain of self-ridicule.

She has claimed that 'I've never sat down and thought, "Oh, I'll play that sensible one as opposed to the sexy, blowsy pub owner." I'd love to do that, but I've never been offered it.' However, the frequency of her recorded disparaging comments about her self-image suggests more than simple modesty. She has been known to protest volubly at being packaged by tabloid newspaper photographers as an attractive piece of meat, so to speak, lashing with her tongue any snapper who attempts to patronise her into a 'smiling bimbo' pose, yet she has seldom made any direct reference to the degree of admiration she elicits in terms of 'the thinking man's crumpet'. In more recent years she has become able to a greater extent to dictate the terms of media attention paid to her, and here too the allusions she makes to herself as a sexual being usually carry a faint tinge of the ludicrous.

Obviously, she is keen to communicate her acting skills, intelligence and awareness as the key characteristics that they are, but this alone probably does not wholly explain her equally obvious keenness to downplay any physical references to herself. This reluctance may be grounded in low physical self-esteem in her childhood – 'body fascism' among girls of such an age was not uncommon even twenty years before the image-laden fashion culture of the present day. At any rate, the bottom line is clear: Emma is willing to be loved first, foremost and almost exclusively for her mind.

Phyllida Law recalled her elder daughter as 'a serious little creature. I remember when we were walking back from school in West Hampstead one day we passed a dead cat in the gutter which was suffering from rigor mortis. She would not be stopped; she picked it up and walked several blocks to give it to a policeman. I will treasure to the end of my days the picture of this child seriously giving this dead cat to a policeman, who had to accept it. Can you imagine being a bobby on the corner and being handed a stiffened cat? Well, of course, she would have been sent up rotten at school for that sort of behaviour.' She also once affectionately spoke of the experience of raising Emma as 'like being run over by one of those things that flattens tar on the road' – an intriguing perspective on someone whose public image today is one of the least steamroller-like of any in her field.

Emma describes her family as having been 'very ordinary, not a bit theatrical', despite having parents who, exceptionally, were both in fairly regular work in the profession. This description, though, does not square entirely with friends' recollections. 'I'd open the door,' said one, 'and Emma would say, "Oh, Uncle Alec's here," and it was Alec Guinness.' In her defence, Emma countered, 'Sir Alec was one of their [her parents'] grandest friends. We weren't a theatrical dynasty in the same way as the Redgraves and the Richardsons.'

Her secondary education took place at Camden School for Girls, a couple of miles east of her home and a few stops on the North London railway line. Camden School, founded in 1871, was rather more fashionable than 'the local state primary' which she had been attending, although it was far from being the kind of establishment which turned out 'gels' ready to take their places in the *haut monde*. Indeed, the school's reputation at the time contained an element of liberality, certainly in terms of the behaviour of some of its pupils. One of Emma's contemporaries at Camden School, the novelist Rose Boyt (daughter of painter Lucien Freud and great-granddaughter of Sigmund), remembered: 'The whole of the school seemed to me to be split into "us" and "them". There were the ones who slept with boys, took drugs, stayed out all night and generally misbehaved. I was in that delightful group. Then there were the others. Emma was just a nice girl, wholesome and hearty, not a neurotic freak like so many others. She wasn't involved in the deviant scene. She may well have gone to lots of parties but not the same ones I went to. Although I saw her as alien, I could also see that she was a well-adjusted, nice person, and I wasn't. She would never have snitched on you.' Emma later and intriguingly commented to a *Daily Express* interviewer, 'My childhood and my adolescence and my early twenties would surprise people enormously, but I'm certainly not going to tell you about it.' The naughtiest recollection of this period she has ever offered is of living near Hampstead Heath and 'snogging in the bushes thereof'.

Classmate Jackie Culpan, now an educational psychologist and one of Emma's oldest friends, described first impressions of her as a girl who was 'enthusiastic and good at everything, which tended to get up your nose. Later on, you came to respect her terrific maturity. She was good with adults. She was the sort of friend you always wanted to take home to meet your parents.' Of the Thompsons collectively, she remembered, 'They were just a truly brilliant family, and incredibly eccentric as well: Mum running around stark naked doing the cleaning, and Gran was always there – she was as deaf as a post – and her dad wandering around in loud checked suits. And food, just food everywhere all the time. How they weren't all grotesquely fat I'll never know.' Perhaps because it wasn't always eaten: on one occasion, tells Emma, her parents settled a dispute by means of a lemon meringue pie fight. A far cry from the conventional nuclear family, but a nurturing environ-ment nonetheless. As a young teenager Emma sometimes seemed a little at sea in a wider social context. 'The girls were outsiders,' agreed Culpan, 'sitting around in coffee bars, ordering one coffee because we couldn't afford anything else, and talking about boys. Emma did quite a lot of going through boys, but in a very tame and innocent way.' Such innocence largely persisted through her subsequent three years at Cambridge.

The Thompson family was not prey to the stereotypical theatrical family impulses of a Mrs Worthington putting her daughter on the stage, and Emma's own theatrical ambitions at this time seemed to come in spasms. She remembered, 'Sophie always knew she wanted to act. I didn't for a long time. Principally I was interested in books. They possessed me. I think I'm short-sighted now [she generally wears contact lenses] because I used to read in the dark with a torch.' Sophie, three years younger than Emma, began her acting career at the age of fifteen in the BBC children's television series *A Traveller in Time*. As a child of nine years old or so her elder sister took a handful of drama lessons with a woman named Sheila Sacks, but they seemed no more than 'jolly things, fun for kids'. Emma later told a reporter that she thought her parents hoped she 'would either marry Prince Charles or become Prime Minister, but definitely not act.' But at her Camden School admission interview no one was more surprised than her mother when Emma, asked what she wanted to be, replied promptly, 'An actress.'

'I almost fainted on the spot,' said Phyllida later. 'It was the first I'd heard of it but that wasn't why I was shocked. I assumed it wasn't the right thing to say to the headmistress. We didn't really talk about it again. I did go to see Emma in a play there once, but funnily enough it didn't strike me that she was hugely talented or anything – she was good, but that was all.'

The play in question was produced towards the end of Emma's years at Camden School; for most of her time there she showed few signs of theatricality, at least in officially sanctioned forms. Away from school, though, she had dabbled in public performance: 'The first monologue I ever did was written by [arts critic and jazz singer] George Melly, called

"Hampstead Liberal", and it was all about this lady standing at a cocktail party and why she'd invited this black man and it is brilliant. It was the early seventies and I was only in my early teens. But I do remember very clearly standing on the stage next to a piano, and I remember the feeling of *power* as people laughed. I suddenly realised what it was, and I supposed I was learning instinctively about timing, and that helped me as I went on.' Plainly, the protestations of a childhood largely devoid of theatrical elements and 'grand' friends were too good to be entirely true.

However, the closest she came to regular dramatic activity in her mid-teens was to lock herself in a cupboard under the stairs during school breaks and rehearse *Monty Python* sketches with Jackie Culpan. 'We'd do a line like "The Right Honourable Patch of Brown Liquid" and just roar with laughter, pee ourselves,' she said. 'Looking back,' Culpan noted later, 'you realise it was a very serious business with Emma. You rehearsed like hell.'

Emma, like many of her generation, was a *Python* junkie. '*Monty Python* changed my life,' she said later. '*Python* is not less important than Garbo; the Marx Brothers are not less important than Ingmar Bergman.' Having been brought up around Eric Thompson's philosophy of making life bearable with a well-aimed quip even about the most grave of topics, it is hardly surprising that Emma not only made her earliest performances (whether 'official' or not) in comedy but believed – as did many of her contemporaries in the early 1980s wave of 'alternative comedy' – that humour can be an immensely useful Trojan horse, allowing trenchant social and political comment to sneak in under cover of laughter. This was to be one of the main strategies of her flawed solo television series in 1988.

She was far from unusual among her contemporaries in being captivated by the bizarre, nothing-sacred humour of the *Monty Python* team. The Pythons, a group of Oxbridge graduates (plus a far-from-token American, animator Terry Gilliam), had gradually coalesced through a number of television comedy and satire shows in the mid-1960s before making the fateful discovery that they encouraged each other's worst excesses in terms of humour. The resulting show – which went through a variety of working titles including *Owl Stretching Time* and *Gwen Dibley's Flying Circus* – was first broadcast in three series between October 1969 and January 1973, with a final six-show series without John Cleese transmitted in late 1974. (Cleese's own latest screen appearance is in Kenneth Branagh's film *Mary Shelley's Frankenstein*, playing the Baron's mentor, Waldman.) The seminal role of *Python* in British humour cannot be under-estimated; the televisual heirs of *The Goon Show* in the 1950s, they proved much more successful at redefining television comedy than ex-Goon Spike Milligan himself in his patchy *Q* series. *Monty Python's Flying Circus* not only moved the goalposts for subsequent generations of humorists but painted obscene hieroglyphs all over the field of play.

In the Thompson household, even watching *Python* became a ritual of sorts. 'Jacqueline would come over to the house [to see the programmes],' Emma explained, 'and we would sit there and my dad would sit behind. I would always wait to see if my dad laughed. I would laugh a lot anyway, but it gave me such joy when my dad laughed. It was just immensely wonderful when we laughed together because laughing with somebody is one of the great pleasures of life.' When Emma wrote her first comedy material, Eric would suggest minor changes to heighten its humorous impact, such as changing 'cherry' to 'cerise' to add a comic note of petit bourgeois pretentiousness.

But Eric Thompson's natural indomitability had been assailed by a string of health problems beginning with a heart attack when Emma was eight, and ending tragically with his death at the age of fifty-two shortly after his daughter had graduated from Cambridge. 'He was ill for three years before he died,' said Emma later. 'He had his first heart attack at thirty-seven which was [due to] fags and working too hard. Even as a child I was always aware he wasn't very well, but he managed to be ill without being an ill person. He was dignified, frightened, but willing to accept what had happened. He was spiritually very powerful. He taught me not to be cruel, always to think before I speak.'

His last stroke, at the end of Emma's first year at university, left Eric Thompson unable to speak. Emma and Phyllida determined to teach him to talk again. 'Em was stunning, really,' said her mother. 'She nursed him and we had classes for him every day. We had a schedule and we split it, fifteen minutes each and then a break, because you can't concentrate intensively for much longer. We learned how to do it from speech therapy at the hospital, and then continued it at home. It took months, but he regained his speech and then he was brilliant – he directed again after that.' Emma remembered, 'He thought his voice had been struck because of his arrogance. I remember him saying once, "You're so thoughtless and selfish, you're just like me," and it cut me to the heart. He used to say, "She's got all the worst and the best of me."' The bluff, no-nonsense approach she had learned from him was employed during his speech therapy, and on one occasion Eric's response led her to a profound and shocking realisation: 'Somehow it was easier for me to teach him than it was for Mum because she was too close. I could push him. I remember pushing him a little far one day and him getting up and running into the study, crying. And I'd never seen my father cry. He wasn't a crier. He didn't show things. And I found myself in that odd position which all people get to at some point, but it is unusual at that age, of trying to parent your parent.' The deep-rooted sense of responsibility she has shown in her adult life – her consciousness of duty as a 'citizen' in the broad social and global sense, her work for and donations to a wide range of campaigns and causes – seems to be grounded in a family upbringing which both imbued her with a highly developed perspective on what was really important and acquainted her at an early age with tragedy and suffering.

However, that sense of perspective prevented the 'serious little creature' from ever becoming irredeemably earnest. The joys of performance and comedy were beginning to make themselves felt to her. The highlight of Emma's 'official' dramatic career at Camden School was a production of *Lady Audley's Secret*, in which 'I played a man [George Talboys] – I thought I looked rather like Cary Grant.' By this stage, through mutual friend Owen Brenman, she had met Martin Bergman, a boy a couple of years older than her who would prove a formative influence and invaluable contact in her early comedy career. Bergman recounted that when he first met her, 'Em had lots of jewellery on and jangled loudly. I thought she was immensely sophisticated. A friend and I asked her to appear with us at a charity show in a couple of sketches we'd written, and Em was immensely polished with perfect comic timing – a stunning, intuitive ability. I also saw Em in [*Lady Audley's Secret*] that year... Had you told the audience that in less than twenty years the girl wearing the moustache would be winning an Oscar, I don't think anyone would have been surprised. Emma always stood out, always looked a professional among amateurs.'

Gradually it began to look as though the ambition she had declared to her prospective headmistress years earlier was manifesting itself. At the age of sixteen Emma went to the Avignon Festival, which included a production of Racine's *Andromaque*, one of her French O-Level texts, 'and I went to see the production five times and met the cast and so on. I wrote a letter to my father at about three o'clock in the morning, saying, "I think I'm going to have to go into the theatre."' She also spent some time in the school holidays working in the stage crew at Manchester's Royal Exchange Theatre. The production at the time was *Hamlet*, starring family friend Robert Lindsay (a far cry from his starring role at around the same time in the BBC television sitcom *Citizen Smith*, in which he played the leader of the four-man revolutionary movement the Tooting Popular Front).

But by the end of her schooling Emma had still not committed herself to the stage. She briefly considered a career in hospital administration, but was largely uncertain what professional direction to take. A report produced for her by a top-drawer Harley Street careers consultancy concluded, said Phyllida Law, that 'they thought she might do rather well in the Church.' At any rate, after obtaining nine O-Levels at A and B grades and A-Levels in English, French and Latin, rather than choosing a drama school Emma applied to Oxford University. Oxford did not offer her a place, but at that time the joint 'Oxbridge pool' was still in operation, whereby colleges at Oxford or Cambridge could make offers to prospective students who had been declined by their first-choice college at the other university. Dr Jean Gooder, director of studies in English at Newnham College, Cambridge, says she 'had no hesitation whatever in picking Emma out.' The first member of the Thompson and Law families to go to university went up to Cambridge, home of the Footlights Comedy Club, and cradle nearly two decades earlier of several Pythons, in October 1978.

2

Across the Water

It's difficult to avoid lapsing into biographer's cant at this point, and saying, 'Everything that Emma Thompson's childhood was, Kenneth Branagh's wasn't.' Yet his isn't a story of squalor, degradation and discontent, simply of an industrial working-class childhood. Their family ties were every bit as close: Ken's paternal grandparents, not to mention a raft of aunts and uncles from the large Branagh and Harper families, all lived within easy reach for the first nine years of his life in the terraced streets of the York Street district of north Belfast.

Belfast in the early 1960s was not the hotbed of strife it has been for the past twenty-five years. (Come to that, it behoves every Northern Irish expatriate to point out that neither is Belfast as bad as is often imagined today – its murder rate is a fraction of that of any major American city.) Harland and Wolff shipyard, from which the *Titanic* had left on its sole voyage half a century earlier, had full order books; the neighbouring Short Brothers Aircraft Works were developing their Skyvan; engineering and tobacco factories, and the last of the old linen mills on which the city's fortune had been built in the nineteenth century, had not yet fallen victim to the twin plagues of the UK's later shift in industrial focus and the flood of disinvestment which the 'Troubles' would bring after 1969. Northern Ireland's capital was a major port with a separate harbour police force. It was no coincidence that young George Ivan 'Van'

Morrison in Belfast, like John Lennon and Paul McCartney in Liverpool, discovered rhythm and blues music through American records brought back by returning sailors. All in all, the city and province were on a more than sound economic footing.

The rosy surface, of course, disguised a more iniquitous social structure. Since Ireland's partition in 1921, the six counties of the north had enjoyed dominion status within the United Kingdom, and with it a large degree of autonomy which would be lost only on the imposition of direct rule from Westminster in 1972. The government of Northern Ireland at Stormont on the eastern outskirts of Belfast had run the province in the interests of the ascendant Protestant community – indeed, almost at times like a family business. Catholics were systematically discriminated against in terms of employment and housing; the economic oppression, coupled with a property qualification on voting, meant that the half-million-strong Catholic community had no hope of altering the situation through an electoral process weighted against them – Stormont was a self-perpetuating oligarchy. For bewildered observers of the Northern Irish tragedy beyond the shores of Ireland, it is easy to forget that the Troubles arose out of militant Protestant opposition to a Catholic civil rights movement inspired by that of Dr Martin Luther King. British troops were originally put on the streets in order to protect Catholics, and welcomed with cups of tea and cakes before they became just another agency of the Protestant civil authority.

Despite such an entrenched (and dearly held) two-tier social system, the reality was that the Protestant working classes, although nominally in a favoured position, were often little better off than the Catholic minority. Many communities depended on casual work, of which there was seldom enough to go round. Dock labourers would queue each day in the hope of obtaining work for that day only (longer contracts were unheard of), and were themselves divided into 'castes' under a preferential system of assigning labour. Those who could not get work tried to subsist on the 'buroo' (the dole), and gained what comfort they could from a different kind of 'brew' in the pub. The dockside neighbourhood in the area around York Street lived a precarious existence, but community spirit was strong and mutually supportive. It is tempting either to pity such a way of life condescendingly or to romanticise it from the safe distance of decades, miles and pounds away. The people of York Street and others like them were neither paragons of earthy nobility nor 'proles' waiting for schemes of improvement to be bestowed on them by their betters, but simply a community living as best they could.

The Branagh and Harper families lived in the York Street district. Now largely wasteland and motorways, with a huge artificial shopping centre erected in the middle to serve no particular catchment area but simply to make the civic statement that that quarter of town isn't dead – a freeway-and-mall sprawl redolent of American suburbs in what used to be the heart of an industrial city – York Street was then a network of back-to-back terraced streets: two-up two-downs owned by the City Corporation and rented by the extended families of dockers, 'millies' and the like.

William Branagh did not work on the docks (nor, by and large, had his father), but as a joiner in a building firm; Frances Harper Branagh, the daughter of a 'blue button' stevedore, the most exalted group of dock workers, was a mill girl. Unable to keep up the mortgage repayments on a home of their own in the more prosperous Cavehill district, they slid back down the hill to a council estate of prefabricated asbestos bungalows, where their second son, Kenneth Charles, was born on Saturday 10 December 1960 (brother Bill junior was five years his elder). Shortly afterwards they were relocated to a three-up three-down house in Mountcollyer Street. The street and the house at number 96 are unchanged: dog-legged, unprepossessing terraces strung between North Queen Street and the Antrim Road, hard by Alexandra Park and near the Grove Primary School which young Kenneth attended and the Grove Baths where he learned to swim.

The Grove School was notable, in Ken's memory, primarily for his bizarre phobia about puddings at dinner-time. In order to avoid being made to eat them, he took to pretending that he was going home for lunch and throwing his school dinner money down the toilet, where it failed to flush away. When this ruse was discovered, his parents realised why young Ken had been losing weight and excused him from school dinners. Instead he would walk to his paternal grandparents' home for lunch each day. His teacher, Mr Gribben, was a strict disciplinarian, rearranging the class's seating plan weekly on the basis of pupils' performance in their last English and Maths test, and keeping order by means of corporal punishment – smacks from a pair of gym shoes upon which he bestowed the unlikely pet names of Zebedee and Dougal after characters from *The Magic Roundabout*. A more surreal early connection with the work of Emma Thompson's father it is hard to imagine. Dougal, the right shoe, wielded with Gribben's right hand, was especially dreaded.

Money was always tight, but juvenile crime was simply not an option for young Ken: a clip round the ear from his mother after a shopkeeper recognised a certain young shoplifter was enough to discourage him from trying it a second time. In an early flare-up of unrest on the streets, he joined a gang looting a local supermarket. Once again, maternal retribution was swift and physical, and a terrified Ken was made to return the loot – unaccountably a box of Omo washing powder and a tin of Vim kitchen cleaner – before the police arrived on the scene.

Although the family just about managed to keep their heads above water financially, it was seldom easy, and William Branagh senior's attempt to set up his own business (which grew from such early enterprises as creating new wooden fireplaces to replace the old tiled models which his own father removed for families anxious to keep up to date in home furnishings) eventually failed. When Ken was six his father joined the tradition of Irish migrant workers on the British mainland, flying back once a month with housekeeping money for the family and a small gift (usually a Matchbox toy car) for his younger son.

By now the tension which would soon erupt into the now all

too familiar Troubles was growing. 'Even at that age – seven, eight, nine – I was conscious of the dial moving, the tension building,' remembers Ken. 'It was actually a very exciting place to live, which is why it's still etched in my memory. I remember that there was this wee wall near our house, which used to have incredible numbers of people in different groups sitting there for long periods, debating what was going on, giving out all the gossip about Sandy Row or some other hot-spot – places which really, even though they were close, were as foreign as Florida. Bar the gossip, all they really knew was what they saw on the TV news, but it was still an ongoing adventure, a kind of drama.' His first television role over a decade later would, in fact, be set in a hot-spot a stone's throw from Sandy Row, and at a time when plenty of stones were being thrown.

The Branaghs, although Protestant, were far from being what the media of the time euphemistically called 'staunch Loyalists' (that is, militant bigots). It's hard to have a more 'Prod' name than Billy – King William of Orange is still revered every 12 July for defeating the army of the Catholic James II at the Battle of the Boyne, and is known familiarly as 'King Billy' – but William Branagh declined to join the triumphalist Orange Order, whose lodges organise the annual marches, and York Street was not seen as the particular preserve of either community. 'Both my parents, I think, were actively in pursuit of living in a mixed area. They had no innate suspicion of Catholics – of the Catholic Church, yes, but not of Catholics. Then again, they were suspicious of Protestant churches as well, very anti any level of organised division. There was a pragmatism, a realism, a desire to get on with living together.

'It's not that I wasn't aware of the divisions. You learned it as one of the tools for living. I discovered early on what Catholic names were and which were the Catholic areas. You knew that there were areas you didn't go on your own, and you knew "If he's called Sean, he's not a good Protestant boy." But I still played with Catholic kids and my parents would have thought of a lot of paramilitary types as silly folk – the kind of people who'd be a pain in the arse whatever they were involved in. So I was equipped with a basic rule of thumb for survival, but also actively told to give people their due. I'd have been hit at home if I'd called someone a Fenian bastard.' That kind of level-headed realism is all too rare even a quarter of a century on; despite weariness and frustration at the Troubles, religious like sticks more closely than before with like, and friendships or relationships which span the divide meet with unthinking prejudice and hostility.

Such sectarian intolerance wasn't in Ken's nature. His experiences of the rigorous puritanism of the Presbyterian Church in Northern Ireland, both in its services and in Sunday School, had given him an early and abiding hatred of the kind of organised religion which sets more store by obedience than love. Even in recent years, the extremity of Ulster Presby-terianism has led to such absurdities as a town council chaining up the swings in its children's playgrounds every Sunday to prevent youngsters from disporting themselves in an unseemly manner on the Lord's Day. But many others still fostered the conventional 'orange and green' prejudices. The first sign of trouble in Mountcollyer Street was a horrific one: a mob from the nearby Protestant Shankill Road area surged down the street, breaking windows in each Catholic house to warn those families that they had been identified and should get out of the neighbourhood while they still had the choice, such as it was. When Ken's father next returned to Belfast and was warned by the Catholic staff of his local pub to stay away in future, he went straight back in for another pint. The polarisation which would lead by the 1990s to most areas in Belfast being more or less exclusively inhabited by either Protestants or Catholics had begun. Today, the kerbstones of Mountcollyer Street are painted red, white and blue to mark out the district in a primitive fashion as Protestant territory; the mixed area of Ken's childhood is no more in that respect.

As the barricades went up and soldiers were seen for the first time on the Branaghs' street, the family felt it had no alternative but to set about leaving Northern Ireland. The authorities in Canada, the first choice of so many Ulster exiles, including Frances Branagh's sister Rose and her husband, would not offer William's family the assisted passage afforded to workers whose skills would be a particular asset to the country. The obvious next option was England, where the new owners of the firm that employed Ken's father had offered him a house at low rent. The family took up residence in Reading in the Royal County of Berkshire, a town in the process of being reborn as a dormitory for London, and home of the Courage Brewery and Huntley & Palmers biscuits.

Reading today looks like a hundred other boroughs in the south of England: an anonymous, modern town centre serving to bind together a number of nineteenth- and early twentieth-century residential areas which accreted for no obvious commercial or geographical reason. The town had been the first major stop beyond London on the Great Western Railway line to Bristol, which opened up the possibility of conducting a business at an accessible distance from the capital. The process was duplicated over a century later when the M4 motorway extension made it possible for workers to commute by road to London while enjoying the advantages of living away from the smog and bustle. This metamorphosis was imminent when the Branaghs – William, Frances, the teenaged Bill junior and nine-year-old Kenneth – arrived in Reading.

Each member of the family came to cope with their new environment in a different way at a time when simply being Irish in England, and especially in a town with many of its young men in the Army, led to tensions of its own. The prejudice was minuscule compared to that which led to the notorious miscarriages of justice against Irish people in England a few years later (one of which would be filmed in 1993 as *In the Name of the Father*, with Emma Thompson in a featured role), but ignorance fostered suspicion, and Northern Ireland is a topic about which it is scarcely possible ever to be fully informed – still less so in the early 1970s, when an opinion poll conducted in England revealed that a majority of those questioned believed that militant Protestant demagogue the Reverend Ian Paisley was a leader of the IRA. To be Irish, whether from north or south, in England at the time was a handicap in itself.

Just fitting in socially, with an accent which can be one of the most impenetrable in the English language to those unused to hearing it, posed further problems. William Branagh's three years of working in England had already led him to modify his speech to the small extent necessary to smooth his way. Bill junior rapidly acquired a classless, regionless Home Counties twang, as if jettisoning all evidence of his birth and upbringing; he reacted against his guilt at this transformation by criticising the speech of his mother, who was suffering most from the loss of family and community that the York Street way of life had given her and was becoming diffident and withdrawn, with only the family's new arrival – daughter Joyce, born in 1970 when Frances was thirty-nine – as a source of comfort and purpose.

Ken, facing peer pressure at school and with a keen urge to make himself unobtrusive, acquired a chameleon accent in the course of his first year in Reading – he was English at school, Northern Irish at home. It was the first sign of the continuing complications that his sense of cultural identity would pose both in his career and in his private life later on, which were dispelled only when his own name became a bigger and more defining label than any national description. His sense of himself as a Belfast boy remains strong, and as well as his many remaining family connections he has fostered a number of links with the province in his subsequent career – probably through the inextricably combined senses of homeland, exile and, to a slight extent, betrayal because of his early desire to be assimilated into English life. Every film that he has directed until *Frankenstein* has been previewed in Belfast, with the proceeds going to local charities including the housing trust which cares for his grandmother, and he plays adeptly to the press's understandable 'local boy made good' fervour on his visits there. The Irish side of his character is still obvious: the charm, the gift of the gab which has enabled him to recruit so many famous names for his various projects, and – perhaps most dominant of all – the Protestant compulsion always to be doing something.

Socially and culturally, though, he seems to have become as English as he could: an acting and directing career more or less founded upon Shakespeare, the role foisted upon him as the latest saviour of the British film industry and the persistent, hated Olivier comparisons all define him in terms of being 'the other side of the water' from his native land. Apparently he still yearns to fit in. In a rare lapse into preciousness, he once mused: 'Actors are beggars, always will be. Our home is really where we work. Belfast is important to me, and I am always moved when I go there. I remain steeped in a working-class Protestant Belfast philosophy. But it's my job to change my voice, become other people, so I have what Olivia Manning describes as the Anglo-Irish sense of belonging nowhere.' His way of coping with that sense has been to try to belong everywhere.

Ken completed his primary education in Reading at White-knights Primary School. It was not the *gulag* that the Grove had been in Belfast: the classrooms (incredibly to him) had play areas rather than slippers prominent on the teacher's desk, and Ken was quickly assimilated into his new milieu through his passion for football. Less significant at the time, though much more so in retrospect, was his first appearance onstage, in a fringed brown blanket, playing the animated dog created by Eric Thompson. The role of Dougal in *The Magic Roundabout* didn't signal the awakening of Ken's instinct for acting, but it was an enjoyable project and typical of the less authoritarian regime at Whiteknights which alleviated his sense of aliena-tion in this new town and country. However, the family's enforced move in 1972 (when their house was scheduled for demolition to make way for an access road to a new super-market) meant that Ken could not graduate from Whiteknights to Maiden Erleigh School with the rest of his year, but moved instead to the new 1,200-pupil Meadway Comprehensive. Meadway was large (spread over two separate sites) and impersonal, and despite the comforting realisation that the rest of the year's intake were as nervous as him about their new school, his social defences were once again heightened.

The young Ken's attempts to fit into his new suburban environment assumed an edge of desperation. 'I had to start listening to what was said with a kind of keenness that was new. If we were going home from school, and the other kids were talking about what they'd had for lunch or supper, I'd listen carefully so I could say the same thing. I remember them talking about "cold meat salads" and trying to imagine what this could be. I reckoned it must be much more exotic than the salad tea that we would sometimes have on a Saturday night: lettuce and beetroot and hard-boiled eggs. So when they'd say, "What did you have for lunch?" I'd say, "Cold meat salad, actually." One particularly vicious kid had me rumbled, he rumbled the fact that I didn't know what I was talking about, didn't know what a bloody cold meat salad was.'

This 'particularly vicious kid' made Ken's school life a hell for several weeks; like countless children before and since, Branagh found himself on the receiving end of merciless bullying. As with most bullies, the terror lay less in the acts themselves than in the constant looming menace; Ken lived in dread of the thug's next opportunity to humiliate him. He took to avoiding the school playground, even cutting classes on occasion. The extremity of the situation became apparent when one morning he tried to throw himself down the stairs at home in the hope of breaking his leg and having to stay off school for a few weeks. His bones, however, remained intact, and his attempt to fake the injury cut no ice with his laughing father. Ken at last confided the reasons for his change in temperament to William Branagh (himself the victim of bullying by a sadistic teacher in his school days), who paid a visit to the headmaster of Meadway. The word got out, Ken's fear of the bully was confirmed and the problem worsened.

Salvation came about through physical education classes. When organised rugby joined the PE schedule, Ken launched himself with a fervour into the game and particularly into his tormentor; his retaliation against the bullying was, as it were, officially sanctioned when it took place on the rugby pitch. The thug, realising that Branagh was less of a coward than he was himself, eased off.

Ken's way into the school community in general came through sport, albeit with a histrionic bent. 'I was a very theatrical footballer, all shouts and gestures and things. It made me appear better than I was.' He became captain of the soccer and rugby teams, and remains passionate about 'the old footer'. In the early days of his Renaissance company he confessed, 'I had this idea that if I was a success as an actor I might be asked to be part of a charity team. Nobody ever asked me. Perhaps they think that because I do Shakespeare I wouldn't be interested in anything as common as football.' When sports results are broadcast he still professes to listen first for news of the Northern Ireland team, then for the Republic, with England coming third – certainly a better bet in the light of the 1994 World Cup, when millions of English people discovered spurious Irish connections to give them an imagined stake in the fortunes of Jack Charlton's team.

The adult Branagh, trying to explain his early life neatly, claimed that his persecution at school was due not to his 'otherness' but rather the reverse – the fact that he sought attention as the class jester: 'It wasn't because I was Irish so much as because I stood out as an extrovert. In Ireland I'd had a huge extended family, had known everybody for several streets, and I'd developed into this larky person, an embryonic actor, I suppose. So when I got to Reading, as soon as I was comfortable, this is how I was. I tried to make people laugh. It was enough to mark you out, wasn't it?' His initial extroversion was seriously damaged by the bullying episode, and would not re-emerge until later in another form, although he apparently still distrusts extroversion when one can't control how it is perceived. There is a significant contrast between his stage and screen career (and his seemingly indefatigable dedication to publicise a given project at the appropriate time) on the one hand and his continuing hunger for privacy on the other, characterised by his release of only such personal details as he feels are necessary or may be useful at that moment. After the horrors of bullying, Ken spent his years between the ages of twelve and fifteen as a primarily solitary boy, hardly socialising outside school, devoting himself instead to reading and to following television and films.

In Belfast Ken had discovered the magic of movies, watching old films on the black and white television in the front room in Mountcollyer Street (it was *The Birdman of Alcatraz*, with Burt Lancaster, which first fired his enthusiasm). This passion, too, later torqued into another approach towards bluffing his way into the Reading crowd. 'I remember when the James Bond film *Diamonds are Forever* came out. I really wanted to see it, but it just wasn't the sort of thing my parents did and we didn't go. I watched clips of it on TV and memorised all the details. Then I had these long conversations at school about how I'd seen it. They'd ask suspiciously what was my favourite bit and I'd go through the clip I'd seen. I desperately didn't want to admit I hadn't seen it.' His interest took a genuine hold, though, and he became something of a trivia buff on supporting players. When, in rehearsals for *Another Country*, he first met his future partner in Renaissance David Parfitt, Ken recognised him at once from the ITV sitcoms *And Mother Makes Three* and *And Mother Makes Five*.

As his parents were not partial to evenings out of that kind, Ken had been taken only once or twice to the theatre for Christmas shows. He was to pinpoint one of these occasions, watching Joseph Tomelty as Marley's ghost in *A Christmas Carol* at Belfast's nearby Grove Theatre, as the moment when he first realised from a spectator's point of view the magic of live theatre, of sharing the same space and time with an actor in an unrepeatable event. 'I was hooked; I've never forgotten that performance.' In terms of direct experience, his first real acquaintance with the idea of performance was watching his parents, aunts and uncles gathered in the pub in York Street of a Saturday night, revelling in the 'crack' and doing 'turns', his father usually coming out with strings of jokes, his mother singing. He had watched brother Bill preparing for his own 'turn' at a Grove School concert, as a blacked-up minstrel (truly, the past is a foreign country), and missed the point of the act when he finally saw it on the stage, wondering why anyone would volunteer to go through such an ordeal.

In Reading, though, he at last succumbed to the twin delights of acting – showing off and pretending to be somebody else. His first performance, as Dougal in the Christmas production of *The Magic Roundabout* at Whiteknights Primary School, made for a more pleasant association with the programme than had been the whacks from Mr Gribben's slippers at Grove School in Belfast: 'I was quite an old pro even in those days. We took it round the nurseries – our first tour!' He went on, 'When I did the plays at school, I thought if only I could do that as a job. I couldn't imagine doing a job that was dull and stuffy. Acting was a job that was all fun.' After his self-declared triumph as Dougal, he wrote a brief social parable for a harvest festival (in which young Lord Ponsonby-Smythe becomes a good and generous landlord after seeing the squalor of his tenants' lifestyles) and took a minor part in Richard Rodney Bennett's *All the King's Men* produced by Thames Junior Opera.

In fact, Ken developed fixations on just about every medium at the time: 'I used to write to a lot of people,' he later recalled, 'Morecambe and Wise asking if I could have tickets to see their television show, to actors asking about their jobs and to the BBC suggesting a chat show for children. I was fourteen and they wrote back suggesting a meeting, but I lost my bottle and didn't go.' His breakthroughs often seem to have come about through letters rather than speaking to people. He claims that he chooses this option 'because I've always found it extremely difficult, and still do, to pick up the phone when you have to ask someone more famous or experienced than you to do something. It really does require a great deal of courage from me, and I usually have to write some kind of script down. When I approached Judi Dench and Derek Jacobi to work with

Renaissance, it took me days just to pick up the phone. My voice rises an octave and I get all breathless, and that still goes on.'

Although often gripped by failures of nerve after making initial contact, the would-be media phenomenon did manage to follow through on a less exalted front, and succeeded in swinging a spot of local teenage journalism. The children's page of the *Reading Evening Post* of 3 August 1974 carried the first 'Junior Bookshelf' column by thirteen-year-old Ken Branagh, complete with his picture at the head of the copy. He was announced as 'Junior Post's own book reviewer ... His favourite authors include Malcolm Saville and Robert Bateman.' The only other reference to Ken's non-theatrical reading tastes came in 1989, when a newspaper feature on the current reading of various personalities revealed an eclectic Branagh selection: Graham Greene, *The Wind in the Willows* and Robert Ludlum. Emma Thompson, in contrast, has been known to spend her time on set reading such volumes as William L. Shirer's *The Rise and Fall of the Third Reich* and Edward Said's *Culture and Imperialism*, and for many years kept in her handbag a copy of Virginia Woolf's polemical feminist essay *A Room of One's Own*.

One early press appearance about which Branagh has remained largely silent was in the 3 September 1977 edition of teenage girls' magazine *Oh Boy!*. The magazine carried the usual mix of photo love stories, innocuous advice on fashion and boys, and a centre-spread pin-up which seemingly every other week was of Paul Michael Glaser from *Starsky and Hutch*. On this occasion, though, its 'Oh Boyfriends!' section on the inside front cover – 'Like a chappie to cheer you up? We've got loads of great guys who'd just love to write to *you*!' – carried the entry 'Sixteen-year-old Ken Branagh is a sports fanatic, but in between huffin' and puffin' he also finds time for a bit of guitar-playing and listening to music (his fave is Wings)! He'd like to write to a young lady of fifteen plus, over 5ft, not fussy about looks but please send photo ...' accompanied by a photo-booth picture instantly recognisable even today. Clearly, by this stage Ken was beginning to re-emerge from the shell he had built around himself in the preceding years. When a fan rediscovered the ad in the early 1990s, Branagh pleaded innocence: 'I was set up. A mate sent two photographs to the magazine. I knew nothing about it until about 150 letters landed on the mat. They kept arriving at fifty a day for the rest of the week. It's slightly galling that it was far more than the fan mail I receive now.' The reference to Wings squares with a later admission to enjoying 'messing about with old Beatles songs on my guitar', and obviously stood Ken in good stead when it came to securing the agreement of Paul McCartney to allow one of his songs to be adapted for use in the Renaissance Theatre Company's first Shakespeare production, *Twelfth Night*, in 1987. It sits oddly, however, with his more recent confession to have been a fan of punk rock!

Schoolfriend Steve Butler – according to *Oh Boy!* 'a bit more fussy about his girls; he doesn't like 'em to wear too much make-up!' and a self-confessed Cockney Rebel fan – now a British Telecom engineer, revealed: 'I sent [the ad] in for a laugh, with one for myself. He got more replies than me, even though I was better-looking. Ken was never short of women; girls used to flock round him during the last two or three years at school. I don't know what it was about him but he was very commanding.' Whether or not Ken was 'set up', Butler's testimony is evidence that even at such an early age, Branagh possessed magnetism offstage as well as on it.

It wasn't all smooth going, however: on one occasion a former girlfriend exacted revenge upon him in quiet but effective style. Ken had been to a party at which, he claimed, in order to get up the courage to sing some of those songs that so impressed the readers of *Oh Boy!*, he had got hammered on unfamiliar liquors. In the course of the evening he managed to lose his shirt and reel through a hedge before being rescued by friends and put away to sleep it off. At this point his ex telephoned 'to grass to my parents, feigning concern that I'd throw up and choke myself'. His father found the sleeping Kenneth half naked, covered in scratches, in a dog basket.

'I'd told my dad I'd be staying with friends all night, in case of just such an eventuality,' he recounted, 'but he came and helped me to stagger into the car before saying very quietly, "Well, you've let yourself down tonight, lad, haven't you?" Next day I came downstairs with the most godawful hangover to find my mother calmly peeling sprouts. I went over to apologise and, without looking up, she just said, "I never want to see you like that again." I felt this quiet Exocet of disapproval.' Years later, the drunken, profane 'arsehole' he played in his film *Peter's Friends* would evoke memories of the 'stocious' teenager.

Ken has never claimed to be a 'roaring boy'. 'I used to think there was something wrong with me because I wasn't on a bottle of whiskey a day,' he said years later; 'I like to eat, drink and be merry, but I couldn't take myself seriously as a hellraiser. It's too absurd, and what would I do it *for*? Also, I'd get such a wigging from my parents – crikey, yes – and life is easier without that.' That early experience in the doghouse evidently made a lasting impression on him, and family approval is still important in the midst of his professional success.

Moreover, despite his conspicuous lack of difficulty in the girlfriend department, the social insecurity persisted. 'I remember a terrible time when I went to a restaurant with a girlfriend and her parents. They ordered trout, so I thought I'd better order trout as well. When the meal arrived, I just started hacking away, and had to spit out all the bones. I looked up. They weren't eating. They had all carefully sliced along the fish, filleted it and were in the process of removing the entire skeleton. [Other] people knew the rules. I didn't.'

His lack of self-confidence persists to this day, coupled with a perceptible degree of superstition. When he appeared at the National Film Theatre in the summer of 1994 to talk about Shakespeare (and indirectly to publicise the forthcoming *Frankenstein*) he not only observed the standard actors' custom of refusing to name *Macbeth*, but more than once leaned forward surreptitiously to touch the wood of the table in front of him for luck. Such insecurity had caused Ken to spend three years or so as the isolated teenager keeping to his room, with books as his main company. It seemed natural at the time that the occupation most suited to his teenage temperament was writing – he had talked his way on to the 'Junior Post' page of the local paper after all, and had even been invited to the BBC to discuss his idea for a kids' chat show (even if he bottled out of actually going). There was football – there was always football – but, one way or another, he was determined to avoid the workaday grind.

Paradoxically, it was through football that the sixteen-year-old Ken rediscovered acting. Meadway's drama teacher, Roger Lewis, trawled the soccer team for volunteers to act in a Christmas production of *Oh! What a Lovely War* for which few people had signed up. Ken was among those who responded to Lewis's renewed appeal, and as his team-mates gradually dropped out (concerned that queening about on stage might compromise their macho sporty image) he grabbed an armful of parts and threw himself into creating a host of characterisations, if not with subtlety or detail then at least with great *brio*. The roar of the crowd, the smell of the greasepaint and above all the sense of community which had been missing throughout his early teens were a revelation to Branagh. Roger Lewis delivered the *coup de grâce* by asking if the lad had considered acting as a profession. Ken quickly realised that he had not just a career possibility, but a calling.

Sixteen was too early an age, he felt, at which to apply for a drama school. Ken elected to stay on at school (taking English, History and Sociology A-Levels) rather than join his father's company, and was adamant at his school careers interview that he wanted to be an actor. Formal career advice in the field was hard to come by – acting was, and still is, thought not to be quite 'real work', and Ken's own parents 'were frightened that acting was a profession full of people who were gay, or out of work, or both'. Nevertheless, his growing collection of books included both plays and an antiquated handbook on theatre as

a career, and, whenever he could find a copy on the news-
stands, *Plays & Players* magazine. But the printed page was no
substitute for practical experience.

Luckily Reading had, in the Progress Theatre, one of the
country's foremost amateur dramatic companies, with its own
theatre, a dozen or so productions a year and an active youth
and student wing. Current Progress chairman Chris Bertrand,
who ran the student group at the time, remembers, 'The
company [proper] was auditioning for a production of *Who's
Afraid of Virginia Woolf?* and Ken came along to try out for the
part of Nick. He was very nervous about coming in the first
place, spent some time standing underneath the ash tree
outside and then went home again before he actually plucked
up the courage to go into the audition. The director was
worried about giving him the part because he was so young, as
it was playing the role of a stud. She spoke to his mum, who
said, "It's all right, he's quite a mature lad, he'll be able to cope
with it." So she cast him, but before rehearsals got properly
underway the production collapsed anyway.'

His first appearance with Progress was in a Victorian
melodrama entitled *The Drunkard, or Down With Demon
Drink*. Ken played William Dowton, a country bumpkin
complete with rustic smock and neckerchief, and although
Chris Bertrand remembers his performance as 'excellent',
surviving pictures of the production suggest that his portrayal
could euphemistically be described as enthusiastic – in other
words, he's visibly 'mugging' in every shot. 'I think because of
his approach to acting he's always likely to be better at comedy
than at serious things,' says Bertrand. 'He has a lovely sense of
timing and can create accents at will – his vocal control has
always been remarkable. At school when he did *Oh! What a
Lovely War*, it wasn't the material or the meaning that got him
going, it was the ability to take on lots of different roles and try
out different accents. I don't think he ever took to improvisation very comfortably – he was much more interested in the
technical aspect of performance than in baring his soul or even
thinking about it.'

Progress members got involved in all aspects of production, and on one occasion Ken, working backstage, saved not just the show but the entire building. The play was a Christmas production of *The Rose and the Ring*, directed by Bertrand. 'We tried to make it a traditional pantomime, with lots of flashes and bangs and things, people appearing and disappearing in smoke and so on. Ken was stage-managing, and one night a flash went off and set the curtains on fire. Ken, being a very quick-thinking chap, rushed on to the stage, pulled the curtain down off its fittings, opened the back door and threw the curtain into the yard. If it hadn't been for him we probably would have been able to claim on the insurance and build a nice new theatre! That was his first experience of stage-managing – I don't think he's ever done it since.'

Branagh went on to appear in a number of small Progress shows, and also in the Berkshire Shakespeare Players' production of *Othello*, as Cassio. The play was staged in Reading's Abbey ruins, and went on to perform at the Viscounts Astor's former country home, Cliveden House (now owned by the National Trust) as part of the Cliveden Festival. He soon learned the problems of open-air theatre: extraneous noise (Cliveden is on the Heathrow flightpath), unpredictable weather (the final evening performance was rained into a marquee, where hasty restaging left Othello dying climactically against the tent's central pole) and the alternative attractions of other summer events. At that time the men's singles final of the Wimbledon tennis tournament took place on a Saturday afternoon. 'We outnumbered the audience,' remembers Chris Bertrand, who played Iago. Furthermore, the seventeen spectators who did turn up could still hear the tennis match on a television set in the nearby bar tent. It would take a great deal to entice Ken to perform in the open air again – in fact, only the chance to play Hamlet at Elsinore Castle would succeed. However, his memories of Cliveden itself were idyllic enough for him to choose the estate as the venue for his wedding to Emma Thompson twelve years later.

Friends of Branagh have observed that he seemed to have a

tendency to fall in love with his leading ladies. Sometimes it worked the other way round, and he would cast – or try to cast – his current *inamorata*. Chris Bertrand recalls a Progress production of Strindberg's *Miss Julie* directed by his wife Jacqui. 'Ken was obviously the prime contender for the part of Jean, but there were a number of people who could have played Miss Julie. He was going out with a girl called Tracy Newson at the time, and would only be in the play if she were to be cast as Miss Julie, so he started very early with that! On this occasion it meant that he wasn't cast. Tracy went out with him for about five years. It was always coming very much from her to him rather than the other way around; he was quite an attractive sort of chap even at that stage.' Tracy Newson is a likely candidate for the Reading girlfriend Ken refers to as 'Sandy' in his memoir *Beginning*, whom he berates himself for breaking up with when he went to RADA. As for his acting, Bertrand said: 'At that time one thought, well, he's quite a capable and aspiring young lad, but there are plenty of others around of equal talent.'

In addition to his Progress activities, Ken went to see plays at every opportunity, camping at Stratford-upon-Avon during the school holidays when he was sixteen in order to attend the Royal Shakespeare Company's productions, and travelling with a girlfriend to Oxford to see Derek Jacobi in *Hamlet*. He found the latter a tremendous experience, and Jacobi became one of his theatrical idols of the period. Unsurprisingly, a decade later when Ken was organising the first full season of touring Shakespeare for his own Renaissance company, Jacobi was one of the actors he approached to direct a production. He also devoured every memoir, biography, manual and criticism collection he could lay his hands on, and was delighted to be given an extensive collection of 1950s issues of *Plays & Players* and other theatre magazines. Schoolwork began to come a poor second to his theatrical passion. Although he enjoyed class work (especially in English, where teacher Stan Grue shared his dramatic bent and went as far as to cast Ken in the title role of the Christmas production of *Toad of Toad Hall*), homework went by the board as all his efforts focused on securing a place at drama school.

He was offered auditions at the Central School of Speech and Drama (at Swiss Cottage, just down the Finchley Road from Emma Thompson's neighbourhood) and the Royal Academy of Dramatic Art (RADA) for the September 1979 intake, and cajoled friends from Progress to coach him through his audition speeches: one from Shakespeare, one from a modern work. Colin Wakefield, who later became a professional actor himself, worked with him (as did Stan Grue) on the 'What a piece of work is man' speech from *Hamlet*, whilst later Progress membership secretary Pauline Gray and her husband, Harry, cast critical eyes on his rendition of a scene from Pinter's *The Caretaker*. After the auditions in January, both schools recalled him for the second round of auditions, but in the case of RADA principal Hugh Cruttwell had reservations. Extraordinarily, Cruttwell invited Ken to return with a different audition speech and work on it with him.

Having worked up the 'gentleman caller' speech from Tennessee Williams' *The Glass Menagerie* with the Grays inside a week or so, Ken went back to RADA. Cruttwell made no bones about his view that the would-be student was a proficient technician in terms of acting, but repeatedly criticised him for attempting to do too much, to convey the entire character in a two-minute speech. After several attempts at the Pinter speech, Ken was astonished when he forgot the words – 'dried' – after only a few seconds. This, said Cruttwell, was a breakthrough; he had unlearned enough of his painstaking preparation to be ready actually to work in the required manner with a director on the piece. Branagh, too, felt the difference, and was invigorated by the remainder of the session. At the end, however, the principal still did not offer him a place, but merely wished him luck at his recall for Central the following day and asked to know their verdict.

Ken had already decided that he vastly preferred the atmosphere of RADA to that at Central, and had told Cruttwell as much. His second session at the Swiss Cottage school confirmed him in his choice: it was a gruelling day of movement, speech and song auditions interspersed with a series of interminable waits. At each stage, a batch of hopefuls was weeded out and sent packing, and at each stage the tension among the remaining students grew more palpable. When the two last auditionees, Ken and an American girl, were offered places, he knew that the rancour and humiliation of such a process had put him off accepting it; he thanked his interrogator-in-chief, went back to Reading and wrote a polite letter of refusal, then prepared to apply to other schools when the anticipated letter from RADA arrived declining to take him on. After school that Friday, the terrified Branagh found a letter from the academy. He had been offered a place. If Ken was ecstatic, the Branagh family dog was less pleased at being subjected to a three-hour celebratory tramp through the January snow.

There remained the question of finance. In 1979 no drama school course was recognised as being of degree status, and grants to students were discretionary rather than mandatory. Consequently, all drama, music, dance and art students had to submit to an assessment by the local county council, which would reach a decision on the basis of both desert and talent. Government money has never even approached sufficiency in terms of funding students in the arts (horror stories are rife of students attempting to finance themselves and collapsing from exhaustion after a string of eighteen-hour days spent in college and at 'real' work), and any one hopeful would have only a minute chance of winning a grant. Ken applied to universities, although his experiences of the burden of tradition and the persisting social élitism on brief visits to Oxford and Cambridge dissuaded him from Meadway's suggestion that he consider the Oxbridge option. Manchester University's drama course had a fine reputation, but even that seemed the wrong path to one who already had his heart set on RADA. Months of suspense until the council audition in May were filled by a growing conviction that the route he had chosen was the only one possible for him, followed by continued uncertainty as the council would not announce its decision until July. Not knowing whether or not he could afford to take up his place at drama school, Ken was confronted by the imminent prospect of his GCE exams. But by the time he applied himself to revision for his A-Levels, there was an air of sad recognition in the Branagh household that he really had left things too late on the academic front. Although his parents were pleased at his acceptance by RADA, which was the only drama school they had heard of, they were still frustrated that even a couple of months before his exams Ken was learning lines for the part of Noah Claypole in *Oliver!*, and then that the Berkshire Shakespeare Players' *Othello* secured a transfer to the Cliveden Festival during the examination season itself.

The news that Berkshire County Council would pay fees and maintenance for Ken's three-year course (the only drama award made in the county that year) left him the summer to make some money to top up the grant by working as a porter in the town's Battle Hospital, and to devote his days off to searching for accommodation in London. He found a room in Clapham in a house occupied by the widower of Dorothy Reynolds, the co-author of *Salad Days*, who was the first 22-carat, drawling 'act-*or*' Ken had ever encountered. The exotica of the house with its theatrical memorabilia went some little way towards offsetting the news that afternoon that his A-Level results were no better than he had any right to expect. He had effectively burned all his academic boats: the only course open to him was acting.

3

'The Most Colossal Talent'

Oxford and Cambridge differ from other British universities in more than simply their golden reputation, although the prestige of an Oxbridge degree is given official status by the system of taking MAs: no Master of Arts courses are taught, but holders of Bachelors' Honours degrees can simply wait until a set period after their original matriculation, pay a nominal fee and convert their BA degree into an MA, a tradition which provokes cries of iniquity or complacent smirks, depending on whether or not the person in question has enjoyed such a privilege. The two universities' collegiate structure, too, sets them apart from all but a few other institutions of higher education. University-wide faculties administer examinations in the subject courses (known as the Tripos, but confusingly arranged into two rather than three parts), lectures and some classes, but the tutorial supervisions which form the core of learning are set up by the individual constituent colleges. Similarly, prospective students sit entrance examinations organised by the university as a whole, but apply to and are interviewed by specific colleges.

In 1978 few of Cambridge's colleges were co-residential. Newnham College, at which Emma Thompson arrived to read for the English Tripos, had been established in 1871 (the same year, coincidentally, as the Camden School for Girls which Emma had been attending), during prolonged and heated debate as to whether Oxbridge should admit 'ladies'. A group of Victorians seriously suggested that, rather than opening Oxford and Cambridge to women, a centre of female academic excellence should be established at the geographical midpoint between the two universities, in Bletchley. For another three-quarters of a century the women's colleges at Cambridge functioned in parallel with the male-only university structure, only becoming fully incorporated into the university in 1949 – a mere ten years before Emma's birth – and as late as the 1960s neither the Cambridge Union Society, the self-important debating club which has spawned a committee-roomful of Tory ministers, nor the Footlights Comedy Club would admit women as full members.

Newnham was and remains all-female (its charter in fact prohibits the college from admitting male students until such time as women constitute more than 50 per cent of the university's student population as a whole), and it was there that Emma began fully to articulate her passionately held views on women in art and in society. This awareness manifested itself in both her studies and her extra-curricular activities: her final-year dissertation on George Eliot puzzled over how the authoress could write such complex female characters but never dared create a female protagonist 'as heroic as she was'; a year earlier she had appeared in the Cambridge Footlights' first all-female revue.

The director of studies (head of department) in English at Newnham, Dr Jean Gooder, remembers, 'It was always quite clear that she was going to act, and act seriously – she was in multiple dramatic activities from the word go, but emphatic-ally not at the expense of her work. She was one of the more remarkable people who could manage both. She was ill in her first year, and got a bit behind in her work because of that; but in her final year when she was really firing on all guns she never let her supervisor down, and was handsomely com-mended. It took me some while to realise that Emma was her father's daughter, so to speak, and our kids were of the generation to have avidly watched *The Magic Roundabout* and were deeply impressed that Emma Thompson was one of my students.'

Despite the energy with which she entered the worlds of both work and play at the university, Emma later said that Cambridge 'stunted me for a while. It's hard to explain it without sounding ungrateful for a wonderful experience. I was the first member of my family to go to university and felt quite lost in it. When you arrive the whole image of the place wipes you clean. I found the female teachers at my college wonderful – enjoyment is always the best teacher. But I found that very enjoyment marred by the great weight of what other people had thought about it.' When she took Ken on a trip to the city years afterwards, 'he had that sort of reaction that people generally have who haven't been, to feel excluded. Not a very nice feeling.' Her 'project' at Cambridge seemed to be neither academic nor career-orientated, but simply to realise her potential as a person to the utmost in as many avenues as possible, taking full advantage of an insular environment strongly conducive to self-discovery and, where necessary, self-reinvention. Years later, when asked in an interview whether she had had ambitions at the time to be rich and famous, she replied, 'No – human. It's not as stupid as it sounds. I think we all start off pretty awful. It's that wonderful thing of learning tolerance ... how to be wise ... how to be kind.'

Too often, wisdom comes through suffering. In the summer between her first and second years her grandmother and uncle both died, and shortly before these bereavements Eric Thompson suffered the stroke which deprived him of his power of speech. Dr Gooder still has 'a very moving letter from her mother written with extraordinary tact to say that she thought it would be better if somebody knew quite what Emma had been through that summer. I thought she coped absolutely magnificently.' Dr Gooder's supervision report for the following term testifies to this fortitude: 'Emma's work is of a different order from last year: she has all the naturalness, frankness and energy which made her so attractive a member of the group, but she has come to some inner decision to put more into her work and has simply deepened humanly, I suspect as she has had to face a succession of family tragedies.' According to the director of studies, 'The word "humanly" was a coded way of recognising that she'd been through a lot.'

The report continues: 'She has contrived to keep up her astonishing dramatic and cabaret performances throughout the term without failing of a single academic commitment... She has been a pleasure to work with: she makes everything she does worthwhile. Her contributions to classes have been characteristically generous, open and fearless.' Yet Dr Gooder recalls that although Emma had 'immense, vivid vitality... I don't think she suffered from over-confidence, certainly intellectually speaking – she had to be shown that she was as good as she could be. Her mother's letter, which is very touching, said that she thought Emma needed to achieve in her work, not simply onstage, for her own self-respect: I think there's a real truth in that.'

Against such a tragic background, Emma had quickly carved out a place for herself in the student culture of performance, where it soon became apparent that her pre-ferred avenue was comedy. She later called such a career path 'a great way to do it. I never had that thing of thinking, I *must* act. I never wanted it badly. Even at Cambridge, none of us did anything on the dramatic side, which was more serious and career-orientated. The Footlights ethos was self-deprecation: "I'm not really here".' It's a slight exaggeration to say that she was involved in no theatrical productions as such: her contemporary Stephen Unwin, now director of the English Touring Theatre, remembers her as 'a brilliant Helena in *All's Well That Ends Well*, in the cloisters of Queens' College', which also featured Stephen Fry and, exceptionally, an actor brought into the production from outside Cambridge – Sophie Thompson. However, the vast majority of Emma's dramatic roles were in comedies and with friends from Footlights or elsewhere.

Footlights has for many years enjoyed an unsurpassed reputation as a crucible of English comic talent. Its high-water mark came in the 1960s: Jonathan Miller and Peter Cook, half of the *Beyond the Fringe* team, originated in the Cambridge club, and a few years later a number of performers including John Cleese, Michael Palin and Tim Brooke-Taylor emerged to change the face of British television comedy with *At Last the 1948 Show, Do Not Adjust Your Set* and finally the seminal *Monty Python's Flying Circus.* The Footlights label was both a blessing and an albatross. The annual Christmas pantomimes and summer revue tours around the country, culminating in a run on the Edinburgh Festival Fringe, drew healthy audiences but also a gaggle of critics keen to be among the first to spot the next batch of comic geniuses – and equally keen to be ostentatiously disappointed if no such marvels were apparent. All that any Footlights generation can do is pursue their own notions of humour and hope that, when their time comes to endure the minute scrutiny they inevitably attract, they will strike a chord. By a stroke of great good fortune for both the performers themselves and the outside world, the circle of 'Footies' who would become the class of '81 constituted the most remarkable group since the *Python* era.

Stephen Fry, a student of English at Queens', was a major figure in their circle in every sense. He stood 6ft 4ins tall and was a couple of years older than the others in his academic intake, having been a guest of Her Majesty's prison service after stealing a batch of credit cards and going on a fraudulent three-month spending spree as a teenager. Fry combined a startlingly acute intelligence with a delicious sense of the absurd. One of his supervisors tells of receiving an essay from him on James Joyce's *Finnegans Wake* which succeeded in putting forward several perceptive points whilst being written entirely in a pastiche of the book's multilingual, densely punning style. His exceedingly English deadpan manner of performance became one of the greatest assets of that generation of Footlights comedians, allowing him to bring off the most absurd lines and situations with an urbane gravitas ludicrously at odds with the material. In addition, the president of the comedy society in Emma's first year was her

49

old friend Martin Bergman, who had gone up to Cambridge before her. Bergman was later to marry the American comedienne Rita Rudner and co-write with her the script for Kenneth Branagh's third film as director, *Peter's Friends*, recycling along the way some of his old Footlights material.

Aided perhaps by this personal contact (although rumours that she went out with Bergman were untrue), Emma secured the title role in the Footlights pantomime *Aladdin* at the end of her first term. This was not as unprecedented or nepotistic as it may sound: 'freshers' were habitually given such major roles in Footlights pantos, particularly as principal boys. The Cambridge student newspaper *Stop Press*, previewing the show, hedged its bets by commenting, 'The tradition of always casting a first-year as the lead could prove disastrous, but Emma Thompson as Aladdin is a most successful find. Her dancing, singing and acting ability should combine to produce an extremely competent performance.' All such reservations vanished when the play was finally seen – *Stop Press* rated Emma 'particularly difficult not to laugh at.' Both Cambridge panto in general and Emma's showing in particular were revelations to her parents. 'I adore panto,' said Phyllida Law, 'but I thought at Cambridge it would be terribly intellectual and they'd all look like Bernard Levin. We were a little bit frightened of them, to tell the truth. But it was wonderful. They got it all wrong, they corpsed and so forth, and I remember Hugh Laurie giggling a lot. But in the middle of it all was this magical girl with a wonderful presence and dancing style and singing voice. It was all I could do to stop her father getting up out of his chair and start giving her director's notes.' The intimation of Emma's talent really did come out of the blue: 'You just looked at her and thought, my God, where did she hide all that?'

Hugh Laurie was the first of only two student romances which Emma is known to have conducted at Cambridge. An Old Etonian whose comic forte (both at Eton and Cambridge and in the years since then) has been ringing subtle changes on the theme of upper-class twithood, he went out briefly with her during her first year. Laurie had an odd combination of social shyness and professional confidence. One friend recalled that if you met him on the street in Cambridge, 'He would be hanging about on the edge of a group of people, clutching a plastic bag,' whereas a theatrical agent recalls his and Stephen Fry's assurance on stage. Emma reminisced about 'walking home with him through the Backs, his arm around me, and he'd be dead on his feet, fast asleep. And you have to realise he was gigantic in those days – six foot two, and a rowing blue who'd eat seventeen steaks a day.' However, after he rowed in the Oxford and Cambridge Boat Race, a prolonged bout of glandular fever kept him off the river for several months and during that time he became more involved in stage activities – particularly in tandem with Stephen Fry – and with Emma. They parted on good terms, and continued to work together in Footlights, culminating in the watershed 1981 revue. Laurie would later play a member of the 'Footlights College, Oxbridge' quiz team in a 1984 television comedy show with Emma and, in 1992, one of the fictional Oxbridge student revue company reunited ten years later in *Peter's Friends*. He is perhaps best known for playing the character of Bertie Wooster to Stephen Fry's 'gentleman's gentleman' Jeeves in several television series of the P.G. Wodehouse stories.

Emma played as little a role in Cambridge's 'deviant scene' as she had at Camden School. Here, too, she is remembered as being above all *nice* – indeed, almost suspiciously so. One contemporary recalled, 'We decided that she must be putting it on because she couldn't decide which one of us would become really successful and useful to her in later life, and so she was being amiable to everyone just in case.' This was largely an application of student cynicism to Emma's 'think before you speak' attitude. Once at Cambridge, it is hard to believe that she wasn't conscious of the career potential offered by being seen in a good Footlights year, but there is little to suggest that she took such a calculating approach to life in general.

There was no sign, for instance, that she either used her

sexuality for advancement (a phenomenon far from unknown in Cambridge, as in the outside world) or indulged in the stereotypical student promiscuity. 'She didn't sleep around, I know she didn't,' said unsuccessful suitor James Gale. 'I certainly had a crush on her. Didn't everybody? She had morals. You didn't try to seduce Emma Thompson, you fell hopelessly in love with her. She had a killer smile. She was a bit dumpy, the individual bits weren't all that stunning, but the whole package was pretty impressive. Everything together, she was very beautiful. I drove a motorbike into her study at Newnham once, with a guy called Tony McCaffrey. We drove through the double doors, along the corridors, up the stairs and right into her study because Tony was madly in love with her. It was an amazing protestation of love and flattery but I don't think she took it in quite the right way. I remember it didn't impress her that much. The bike was an MZ 250, the ugliest bike ever built. We had to leave it in the study to hide it and I think she was terrified she was going to get caught.'

Her other stage outings included a performance 'head and shoulders above other recent Stoppard productions' as Gwendolyn in *Travesties* (Tom Stoppard's Joyce/Lenin/Dadaism parody of Wilde's *The Importance of Being Earnest*) in May 1979, co-directed by Annabel Arden, who would later become one of the founders of experimental performance company Théâtre de Complicité. 'She was bliss to be on stage with,' enthused one of her fellow actors in *Travesties*. 'You felt lifted up, but incredibly secure. If you made a mistake she could cover it up and make it all look deliberate.' In the summer of her first year she joined the company of the touring Footlights revue, *Nightcap*. 'The boys were fairly blokish,' she remembered, 'and it was difficult to break down the reservations they had about me writing for them.' Nevertheless, *Nightcap* was the show in which Emma was first noticed, both by agents and by television producers. 'Brian Wenham, head of BBC2, saw *Nightcap* in Edinburgh and sent producer Iain Johnstone to watch it,' Martin Bergman explained in his annotations to the Footlights club archive. 'Iain came backstage for a chat. I had left Edinburgh by then, though, with chronic toothache [an excuse which Bergman dignified in a later note as being in order 'to concentrate on directing and writing']. When in London I was suggested as a possible front man for Iain's latest show, *Friday Night, Saturday Morning*. On seeing a film of me, Iain suddenly linked my name with Footlights. They were booked to appear in the programme as well with a sizeable extract of *Nightcap*. The revue went much better without me and some dodgy material in it, and the acclaim for Emma began.'

Her biographical blurb in the programme for *Nightcap* flatly contradicted the universal recollections of her as essentially virtuous in sexual matters: 'We're very worried about Emma – the tour involves her going out with six men over a period of eight weeks – might not be enough men.' The company included Simon McBurney, also a founder and now the driving force behind Théâtre de Complicité. McBurney's blurb included the line, 'Ideal holiday: an hour away from Emma Thompson.' This was disingenuous: by now the two were a couple. In Emma's second year they shared a house with Annabel Arden and Jane Grenville (now an archaeology lecturer) off Cambridge's Mill Road, beyond the local landmark 'Reality Checkpoint', a heavily graffitoed lamp-post which marked the unofficial boundary between the university-dominated town centre and the outside world. McBurney is credited by cynics with being a major force in Emma's development as an artistically and politically aware performer, but the truth is that the Svengali card is wildly overplayed in respect of their relationship. 'I think what he did do for her,' says Dr Peter Holland, former senior treasurer of Footlights and a major figure in the university's dramatic culture, 'was to suggest the seriousness of theatre as a skill – although she was never seen as being likely to go on to do radical theatre work like Simon.'

Dr Holland believes that, both at Cambridge and in her subsequent career, Emma has relied on her inherent abilities rather than taking up substantive challenges. 'She's someone who hasn't quite learned to push herself, then and now.' He explains that Cambridge performers generally follow one of a small number of more or less standard paths into the theatrical profession: broadly speaking, straight actors graduate at first to minor parts with the Royal Shakespeare Company or whoever, theatre 'radicals' like Simon McBurney or Tilda Swinton (another contemporary) set about carving their own niches within that field, and Footlights veterans gravitate towards radio light entertainment. 'With Emma it was a bit of stage work, a bit of screen work, but she always seemed to be heading towards big art movies with a lot of kudos.' In this respect, her Footlights activities represented an area in which she was safe, professional and in a greater degree of control. James Gale agreed that the Footlights route 'was a career decision. She was clearly talented, there wasn't any question about that, but there was definitely a feeling that the quickest route to success – which I think was important to her in view of who her mum and dad were – was through light entertainment, and that meant the Footlights.'

Whether or not her political views owed part of their genesis to her association with McBurney, it was at this time that she came openly to hold the committed socialist and issue-centred beliefs which would later lead her both to take part in a number of benefit performances for deserving causes and to act as a private benefactor for such bodies as a women's refuge and women's radio station in London. 'I don't know where she gets it from,' said Phyllida Law, relishing the cliché, 'certainly not from us.' Cambridge contemporary Kim Harris, Stephen Fry's room-mate at Queens', recalled that when he met Emma in her second year, 'She seemed to have a full set of political principles and she was never a grinding bore about it, either. She didn't do a Vanessa Redgrave and melt your ears with it.'

More striking was the change in Emma's outward image. After her first term at Cambridge, a schoolfriend remembers her 'waltz[ing] in, all flowing scarves and fantastically theatrical'. But now she was habitually to be seen in Doc Marten's, a leather jacket and taking pillion rides on McBurney's motorbike. She also adopted little round glasses and, most radically, shaved her head. She described the net effect as making her look 'like John Lennon, only bald'.

Several differing theories emerged as to why she took such a drastic step with her hairstyle. Dr Jean Gooder was told by Emma that 'she wanted to see what difference it would make to how people perceived her. She had done something which looked extraordinary, for reasons which were perfectly accountable. A lot of her gestures have something much deeper behind them.' It sounds suspiciously like a post facto rationalisation, and indeed Phyllida Law put the act down to youthful bravado. 'I must say I was pretty taken aback. It shows she wasn't always mature. She had to wear a woolly hat. She used to say, "If you don't behave, I'll take my hat off."'

Jane Grenviile remembered that it wasn't a particularly sober decision. 'They got drunk one Saturday afternoon. For some reason I didn't have any sheets and was lying in my sleeping-bag. They were being silly and got hold of the razor and shaved each other's heads. Then they came bounding into my room yelling, "Your turn." I pulled the sleeping-bag over my head. They did it to see what it would look like. It made me realise how good-looking Emma actually was. It looked wonderful. It wouldn't look odd now but at the time it was really outrageous.' Grenville also sides rather more with Jean Gooder's version than Phyllida Law's: 'Once or twice, for social events, she put a hat on, but she didn't go running out to buy a wig. She wouldn't be a great actress if she didn't thrive on people's reactions.'

In a 1993 interview, Emma gave a less sanitised version of events: they hadn't been drunk, she explained, but stoned on home-grown marijuana. Dr Gooder, invited to reconsider her opinion in the light of this confession, laughed, 'I thought I was scrupulously reporting Emma's version of the matter. These are the kind of things, of course, that one prefers not to be too aware of.'

James Gale believed simply, 'She shaved her head because Simon shaved his.' There was a strong element of togetherness to the relationship. Dr Peter Holland recounts that once at a party, bursting not so much with youthful rebelliousness as with alcohol, they asked him whether they could borrow his two-year-old son for a few days, because they thought they'd quite like to have children and wanted to find out what being a parent felt like and involved. 'I agreed with alacrity,' laughed Dr Holland, but naturally sobriety intervened and young Adam was not in fact taken under the couple's wing.

Emma was now one of the hard core of her Footlights generation, and her comedy appearances were regular affairs. Early in 1980, Bergman's successor as Footlights president, Jan Ravens – the first woman ever to be appointed to the post – directed what was surprisingly Cambridge's first all-female revue, *Woman's Hour*, in which Emma featured along with Ravens and Sandi Toksvig. Emma had scalped herself the day before the show opened. 'Jan Ravens was quite appalled,' according to long-time Footlights choreographer Jenny Arnold. 'She hadn't banked on Emma looking like that. But she did the show, and in fact looked terrific in it.' However, its earnest *Stop Press* write-up was a sad demonstration that not all of Cambridge was yet ready to accept women on their own terms. 'It *is* very funny,' granted Paul Clarke. 'What is less certain is whether this sort of show really helps women achieve equal status on a broader dramatic level. Most of the humour was related to women and their stereotypes. Is there not a danger that this will isolate them from mainstream humour by leading us to think that women can only put on good shows about women?' When Emma came to write her own television series, she would attempt to integrate material about 'women and their stereotypes' into a broader range of comic material, sadly with little success.

At the time, though, praise for her was unstinting. She was a success in a supporting role in the 1980 Footlights panto *The Snow Queen*, playing the Wise Old Woman, a queeny actress type who saw everything in theatrical terms. In the non-Footlights revue *An Evening Without* in January 1981, she was deemed 'brilliant as the Queen in a rendering of the Frankie Howerd version of the Christmas message'. Two weeks later she appeared with Stephen Fry in a lunchtime production of one of Chekhov's funniest short plays, *The Proposal*. Her Natasha was described in *Stop Press* as 'full of bristling vigour ... [with] the beady eyes and confident stride of those withered English huntswomen: argumentative, intolerant, blind to any serious opposition, except in one magnificent moment; a flustered, clucking pause that is over almost before it has time to move, where she realises that her temper has just chased off the only suitor she is ever likely to have.'

Academically, Emma herself was suffering from rather the opposite complaint from over-confidence. Although in classes and tutorials she was 'open and fearless', the topic of George Eliot and her heroines seemed to daunt her when working on the 10,000-word dissertation which would count towards her final-year degree result. Her supervisor's report noted: 'The weight of existing Eliot criticism seemed to inhibit Emma from putting her own thoughts on paper. She felt that what she had to say could not be novel and must not be radical. In the event I believe her critique of George Eliot had both these qualities ... It is in general in the conduct of argument that her weakness lies. Her sweetness of character (which makes her a delight to supervise) perhaps prevents her from being sufficiently combative to develop a full intellectual rigour.' Despite these reservations, the examiners awarded Emma a First in her dissertation; overall she emerged with Second Class, First Division Honours in her BA before embarking on the Footlights summer tour.

The 1981 Footlights revue featured Emma, Stephen Fry, Hugh Laurie and Tony Slattery, now a major comedian, actor and 'television personality' – all of whom would appear in *Peter's Friends* – along with Paul Shearer (still an actor and writer, but not a charter member of the old Footlights circle which continues periodically to reunite in varying permutations) and Penny Dwyer (now in the personnel department of a London consulting engineering company whose last major engagement was on the Channel Tunnel). Fry's room-mate Kim Harris was business manager for the tour. Emma's programme entry described her thus: 'Wears baggy trousers and little round glasses. Protests regularly. Votes SWP. Refuses to be stereotyped. OK?' Beneath the parody was a kernel of truth: Emma would, then as later, argue out any suspect ideological overtones in a piece of material. But whether such rigour helped or hindered the end product, *The Cellar Tapes* was the most acclaimed Footlights show since those of the *Python* generation.

Watching the BBC Television presentation of the show a decade later, the primary impression is of the company being composed of Stephen Fry and some other people. Fry's very English poker-faced style, into which he somehow contrives to inject a degree of low camp, was perfect televisual fare. Even at the time, his 'Shakespeare Masterclass' sketch with Hugh Laurie was recognised as wickedly sharp parody, with its exhortations to an aspiring actor to 'gather from the buttocks' before delivering his lines. In the Dracula story sketch, 'The Letter', Fry held the camera simply by sitting in a high-backed chair, reciting an unpredictable, absurd monologue. A typical extract recounts the narrator's first meeting with the Count's manservant: 'Of all the hideously deformed spectacles I have ever beheld . . . those perched on the end of this man's nose will remain forever pasted into the album of my memory. He introduced himself, "Travolta, sir, at your servile."'

This domination is partly a consequence of the cuts imposed upon the stage show for the television version, partly the nature of the medium. The camera loved Fry from the first whereas, for instance, Tony Slattery seemed to veer between the manic and (as in the song 'I'm Gonna Shoot Somebody Famous') the unsettlingly sombre. But if Stephen Fry hadn't been there, the press appreciations of Emma Thompson might have taken off a couple of years earlier. She showed a cool assurance in the face of variable material: her spoof Sondheim musical number 'Send Up the Genre', set to the tune of 'Send In the Clowns' (first aired in the revue *Death In the Aisles* in February 1979, and subsequently used in *Nightcap*), hit its target squarely with a resounding twang, whereas a choral offering sarcastically hymning the far-right British Movement seemed at best politically 'right-on', at worst simply a blunt and leaden condemnation.

Emma had a number of unquestionably fine moments in the programme. In a 'Barretts of Wimpole Street' piss-take with Stephen Fry, invalid poet Emma and her suitor Fry discuss their future in magnificently strangled 1940s Ealing dialect: 'My dalling, you ken be well. I read some more of your po-ems – they're ebsolutely fentestic.' It would have been too easy to play the sketch to excess, but the performers were skilful enough to rein themselves in and let the ridicule emerge naturally. But the routine which makes a journalist's dictionary of clichés fall open at 'eerily prophetic' was the stage actress Juliana Talent (a 'luvvie' years before the term was coined) accepting an award. Beginning with false-modest simpers and a husky 'this award doesn't really belong to me', Emma managed with deadly accuracy to cram in virtually every acceptance-speech line ever to make an audience wince in anguish. 'And of course I'd like to thank from the bottom of my heart, my husband Lindsay,' gushed Juliana (fractional pause), 'the director.' It's hard to resist remarking, 'Little did we know . . .' – and indeed, after one of her numerous awards in later years she admitted to having been overcome with embarrassment on her way to the podium at finding herself turning into the target of her early satire. She has, though, always been too self-deprecating ever to have plumbed the depths of Juliana Talent's final remark: 'All you need is luck. I was simply lucky enough to have been born with the most colossal talent.'

4

In the Making

'The interesting thing about Ken,' says an anonymous contemporary at RADA, 'is that he turned out to be such a tower of ambition.' The boy from Belfast via Reading was regarded by his fellow students as a fine comedy actor, but less strong at epic drama. He certainly didn't have a 'destined for greatness' label hanging from his collar, but nor did any of his generation at the school who have subsequently become generally known: Douglas Hodge, James Wilby, Kathryn Hunter, Nigel Pivaro, Paul McGann, Fiona Shaw and Mark Rylance were all at the Academy within a year either side of Ken.

The Academy of Dramatic Art had been founded in 1904 (it was granted royal status in 1920), and the Central School (at which Ken had turned down a place) two years later. By teaching acting as a craft, the schools helped the profession to escape from the social stigma which had surrounded it for centuries, of being looked on as barely better than prostitution. Through the twentieth century actors had steadily moved further away from their remarkably long-lasting reputation as 'rogues and vagabonds'. The birth of 'fringe' theatre in the 1960s and early 1970s, with its plethora of small studio venues, often (in London) in spare rooms behind or above pubs, went some small way to countering the decline in the number of provincial repertory theatres and, more importantly, encouraged new dramatic writing, which often required more vigorous, less 'poised' styles of acting.

In the wake of RADA and Central, a number of drama schools were founded in and around London, and a few in other cities. The newer universities, too, included drama departments which combined the academic and practical aspects of theatre. Frustratingly for generations of students, neither Oxford nor Cambridge has ever offered anything remotely resembling a drama course, although in the late 1980s theatre producer Cameron Mackintosh endowed Oxford University with a visiting professorship of contemporary theatre, which has been filled by such luminaries as Stephen Sondheim and Sir Ian McKellen. However, the oldest drama schools remain the most prestigious institutions at which to learn the trade – the Oxford and Cambridge of the profession – with RADA, the senior school and the only one in England to carry royal status, a notch or two ahead in terms of kudos. That simple five-letter word 'royal' can make a small, perhaps subconscious, but vital difference to perceptions of students and would-be students, as Branagh maintained it did with both his parents and Berkshire County Council when it came to attracting permission to study there from the one and funding for his course from the other.

Situated in premises on Gower Street near London's West End, cheek by jowl with a number of the buildings of the University of London, RADA owes much of its finance to a bequest from George Bernard Shaw. When the writer died in 1950, he appointed the Public Trustee to administer income from performances of his plays whilst they remained in copyright for the joint benefit of the British Museum Reading Room (as the British Library then was) and the drama school. RADA thus had a certain amount of assured income above and beyond tutorial fees and whatever other private and public munificence it might attract. The twenty to thirty students of each year's intake received a thorough training in various approaches to acting (improvisation, the Stanislavski 'Method' and so forth), as well as in music and movement to equip them with as comprehensive an arsenal as possible for a career in a large and diverse profession.

Branagh himself, discussing his RADA years, has made the most of the opportunities to ridicule himself: the callowness, arrogance, instinct to overplay. Like Olivier, his confessions are a double-bluff, a strategy acted out openly by his character in *Peter's Friends*. Exhaustively he lays bare all his faults, to his audiences on and off the screen, then in effect pleads, 'But you still like me a bit, don't you?' in the hope that his disarming candour will win us over. The fundamental Ken can't, he repeatedly protests, tolerate all the twee socialising so beloved of theatre types, but the facts and the accounts of those around him give the lie to his protestations. For Branagh doesn't simply name-check or dine with those he admires: he repeatedly and compulsively employs them. His personal rep company ranges from Alex Lowe (who played his public-school 'fag' in his first professional stage engagement, *Another Country*), through his family (wife, mother-in-law and sister-in-law) to early idols (Derek Jacobi and Judi Dench). None of his own stage or screen projects has failed to include a number of people known to him from earlier encounters and subsequently invited on board with him. He has defended himself by saying, 'Despite the notion that I always work with the same people, I try to change at least half of them for new stimulus,' but in the theatre and film worlds even that remaining half is an extraordinarily high proportion to work with on a semi-regular basis.

It was at RADA that he made contact with the first of those he would later enrol: twenty-six-year-old Scottish student John Marshall, who arrived a few days late from the Canadian university where he had been finishing a doctoral thesis in English and who, as John Sessions, would be one of the leading lights in the revival of improvised comedy a few years later (and who described Ken as the worst-dressed student at RADA); principal Hugh Cruttwell, who appeared so underwhelmed by Ken's first audition for the academy but whom, since setting up Renaissance, Ken has used on several occasions as an artistic adviser and second pair of eyes (to direct the director when he's on camera); even Sir John Gielgud, who, as patron of the academy, gave the star-struck student a few tips when he first essayed the part of Hamlet, and was recently cast by Branagh the director in his short film version of an Anton Chekhov story, *Swan Song* (which received an Oscar nomination) and in the title role of a radio production of *King Lear* to celebrate the knight's ninetieth birthday. This behaviour shows the same complexity of motives as his oscillating sense of national belonging; in this case the apparent elements are genuine indebtedness, a desire to be seen to have been assimilated by this world, and (no doubt unconsciously) the old showing-off impulse taken to a more abstract level – he works with such people not just because they are good but also simply because he can.

In order to reach the point where he could make such acknowledgements through his casting, though, he had first to become an actor. Drama school was a round of sweating through movement classes and overcoming embarrassment at having to wear dance tights; of learning his way around a musical score and battling through numbers performed in front of students and staff (a torture from which he fled in terror on the first occasion before gritting his teeth and returning); and of participating in a variety of exercises intended to hone the skills of observation and perception necessary to an actor, from impersonating zoo animals (craftily, he chose to be a crocodile, lying immobile and watching the other goings-on through narrowed eyes) to walking blindfold around the busy streets of central London.

But in a profession where more work is now generated by film and television than stage productions, actual tuition in screen acting was limited, at that time, to spending one day in a television studio. 'Hugh [Cruttwell] said something with which I subsequently profoundly disagreed,' said Ken fifteen years later. 'He said any actor worth his salt can learn everything there is to know about screen acting in a day. *This is not the case!*' He acknowledged that his privileged position as a director had taught him a great deal about screen acting. 'The last year I've spent in the editing room watching a whole disparate bunch of people. I'm only just beginning to discover what the differences are ... There's a sort of vocabulary ... And I'm sometimes guilty – *mea culpa* – of doing too much or of playing to the camera. There's [sic] a trillion things you don't know unless you do it.' With the exception of the inadequate consideration given to screen acting, RADA was in effect dedicated to doing as much as possible and across as broad a range as possible.

Above all, Branagh the student had to learn to accept and use criticism. Being taken apart for essaying too broad a characterisation or for over-reliance on a vocal quirk to define a role and taking on board the notes given by a director instead of remaining chained to one's own original conception is a talent in itself, and one which Ken had discovered with shocking suddenness at his re-audition with Hugh Cruttwell, when his performance was dissected to the point at which he 'dried' and real work could begin. Always a first-class acting 'technician', Ken had painstakingly to learn how to subordinate himself to a role in order to bring out what lay in it, rather than imposing his own performance devices upon it. To this day, director Kenneth Branagh seems more inclined to let actor Kenneth Branagh get away with such short-cuts – it is often noticeable that other directors are more successful at getting Ken to 'do less' on screen, and let the script and the camera do as much of the work as they properly can, than he is when directing himself. Branagh protests that he never knowingly takes such soft options, and works unremittingly to prevent it – another log on the fire of his compulsion to keep working, and working intensively.

He also laboured to overcome his tendency to corpse. It's amusing to see actors collapsing in giggles on collections of film and television out-takes, and it can occasionally enliven a stage production (some pantomimes are even known to include 'rehearsed corpses' to heighten the innocent audience's enjoyment by suggesting that the cast are also finding the show dreadfully funny). As a chronic affliction in an actor, though, corpsing is a curse, not to mention a royal pain to the other unfortunates onstage who have to put up with it. The only possible way to cure it is to shame the perpetrator into keeping a tighter rein on himself by tearing him off a strip every time it happens. This was the method practised by Noël Coward on the young Laurence Olivier in a production of *Private Lives*, and Kenneth Branagh found himself subjected to numerous wiggings at RADA for dissolving helplessly, often with no discernible reason. The sense of embarrassment and betrayal of his fellow actors made him less prone to corpsing, but the trait has never been eradicated: in the mid-1980s, during the filming of Ibsen's *Ghosts* for BBC Television, he suffered such an acute attack of giggles (provoked by a mischievous Michael Gambon) that he was ordered ignominiously out of the studio. Not even on the stage of the Royal Shakespeare Theatre at Stratford-upon-Avon, as the incarnation of lonely majesty King Henry V, would the titters ever be completely banished.

Shakespeare, of course, constituted a sizeable part of the RADA course, both in terms of full productions and of individual scenes worked on in classes. Ken's accounts of his first encounters with the Bard vary from telling to telling; undoubtedly the most bizarre version was given in a 1994 lecture as part of a National Film Theatre Shakespeare season. 'I remember a piece by Peter Sellers on Radio 3,' he said, 'doing "A Hard Day's Night" in the style of Richard III. That introduced me to a series of phrases that had worked themselves into the popular culture, like "Alas, poor Yorick, I knew him well" (although it's actually "I knew him, Horatio"), so I had a second- or third-hand understanding of that.' He claimed his earliest direct exposure was 'in Belfast, aged about nine, seeing a television version of *Hamlet* with Richard Chamberlain, who was known at the time for playing Doctor Kildare; even I remember ITV being very pleased with this, putting on a Shakespeare play over all of Sunday night – something they wouldn't do now, I might add.' The Shakespeare on film which first captivated him had been 'Joseph Mankiewicz's *Julius Caesar*. I thought Brando was marvellous, but Gielgud and [James] Mason were absolutely wonderful.' His initial experience of Shakespeare on stage had been at the age of thirteen, on a school trip to see *Romeo and Juliet* at St George's Theatre, Tufnell Park in north London, with Peter McEnery and Sarah Badel in the title roles: 'There was a lot of miming going on, which was very tough with a bunch of thirteen-year-olds.' At RADA he would find himself on the receiving end of the same experience.

Acting is not simply a matter of technique, but of making contact with an audience. Every actor dreads the mortuary atmosphere of an empty house – playing to 'two men and a dog'. Emma Thompson, in performances during the summer in Cambridge, most likely had to tussle with audiences full of the foreign language students who descend on the town during July and August and insist on supplying voluble running commentaries to shows, usually in high-octane Italian. Probably the most chilling trial is playing to an audience who don't actually want to be there, as Ken found when RADA toured *The Merchant of Venice* around comprehensive schools in north London. Silent indifference to a play is one thing, outright bored hostility quite another. The horrific experience would be filed for future reference when Ken formulated the approach of Renaissance, with its priority of making Shakespeare popular and accessible.

His contacts with the great and the good continued. With typical audacity, Branagh wrote a letter requesting advice on his interpretation of Chebutykin in Chekhov's *Three Sisters* to no less a personage than Lord Olivier. He was astonished to receive a reply; no matter that the great man offered no practical pointers – the fact that he had simply bothered to write was enough to give an enormous boost to Ken's confidence.

When a visit by Her Majesty the Queen and the Duke of Edinburgh was announced to commemorate the academy's seventy-fifth anniversary, Ken and John Marshall were

67

among the first to volunteer to perform in the concert to be presented before the royal couple. The future John Sessions' proposal to perform a three-minute improvisation was hastily rejected – Hugh Cruttwell explained, choking back his laughter, that he couldn't risk an item which had every possibility of jumping the rails of decorum – but Ken took the opportunity to request that he perform a soliloquy from *Hamlet*. Cruttwell agreed, and after detailed rehearsals told the would-be Prince that the academy's president, Sir John Gielgud, might be prepared to look over his rendition before the 'command performance' itself. Nerves took over, and Ken gave a wildly exaggerated, crass performance of the 'rogue and peasant slave' speech before the knight, who was nonetheless gracious and generous in his advice afterwards. The final concert performance was more controlled, and when the students were presented to the Queen and Prince Philip, Gielgud also passed on his congratulations.

At RADA Ken also made the acquaintance of the man who would later direct his own first play, *Public Enemy*. Malcolm McKay directed him in three shows at the academy, beginning with *A Midsummer Night's Dream*, in which (as in the later Renaissance production) he played Peter Quince, the leader of the group of 'rude mechanicals' who stage the play within the play. 'He was brilliant as a sort of Ronald Coleman, with a cigarette and a little satchel and notebook. It was a very, very funny production – John Sessions was Snout. But it was a small exercise, really – we cut it down to an hour and a half – and there's not an enormous amount to say about it.'

Their next show together, a stage version of James Hadley Chase's *No Orchids For Miss Blandish*, was 'much more violent', according to McKay. 'John Sessions played a New York cop, one line and very serious about it. Ken was very sharp, very hard-edged' as Eddie Schultz. Branagh himself describes his performance as a homage to Al Pacino in the *Godfather* movies. ('I hadn't noticed the Pacino myself,' says McKay, 'but if that's what he says he was doing...').

Ken's first serious love affair, with a fellow RADA student, was by his own account as fraught as most student relationships, with the added dimension of the pair having to use their emotions in classes together, to the bemusement and embarrassment of class-mates and unknowing teachers. (Unlike Olivier, the confessional impulse fails Branagh in personal matters.) They moved into a flat in Willesden Green together towards the end of Ken's first year at the school, and stayed together on and off until 1983, when they admitted the relationship was doomed due to his non-stop working.

Branagh's autobiography *Beginning* names the woman in question as Wendy Seagram. However, neither RADA, the Royal Shakespeare Company nor Equity has ever had a Wendy Seagram on their register. Ken had given her a pseudonym to protect either her or himself. However, once again this impulse to keep the private life of a public figure private backfired, and 'Seagram's' true identity became a topic of contention in itself. *Today* newspaper in 1989 speculated that she might be one of Vanessa Redgrave's daughters, Joely or Natasha Richardson. Natasha was a blatant example of fabrication arising from a desire to generate for Ken a knotty, involved history. She later went on to live with Robert Fox, the producer of the play in which Ken made his first professional stage appearance, *Another Country*, breaking up his marriage to casting director Celestia Fox. Natasha also appeared with Branagh in a BBC television version of Ibsen's *Ghosts* and in the film *A Month in the Country*, although she shared scarcely a scene with him in the latter. She is now married to Ken's compatriot, Ballymena-born Liam Neeson. Ken was involved with Joely Richardson for a while in the mid-1980s, a relationship which broke up with some acrimony, but this postdates his time at RADA and the RSC.

'Wendy Seagram' is in fact actress Katy Behean, a contemporary of Ken's at RADA, who played Lady Anne to his Richard Crookback in *Richard III* in class work and, according to Malcolm McKay, was 'brilliant, fabulous – she stole the show' as the fearsome Ma Grissom in *No Orchids For Miss Blandish*. Behean refuses to discuss the relationship, but it is

69

noticeable that despite a reputable acting career including a good deal of work at the Royal Shakespeare Company she has never worked professionally with Branagh.

Life in Willesden Green was not exactly idyllic: in winter the flat was an icebox, and meals often consisted of casseroles cooked all day on low heat while Ken and Katy were at the academy. Although he claims to like cooking, few other people have testified to cuisine being a Branagh forte. When he and Emma Thompson were in Hollywood to make *Dead Again* she once unwisely let him cook her a meal. It began with cream of mushroom soup – sliced mushrooms in a pot of warmed cream; she discreetly refrained from inquiring what he'd done to the main-course casserole. Like virtually all student cooking, Branagh and Behean's meals tended towards the cheap and cheerful, not so much cordon bleu as cordon blimey.

The range of parts and plays at RADA was necessarily eclectic: Ken was an eighteenth-century fop in Congreve's *The Old Bachelor*, a rustic in Edward Bond's *The Sea*, a middle-aged leftie – 'the old queen upstairs,' in the words of another cast member – in Dusty Hughes' *Commitments* (not to be confused with the Roddy Doyle story) and 'a mad animal' in the play which once held the world record for the longest title, *The Persecution and Assassination of Jean-Paul Marat as Performed by the Inmates of the Asylum of Charenton Under the Direction of the Marquis de Sade* by Peter Weiss (universally known, thank Heaven, as the *Marat/Sade*).

However, after his Hamlet soliloquy before the Queen, Ken had argued passionately in a letter to Cruttwell that he should be allowed to play the Prince in a full production. After appropriate thought, his request was granted in the first term of his final year.

The scheduling was a boon: the third year at RADA becomes preoccupied with presentations of plays and speeches before agents and directors as students become increasingly conscious of the dog-eat-dog profession waiting at the end of their course and aware of their need to get on to an agent's books if they are to have any hope of regular work. Ken, while working as a janitor at St Martin's School of Art, spent much of the summer sending copies of his curriculum vitae and publicity picture to repertory theatres all over the UK, whose responses were predictable: perfunctory and non-committal at best, or just plain silent. His performance in *No Orchids For Miss Blandish* had attracted the attention of an agent, but for some reason he felt that she would not be the best representative of his interests. Immediately he heard that his *Hamlet* had been given the green light, he wrote to Patricia Marmont, a former actress who had appeared in, amongst other things, the film version of Tennessee Williams' *Suddenly Last Summer* with Montgomery Clift and Elizabeth Taylor, and who now ran her own agency. Marmont had given a talk at RADA on the actor-agent relationship, and now Ken invited her to *Hamlet* with a view to accepting him as a client.

Again, Malcolm McKay directed, and remembers that Branagh 'took it terribly seriously; it was his big thing at RADA. He did a lot of work at home. He's a delight to work with as an actor: very fast, great facility, very bright – he does things before you have finished asking him to do them. And I would say he was generally quite admired by the other students. He's not a braggart, he doesn't swagger around. He kept himself to himself, and his relationship with Katy seemed to be fairly stable.' In fact, the stresses of living and working in each other's pockets had led Branagh and Behean to stop living together. During this fraught period, according to Ken's memoirs, art imitated life in a most agonising fashion. The two were asked in an improvisation class to pretend to be parting lovers dividing up the property in their flat. After the real-life move, though, matters between them had become easier; they had spent a happy summer together, including a visit to Reading while Ken's parents were off on holiday.

However, rehearsals brought their own problems. One of the other actors seemed to be deliberately intimidating Ken. After having had to put up with being bullied at school in Reading, he was once again reduced to a state of nervous terror for the first week of rehearsal. He didn't confide his fears to anyone involved in the production, and only with hindsight can Malcolm McKay recognise that the air of menace surrounding Mario Arambides, who played Claudius, could so have affected Ken. 'Mario was a very frightening Mexican-American, and to be honest I think he was a bit pissed off that he wasn't playing Hamlet. I liked him very much, but I know he frightened other people; I'd no idea that Ken was in this state of paranoia about him. It was his ferocity – and I'm not talking about "luvvy" ferocity. Mario was the real thing, he'd been in Vietnam . . . he was quite tough to handle.'

And, despite the early traumas, the show went off generally well. McKay compares it favourably to Ken's later Renaissance production of the play directed by Derek Jacobi: 'Although technically the Jacobi was more accomplished, I thought his RADA show was better because he was less confident and more vulnerable.

'The thing to bear in mind about Ken is that he's fantastically talented in all departments but he's not a heavyweight, a great visionary artist. As an actor he's superbly professional, very imaginative. As a film director he has no great art, but he has had one *brilliant* idea, and like all brilliant ideas it's dead simple and dead obvious: that Shakespeare is a popular playwright, and ideal Hollywood material. Ken has always regarded Shakespeare in those terms, and he's absolutely right. That idea of making it clear: people who can fall in love at first sight across a crowded room, people who get angry enough to kill immediately, people who live their lives according to honour – these are old concepts but they still have a great contemporary meaning. Shakespeare's "poetry" has no meaning to anybody, much as the RSC would like to think it does. But his great love of humanity still has a phenomenal meaning, and Ken's realised that.

'As a writer Ken's yet to be proved. But the point about him is the package. You take those three talents and add a phenomenal energy – he gets up at six in the morning, works fucking hard – and an overdose of charm, which can win the world on its own. That's the secret of his success.'

Success – and slotting in multiple commitments – started early, even before he had graduated from RADA. *Hamlet* coincided with the coup of securing the title role in *Too Late to Talk to Billy*, written for BBC Northern Ireland's television drama department by Graham Reid. Ken had spotted the original advertisement for the part in the actors' weekly newspaper *The Stage* whilst in Reading with Behean; chivvied by her into ringing director Paul Seed, he then had to journey to London to deliver his c.v. and photograph to BBC Television Centre. The offer of an audition came that same afternoon. Ken was surprised and elated at the audition to find that his RADA contemporary John (professionally known as Colum) Convey had also been called, for the part of Billy's best friend Ian. However, although the pair made a strong impression, Seed and producer Chris Parr were reluctant to cast Ken if he refused to give up *Hamlet* to make room. In the end, they arranged to begin rehearsals in London to accommodate him and even to negotiate with Equity to secure the temporary union card necessary for the work. Hugh Cruttwell, for his part, excused Ken from his small role in one of the term's other productions, Feydeau's *A Flea in Her Ear*. All he needed in the end was one day off from *Hamlet* rehearsals, and the juggling of schedules was conducted in a low-key, matter-of-fact way. 'One day he came up to me,' says Malcolm McKay, 'and told me, very politely as he always does, had a day or two off; came back, gave me a bottle of Scotch and that was that, it was forgotten.'

The performances of *Hamlet* went off tolerably well, although Ken was tired and distracted on the second night after a day's rehearsal for *Billy*, and fluffed his lines a few times. His delivery had a nervous speed, and he tended to over-emphasise the 'antic' aspect of Hamlet's 'antic disposition', going too readily for the comedy in his portrayal of the Prince's feigned madness. Nonetheless, Pat Marmont invited him to consider joining her books whilst he was in Belfast for the television shoot. Branagh's father had tried to dissuade him from taking the part of Billy, telling his son, 'If you're going to do things like that you'll not get anywhere.' Ken was to prove him spectacularly wrong.

The play, set in the late 1970s in the Protestant Sandy Row-Donegall Pass area a couple of miles south of Ken's early home turf, is a family drama behind which the Troubles are little more than a backdrop. In the play the Loyalist paramilitary UDA (which had not yet been proscribed by the government) is a cross between a social club and a way of dignifying the macho impulses of local Napoleons. The Martin family is not involved in such shenanigans; with their mother dying of cancer and their father Norman a drunken brute, it falls to Lorna and Billy to look after their younger sisters. But Billy's hatred of his father's unthinking selfish cruelty threatens paradoxically to turn him into the same kind of man. Surly and truculent, he spoils for the definitive conflict with Norman which never comes; unable to tell his girlfriend of his love for her, he sulks about middle-class values when she leaves for university in England. Billy is Coolderry Street's rebel without a cause, unable to articulate what he wants but wanting it now.

For any young actor's first professional work, it would have been the luckiest of breaks; for Ken it was astonishing. He brooded magnificently and, although he showed a tendency to be too strident, at other moments this first-timer embraced the idea of screen acting as 'doing less' – he let Reid's script speak for itself and resisted the temptation to fill awkward silences with facial acting and its attendant danger of crossing over into mugging. The central trio of Branagh, Bríd Brennan as Lorna and James Ellis (still remembered at the time as Sergeant Bert Lynch in fifteen years of the BBC police series *Z Cars*) cast against type as Norman drew universal plaudits: the *Guardian* critic described his Billy as 'storing anger like a bomb under his coat, but with an acute sense of duty and responsibility towards his sisters, and a capacity for tenderness that he will not allow to become commitment.' The play became a trilogy and then a tetralogy, and Billy Branagh changed his mind about the wisdom of his son taking the part.

'The script was too near the bone for him,' mused Ken. 'It was taking him back to his childhood, to growing up in Belfast.'

Ken's return to Belfast for filming reawakened the problems of identity. There he was, a native of Northern Ireland, making his living in Northern Ireland as a Northern Irishman, but living in England and speaking with a now naturally English voice – not a true Brit, but too fake an Ulsterman to be able to drink in pubs with old Belfast mates without people querying his accent. 'A regional accent can be a liability in London,' he later said. 'It's wrong, but that's the way it is. I went away from Belfast and lost mine.' Yet he did so more deliberately than the remark suggested, in order not just to get work but to fit in. 'Then, ironically, I had to brush up on my Belfast again for Billy. It wasn't difficult, it was always there in the back of my mind. Afterwards, for a while, I was only offered parts playing wild Belfast fellows.' In Belfast he took refuge in assuming a Billy-like character offscreen as well as on it. 'You can act tough, so long as you've seen enough Clint Eastwood films and been convinced by them. In Belfast, I kept being Billy. People knew that Billy was a surly git, so I'd keep up that look as if to say, "I'll be just about civil but don't you come any closer."' The complexities of nationality would subside only when he had forged an identity for himself as an individual – or, at least, a reputation.

The remainder of his final term at RADA was taken up with a production of *The White Devil*, John Webster's Jacobean tragedy, after the first night of which fellow students bawled him out for his attempts to imbue the character of Antonelli with a kind of villainous *loucherie*. The end of term, the play's last night and his twenty-first birthday coincided. Although none of his year at the academy had work waiting for them, he was at least in a better position than most: he had not only an agent (agreeing to join Marmont Management's client list had been a foregone conclusion), but the title role in a soon-to-be-screened television play. The beginnings of the reputation which would give him a more concrete sense of identity were not yet in place, but, although the insecure graduate could not yet see it himself, lay in prospect. The first phase of that reputation consisted of a double whammy thrusting him into the critical consciousness: *Billy* and the stage production he joined a few months after leaving RADA: *Another Country*.

5

The Sun Has Got His Hat On

Emma Thompson graduated from Cambridge with a good 2:1 in English, a theatrical agent (Richard Armitage of the Noel Gay Organisation had in fact signed her up on the strength of the 1979 revue *Nightcap* at the end of her first year – he also took on Fry and Laurie, and since his death Noel Gay have continued to represent all three through Lorraine Hamilton's semi-autonomous agency) and a frenzy of attention paid to her Footlights generation.

The Cellar Tapes won the inaugural Perrier Award for comedy on the Edinburgh Fringe and, following on from the company's brief appearance on television a couple of years earlier, the BBC filmed a TV special of material from the show (broadcast, misleadingly, as *The 1982 Cambridge Footlights Revue* in May of that year). Thompson, Fry and Laurie then embarked on an eight-week tour of Australia along with Footlights colleague Robert Bathurst, subsequently a comedy actor. This show, *Beyond the Footlights*, subsequently enjoyed a run at the Lyric Theatre, Hammersmith; a brief mention in a *Sunday Times* theatre review named only one performer: 'Emma Thompson will go further,' wrote Robert Hewison with punning prescience, and most major critics singled her out for greater success. It's worth noting in passing that *Beyond the Footlights* also played two nights at the Riverside Theatre, Coleraine, Co. Londonderry, in April 1982 – so Emma performed on a Northern Irish stage more than two years before her future husband played on his native soil.

The idiosyncratic charm that drew so many to her at Cambridge also stood her in good stead professionally; 'a mixture of confidence and innocence and directness' is Robert Bathurst's analysis of this quality in her. 'All sorts of people have just gone completely weak at the knees over her. She is able not to seem too keen for their favours and I suspect that's immensely appealing.'

The Footlights connection certainly did her no harm either. Although both the Cambridge student press and Edinburgh Fringe reviews now have a long-established tradition of bemoaning Footlights revues for not being as wonderful as their illustrious forebears, *The Cellar Tapes* emphatically bucked that trend (to the extent that the class of '81 are now regularly cited as the most recent of the aforementioned illustrious forebears). In addition, Martin Bergman had acquired an early reputation at the university as a 'mover and shaker'. 'He was already being very smooth, wearing leather jackets, going to London and coming back with contracts,' recalled Kim Harris. 'To us, still essentially sixth-formers, he was remarkable.' Moreover, Jan Ravens had by 1981 joined the BBC as the only female radio producer in its Light Entertainment section. Ravens didn't set out to stamp a feminist agenda on to radio comedy – 'I wanted it to seep insidiously into people's brains that women could be as funny' – but she did produce the first series to have more women than men in the cast, *Three Plus One on Four*, the three being Alison Steadman, Denise Coffey and Emma Thompson. *Three Plus One* ran for only one series on Radio 4, partly due to the outcry caused by a sketch about female orgasms which was broadcast at the end of an edition and outraged a number of listeners who had just tuned in for the following programme, the revered radio institution *Desert Island Discs*. Midway through the series, Emma was replaced by Susan Deneker as other commitments left her unable to complete the stint.

It was Emma's good luck to arrive on to the comedy scene just as a new wave of performers was coming to the fore. The Comic Strip Club, then at pornographer Paul Raymond's Revue Bar in Soho, had launched a wave of 'alternative' comedians. Although the 1960s television programmes of David Frost (particularly *That Was the Week That Was*) had more or less rediscovered the power of political satire as a comic form, it rapidly proved too hot for the televisual powers-that-were to handle: *TW3* itself ran for only one series, and the satirical elements of *Not the Nine O'Clock News*, which began in 1979, have generally been exaggerated in the popular memory; they consisted in fact largely of brief mock newscasts in each edition. But a number of young comedians on the live circuit were beginning not so much to satirise the barbarisms of the early Thatcher period as simply to hold them up to ridicule within the format of otherwise normal stand-up routines. Such an awareness, coupled with the post-*Python* generation's heightened sense of the absurd – the comedy of non sequiturs and ludicrous juxtapositions – inspired this otherwise disparate group to combat the frilly-shirted bigotry of the Bernard Manning school of comedy with their own more radical styles

'Alternative' comedy was simply a useful umbrella term for a clutch of fresh performers who happened to emerge at around the same time. Dawn French and Jennifer Saunders, two trainee teachers, began their career at the Comic Strip, as did Alexei Sayle and others; a number of forgotten names concealed comedians now widely known – performance poets Twentieth Century Coyote included Manchester University graduate Rik Mayall, Fiasco Job Job was a double act consisting of Arthur Smith (later author of the hit play *An Evening With Gary Lineker*) and Rupert Gavin, now a senior executive with British Telecom and also the man behind major comedy-theatre producers Incidental.

Television executives knew that something was happening on the comedy scene, but didn't quite know how to package it for mass consumption on the small screen. The absurdity proved easier to televise (or at any rate less discomfiting for producers) than the political aspect, and the mock-spontaneous anything-can-happen 'zoo TV' format which later crystallised on the UK's *Saturday Live* and *Friday Night Live* series with Jonathan Ross had not yet come into its own. Series such as Channel 4's *Chelmsford 123* were erratic, but at least constituted a welcome change from sitcoms set in suburbia. One of the more successful series was Granada's *Alfresco* for the ITV network, which put 'alternative' comedians Ben Elton and Robbie Coltrane together with *Cellar Tapes* alumni Fry, Laurie and Emma Thompson. 'We're trying to play down our Footlights past,' she said at the time. 'We're not trying to deny it, but it has such a powerful aura that when you leave you feel a bit wary about the name. We all grew up on *Monty Python* – the other shows we're too young to remember.'

Ben Elton was already well known as the writer of the BBC2 'students from hell' series *The Young Ones* (with Rik Mayall, Adrian Edmondson and Nigel Planer, who would later be the voice on the 1990s revisions of *The Magic Roundabout*), and subsequently wrote his *Alfresco* colleagues into an episode in the BBC show's second series as the 'Footlights College, Oxbridge' team in a take-off of TV quiz programme *University Challenge*. Stephen Fry had appeared on the show's real-life counterpart in the Queens' College team and now played the part of Lord Snot; one of his team-mates was the bejewelled, braying Miss Money-Sterling, who interrupted the question 'What is the chemical equation . . .' to titter, 'I've got a Porsche – eoh, and Daddy sends hugs.' Emma and the Footlights group weren't exactly playing down their past on this occasion as she bantered inanely with Griff Rhys-Jones, who was parodying quizmaster Bamber Gascoigne. (An unsubstantiated rumour a little earlier had linked Thompson's and Rhys-Jones' names briefly, but no evidence has ever come to light to confirm the whispers.) Whatever Elton's later reputation as the soundest of ideologically sound comedians, his first success came with the exuberantly puerile humour of *The Young Ones*. Its stereotyped portrayal of unwashed, bickering students who wouldn't recognise a set of lecture notes if they jumped up and started nibbling their acne was cherished by the very community it lampooned, and Fry, Laurie and Thompson were happy to poke fun at their own varsity background.

On the subject of *Alfresco*, Elton was candid about the sporadic chaos of the series: 'On occasion scripts weren't finished when we went out to shoot. We spent all day filming one sketch leaving only fifteen minutes for a fight scene that would normally take a day to film. We decided to do it all in one mad go and it was just at the end when I was supposed to fall eight feet backwards that I remembered we hadn't put the mattresses in place. Naturally I refused to fall, stopped fighting and started arguing with the film crew. We've kept that in the show because it's good improvisation.'

Alfresco got off to a shaky start, but gathered critical and audience momentum and ran for two series. The performers, all given their first major television exposure, drew favourable opinions – 'They are all rather good,' puzzled the patrician *Sunday Telegraph*, apparently under the misapprehension common to older viewers that 'alternative comedy' more usually meant an alternative *to* comedy. From the outset, however, Emma was the critical darling: 'She is going to be a star,' noted one perceptive critic on a regional paper, while the *Daily Express* was even more fulsome: 'If Emma Thompson doesn't become the brightest new comedy star of the galaxy . . . there ain't no justice.' She had writing and performing talent, intelligence, the ideological awareness and argumentative stamina to go ten rounds with Elton and could blend them all with an articulacy which proved both attractive and daunting. Emma returned to the Edinburgh Fringe in 1983 with a one-woman show entitled *Short Vehicle*, which included material by Fry, Laurie, Ben Elton and Andy de la Tour. But the bulk of the material came from her: 'It's terrifying,' she confided beforehand. 'I've been trudging round cafés trying to get ideas [by eavesdropping]. I've never been keen on jokes. I like the different ways people speak: they're almost invariably funny.'

Professional ambition overrode her personal life. She had a

brief relationship with singer Red Stripe from an *a cappella* vocal group The Flying Pickets, but there were no major love affairs. 'She used to moan all the time about how she was never asked out by men,' according to an employee of Noel Gay at the time. 'Mind you, she didn't exactly dress to attract – she'd have her hair scraped back and wore leggings, brightly coloured socks, Doc Marten's, big, grungy jumpers and anoraks.'

Emma used her rising profile from *Alfresco* and spots on *Carrott's Lib* and *Saturday Live* (the American show held rights to the full title, so for legal reasons the word *Night* could only be included once the Channel 4 programme had moved to Friday) in order to lend more public support to causes close to her heart. When a benefit music and comedy show, *The Big One*, was staged for CND at the Apollo Victoria Theatre in London's West End early in 1984, she compèred it, though on this occasion she did come across to some as the bourgeois banner-waver: the *New Musical Express* called her 'unashamedly upper-middle-class' and sneered, 'Her monologues, patter and sulphurous rapport with her victims in the audience *were* hilarious, but you couldn't help noticing how high she carried her pert, blasé little nose.'

An ill-advised spontaneous comic routine the previous year had provided her with her first experience of abjectly dying before an audience. Unfortunately, it happened to be at a mass rally. She remembered, 'Absolutely the worst moment I ever had was trying to do five minutes' stand-up comedy on Nelson's Column during a Reagan Out CND march I was co-ordinating in 1983. At the time I was boldly trying to discover for myself if I could do stand-up and whether it was a direction in which I wanted to go. That occasion was gross, the most frightening thing I've ever done. I should have been warned. Beforehand I was standing in a lorry marshalling, doing the "could little Willie please find his mum?" routine. And then I thought, "It's a hot day. They've had a long wait. I'll do a monologue." So I started, and halfway through this woman came up, grabbed me and hissed, "If you can't say something sensible, *shut up!*" It was said so viciously that I apologised.

At eighteen, Ken had already grasped the value of publicity, as shown in this local press shot when he won a place at RADA *(Camera Press)*

A pert young Emma, at the time of *Alfresco* *(Universal Pictorial Press)*

OH BOYFRIENDS!

Like a chappie to cheer you up? We've got loads of great guys who'd just love to write to *you!*

Sixteen-year old **Ken Branagh** is a sports fanatic, but in between huffin' an' puffin' he also finds time for a bit of guitar playing and listening to music (his fave is Wings)! He'd like to write to a young lady of fifteen plus, over 5ft, not fussy about looks but please send photo to:

Steve Butler is Ken's mate and he's a bit more fussy about his girls — he doesn't like 'em to wear too much make-up! He's also sixteen, likes listening to Cockney Rebel and making friends and would like a girl (over fifteen) to write to him at: **62 Virginia Way, Southcote, Reading, Berks.** Send photo please.

An early press appearance in *Oh Boy! (IPC)*

Ken as King Henry V in the 1984 RSC production. *(Siôn Probert)*

Emma with Stephen Fry, linchpin of her Footlights company and writer of
Me and My Girl (Camera Press)

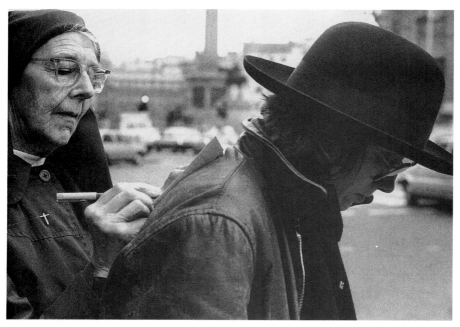

Thompson the campaigner: giving physical support to a CND petition (above) and with Julie Christie and Caron Keating, handing in an Oxfam petition about Kampuchea to 10 Downing Street *(Times Newspapers)*

Ken and Emma as Guy and Harriet Pringle in *Fortunes of War (Camera Press)*

Two faces of Branagh in the Renaissance Shakespeare tour: as Benedick in *Much Ado About Nothing* and (an Archie Rice-like) Touchstone in *As You Like It* *(Camera Press)*

Ken woos Emma
on screen in
Henry V . . .
(Kobal Collection)

. . . and weds her
in real life at
Cliveden House
(Rex Features)

When they married they were playing the ultimate unhappy modern couple in *Look Back in Anger (Camera Press)*

She was there because she was worried about nuclear weapons and quite reasonably thought it was flippant for somebody to do a monologue of a comic nature. It taught me a lot . . . I realise how easy it is to offend if they don't know you and don't pick up on the irony. I just *died*. I was wearing a bright turquoise summer thingy and couldn't change into a disguise or put on a moustache. I would have been quite happy for the bomb to drop on me immediately. That's very sick, very funny, be careful how you put it.'

Emma has never shirked putting both her money and her considerable commitment where her mouth is in terms of important causes. The 'Votes SWP' line in her *Cellar Tapes* programme biography was most likely self-parody – her idealism is consistently tempered with realism, and the mature Thompson would certainly devote little time to such a marginal political outfit. Nevertheless, she is active in the Labour Party, having donated over £2,000 to the Hampstead branch in 1993. It is not beyond the bounds of probability that she may some day follow in the footsteps of another Oscar-winning actress who now sits as the Labour Member of Parliament for the Hampstead and Highgate constituency, Glenda Jackson.

In addition to the CND appearances mentioned above, Emma persuaded her then-fiancé that performances of *Look Back in Anger* in 1989 should be staged for the benefit of Friends of the Earth – Ken went so far in his support as to voice-over a 1990 *Disappearing World*-style television documentary about the gathering wildlife and ecological catastrophe. She was a vigorous campaigner against the 1992 Gulf War, addressing rallies at which she poured scorn on the notion of limited, strategic, 'surgical' bombing. Theatre and politics combined in a 1993 campaign to save the concept of theatre in education, as government cuts and national curriculum prescriptions threatened to send many companies working in this valuable field to the wall. Prominent supporters included the National Theatre's artistic director Richard Eyre, Sir Anthony Hopkins and Emma. Later in 1993 her name was linked with that of the Princess of Wales in an appeal for £1.45 million to renovate London's Serpentine Gallery, a cause with scant ideological dimension to it beyond another indirect comment on the level of arts funding offered by the Conservative government, a topic which constantly exercises Branagh.

Thompson is conscious of the asset that her name can be to a campaign or appeal (although she would balk at being called a 'celebrity', with its connotations of those who are inexplicably famous simply for being well known), and uses that cachet adroitly. Comments such as 'I wouldn't go within a hundred miles of a fur coat' are made in the awareness that she is not only speaking her own mind but keeping a particular cause in the public's line of sight. When Oxfam, Christian Aid and CAFOD organised a petition in 1989 to protest against the continuing representation of Cambodia/Kampuchea in the United Nations by members of the genocidal former Khmer Rouge regime, the signatures were delivered to number 10 Downing Street by actress and campaigner Julie Christie, then children's television presenter Caron Keating and Emma (who had also gone on the Oxfam-organised fast for Kampuchea in 1988, the idea being that instead of eating for a day, people donated the corresponding money to alleviate the hardships in that country). She also supported the Sandinista government in Nicaragua against the American-backed campaign of destabilisation in the 1980s.

However, her beliefs are more than simply a matter of public relations. In 1993 the cover feature of *Time* magazine reported that she tithes to charities, and was probably not speaking figuratively. That represents a great deal of money. Although Emma said at the time of her Merchant Ivory films *Howards End* and *The Remains of the Day* that neither she nor Ken had ever been paid more than $250,000 for a film role, industry sources estimate that her going rate may now be in the $3 to $5 million bracket per film. To commit one-tenth of such sums to donations makes her one of Britain's most generous private philanthropists; to do so without making a song and dance about it is a weighty testimony to the sincerity of her beliefs, not simply in the relevant causes themselves, but in the duty of those who are in a position to help to do what they can.

Her abiding preoccupation is the status of women in society; their continuing marginalisation, whether conscious or not, and their under-representation at senior levels in all walks of life. She would be the first to point out that this is not a 'minority' cause – women form 53 per cent of the planet's population, after all. Nor does she raise the issue by tiresome soap-boxing. Since her years at Cambridge she has thought long and deeply about such matters. Virtually every interview she gives to publicise a particular work will touch upon that particular character's significance as a woman in the broader social context: whether she is talking about the positive image of Kate Lemon, the nurse in *The Tall Guy*, refusing to cry when her relationship breaks up, or of the anger of Beatrice in *Much Ado About Nothing* that she can never fully be 'one of the lads'; whether about the lack of a defined role for Harriet Pringle in the 1930s and 1940s in *Fortunes of War* or for Margaret Schlegel decades earlier in *Howards End*, she addresses the particular instance with perception and insight rather than flipping into a standard set of all-purpose women's-issue sound-bites. This piercing intelligence both informs her approach to her dramatic work and is visible in the final performances.

In a 1988 interview Thompson first came close to a general statement of her belief in the importance of remaining aware of such matters: 'I feel a tremendous sense of gratitude and also responsibility to all the women who fought and got me the vote, who fought for my education, who fought for my right to contraception. What I see missing in my generation is a sense of the past, and a sense of continuity and of being the result of those struggles and therefore our lack of acquaintanceship with those struggles. I don't think that's a good thing. I think you should always be aware where your rights come from and how ephemeral they are and how difficult to protect. I think doing what I do helps women who haven't got as much confidence and haven't got as many privileges to think better of themselves.' The previous year, at the thirty-second Women of the Year lunch (televised by the BBC), she spoke of her own family's experiences of the institutionalised exploitation of women: when in domestic service, her paternal grandmother was made pregnant by her master, and the same 'advantage' had been taken of five other girls. The child was Emma's uncle. That and other kinds of abuse of women are not confined to the past, hence her agreement to be patron of a women's refuge. Returning in a 1994 article in *OK!* magazine to the topic of women in previous generations who had fought for equality, she also wrote of her maternal grandmother's efforts to try to introduce contraception to working-class families in Glasgow, and of her being stoned in the street for her good intentions. 'I want to remember, and celebrate, the women who made it all possible for us,' she wrote, 'women who sacrificed everything – their lives, their comfort, even their time with their own children – so that we modern women can have the freedom that we have. Let's never forget them.'

As well as voicing her own opinions on such issues, Thompson has given help and support to a number of initiatives intended to give other women a voice. Among these is the UK branch of the Emily's List movement, an organisation which aims to get more Labour women elected to the parliaments at Westminster and Strasbourg by helping them with costs such as childcare, transport, etc., and helping their constituencies with election expenses. ('Emily' is an acronym for 'Early Money Is Like Yeast' – i.e., it helps the dough rise.) Furthermore, in March 1994 she made a donation of £7,500 to rescue London's first women's radio station, Brazen Radio, from financial difficulties only a few days before it went on the air under a limited-term community broadcasting licence. 'A lot of women don't get much space to put across their views,' she said, 'and this is a chance to do something a bit more radical than, say, you would find in most women's magazines. Much women's TV has, I think, become too soft. I want there to be scope for women to talk about their experiences of motherhood, childbirth and to be more open and to display more anger.'

The words 'one-nation Tory' would no doubt have Emma releasing the safety-catch on her revolver, but the motivating spirit behind her activities is not dissimilar. She plainly feels it incumbent upon her to use her money and status in avenues of wider benefit; she is conscious of a duty to be as good a citizen as she can, with the qualification that in the modern world, citizenship is not a municipal or national matter – hence her interest in issues ranging from the local, through the gender-based, to the global. Paradoxically, she is a model of Margaret Thatcher's vision of concerned and active individuals of means rather than government-organised aid, even if all Emma's dearest causes are those guaranteed to get up the former Prime Minister's nose as thoroughly as a little finger. All in all, a far cry from that well-intentioned but abortive stand-up spot at a Trafalgar Square rally.

Stephen Fry, meanwhile, had been commissioned to write a new book for the 1930s musical *Me and My Girl*, in which Bermondsey barrow-boy Bill Snibson succeeds to an aristocratic title and country estate, and is naturally reunited with his Lambeth lass Sally Smith just in time for the finale. The show, whose songs had been written by Noel Gay, was now to be revived under the auspices of the Noel Gay Organisation, headed by Gay's son Richard Armitage, who happened to be Emma's agent. Director Mike Ockrent remembers, 'There were two versions [of the script] in existence from the earlier period, the French's acting edition and what was probably the original rehearsal script, neither of which were acceptable to anybody. Stephen had then done a version which I've never seen – and the producers never wanted anybody to see it! Then I went down for two or three days to Chichester, where he was playing some small parts that season, and we sat in his bed-and-breakfast place and cobbled together a basic scenario for the way it would go, virtually constructed the whole script, decided on numbers and so on. He pushed it through pretty fast, in about two weeks.'

The female lead role in *Me and My Girl* was to furnish Emma's major theatrical break. 'We'd been struggling to find somebody for quite a while,' according to Ockrent, 'until Richard Armitage suggested Emma – tentatively, because she was a client of his [as was Fry]. Stephen then said, "Well, you should see her." They were all incredibly young in those days; there was no sense yet of whether she could act it or whatever.' At the time of the production, Ockrent explained the casting – all the lead actors were from theatrical rather than musical backgrounds – in terms of 'looking for a sense of reality behind the comedy ... It's not the normal type of musical casting. We wanted the truth of the play to come through.' He now speaks of Emma's casting in more pragmatic terms: 'I think it was perceived by Richard that it would be a very good thing for her to do, which it was – it plunged her right into the mainstream of British theatre life.' Emma had reservations about the show – 'When I first read the script I didn't want to do it; I thought it was a reactionary piece about class rehabilitation' – but claimed she accepted the part of Sally because 'I wanted to learn to tap-dance.' The flippancy conceals a grain of truth, in that whether or not the show turned out to be a success the experience would at least equip her with another skill which she could later employ.

Having first astounded her parents by revealing herself in the Footlights pantomime to be a talented musical comedy actress, it was now Emma's turn to surprise those involved in *Me and My Girl* – including Thompson family friend Robert Lindsay, who was playing Bill Snibson. Ockrent recalls the difficulties of learning musical theatre 'on the job': 'It was the first musical that any of us had ever done – Bob [Lindsay] had done one "play with music" before, but none of us had really plunged into the world of full-scale musical theatre, and the actors were trying to cope with learning songs, learning to dance and throwing scenes together ... I was the only one who saw the whole scale of it. Emma wasn't obvious casting at all, but she got better and better as the show went on; I think she was nervous at first of singing in public. She did a wonderful job, proved herself to be light on her feet, sang beautifully. The great thing about doing a musical is that it pushes actors to extremes: you have to sing, to dance, to be funny and charming, and she produced the lot. There was nobody more amazed than Bob and Emma on the very first performance of the show in Leicester, with lots of agents and people from London in the audience, that they seemed to like it. I have to say I shared their amazement, but they had such incredible vibrancy between them that they made the show.

'She was incredibly adept, brilliantly smart and sharp-minded; looking back, she had everything that one needs, but everybody then was so light-hearted and frisky that it seemed that the road ahead for her lay in light comedy rather than the more serious side. It's every comedian's dream to be able to play the heavy dramatic roles, but it's given to very few to be able to do it, and Emma's been able to do it brilliantly and while she's still young. She's extremely natural, that's why she was charming – she didn't appear to be working at it, she was just *it*. Her romantic scenes with Bob were absolutely delightful and they were extremely fond of each other.'

When the show opened in the West End in 1985 a generation was reintroduced to songs like 'The Lambeth Walk' and 'The Sun Has Got His Hat On'. The production, and Emma in particular, drew rave reviews. 'Neither Emma Thompson nor Robert Lindsay have got the accent quite right, but it hardly matters,' cavilled *The Sunday Times* in a rare sour note; its daily sister paper, however, was more fulsome: 'Miss Thompson, a big girl in a print frock standing out in maximum gauche contrast to the surrounding company of sour-faced well-corseted swells, contributes a character as real as a pair of old boots and sings with a full-hearted relaxation that gets to the core of Gay's style.' *Me and My Girl* ultimately ran for seven years. Emma left after sixteen months and more than 500 performances, during which time the show simply became a chore to her: 'I used to think that if I had to do the Lambeth Walk one more time I'd commit *hara-kiri* onstage. I became less than human for a while. But I'm proud of having done it and lived.' Stephen Fry was more than proud; the show averaged £80,000 a week in box-office takings, 3 per cent of which went to him for the duration of its run.

Alfresco had also led to an appearance on the Channel 4 comedy programme *Assaulted Nuts* in early 1985 in the unlikely company of such luminaries as Tim Brooke-Taylor and Barry Cryer, and to a commission from Channel 4 for a one-hour solo comedy special from Emma. The three-year-old independent channel had a remit to cater for a broad range of minority interests, and was at the time subsidised by its big-sister network. Emma was exactly the sort of comedian they were looking for. Mike Bolland, senior commissioning editor, was ready to reject the script until Thompson demonstrated its comic potential to him by turning up and performing it to him in its entirety. 'It was quite extraordinary,' he said. 'She did the whole thing in my tiny office and it was incredibly funny. It had never happened to me before and no one's done it since. When she'd finished, I said, "OK, let's do it."' Emma wanted to call the show *Sexually Transmitted*, but the channel wasn't *that* adventurous. Known for a while as *First Offence*, because 'It's the first programme I've written for television, and it's also quite offensive,' it finally went out as *Up For Grabs*, and was buried in the post-Christmas schedule at 12.15 a.m. on 28 December 1985. Bolland maintains that the aired version didn't quite match its office incarnation (which, he said, was the dirtiest thing he'd ever seen), and in the press Emma was 'praised for her brilliant character acting and damned for her frequently filthy script', but it was funny enough to attract the attention of Michael Grade, who had returned to the UK after a spell running the television arm of American production company Embassy, and was now controller of BBC1. Grade commissioned a series of six half-hour shows from her. When *Thompson* was finally seen in 1988 it would turn out to be hideously disappointing.

The transition from comedy and musical performance to straight drama was made by means of the John Byrne-scripted six-part series *Tutti Frutti*, screened by the BBC early in

1987, which mixed all three genres. Glaswegian artist-cum-playwright Byrne's *Slab Boys* trilogy (set in a carpet factory) had first established him as a dramatist who could mix pathos and the blackest of comedy in the same scene, often in the same image; *Tutti Frutti* itself would climax with a grimly hilarious botched self-immolation scene. The series dealt with ageing Scottish rock and roll band The Majestics, whose 'silver jubilee' tour is beset by a plethora of complications. Managed by a small-time clothier and would-be showbiz mogul (played by Richard Wilson in the first of the high-profile roles which would culminate in *One Foot in the Grave*'s Victor Meldrew), they are booked into ceilidh halls, pursued by the married guitarist's possessive young girlfriend, and record an appalling 'comeback' album (whose disgruntled studio engineer was played by actor-musician Patrick Doyle, who, later in 1987, became Branagh's composer on *Twelfth Night* and on all subsequent ventures). The heftiest strike against The Majestics is that their lead vocalist has just died and has been replaced by his younger brother. Robbie Coltrane, who played both new recruit Danny McGlone and (in flashback) his late brother 'Big Jazza', suggested his *Alfresco* comrade Thompson for the role of Suzi Kettles, an art-college contemporary with whom Danny becomes thornily involved twelve years down the line, and who ends up joining The Majestics.

Both the character of Kettles and Emma's performance were virtual templates for many of her future roles. A strong, independent woman with a sharp mind and a tongue to match, Suzi refuses to be another 'chick' or 'doll' letting a man presume his way into her bed. It is she who is apprehensive about Danny's television interview for what turns out to be a posthumous stitch-up of his brother and she who does her level best to keep him in line on the road. When her psychotic estranged husband beats her up and rapes her, she fights back but refuses later to reveal the full extent of what has happened. Emma clicked right into the part, riding the switchback moods of Byrne's script rather than trying to steer it in a direction of her own. Her accent was almost faultless (only a determinedly critical listener can detect the occasional Home Counties vowel), and her Suzi Kettles hammered home the point that, although her greatest dramatic strengths are in middle-class roles for which she doesn't particularly have to stretch herself, her range in fact extends beyond this area. 'I learned a lot from playing the part of Kettles,' Emma said afterwards, 'and from the women of Glasgow, too. They taught me that you don't always have to be terribly polite to people. And that you can just say look, buzz off. Leave me alone.'

The flame-mopped Kettles – 'the first doll I ever come across that didnae look daft in drainpipes,' in the words of one of the band – was the first intimation to the public at large that there was more to Emma Thompson than a talented comedienne with a generous dollop of social awareness stirred in. She ably demonstrated her facility, and indeed predilection, for defining her character as the psychological and moral centre of a drama, even when not the main protagonist. In *Tutti Frutti* and since, Thompson consistently constitutes the intelligent norm against which the transgressions of other characters are measured: not a paragon, but the most comprehensively sympathetic character with whom viewers unconsciously align themselves. Such centring is fairly obvious in later work such as *Howards End* and *Fortunes of War*, when this function coincides with the main character, but it is just as present in, say, her first feature film *The Tall Guy*, in which her character makes the running in terms of courtship and refuses to subside into a mere adjunct to the male protagonist. *Tutti Frutti* set out her stall as a natural portrayer of real, believable people who are admirable on an everyday human scale, a flair which is all the greater for being so seldom obtrusive.

Emma was in the fortunate position of making the shift not so much from stage to screen as from comedy to drama. Being familiar with both performance media already from her Footlights and *Alfresco* days, she could adjust more easily to the necessity of 'doing less' for the camera. Even in comic sketches on television it is easy to go over the top in caricaturing a character or the delivery of a line – most actors (including Ken in his first *Billy* play) find that their initial screen appearances are full of attempts to convey physically, facially or vocally what will be communicated perfectly well with a minor inflection or movement, if even that is necessary. Generally, though, the only way to learn the importance of an economical screen acting style is through trial and error. The 'trust' exercises so beloved of fringe theatre directors, designed to foster company bonding, can't really be played with a camera – actors simply have to take it on trust that the camera will, metaphorically, catch them when they fall.

Logistics are another matter. Although live performance does not allow the luxury of retakes, nor does it involve long periods of sitting around between takes and scenes while the next set-up is being prepared. Likewise, screen acting does not need the often-prodigious feats of memory required for a live role, but it does demand both the ability to clean one's mental slate repeatedly in order to accommodate a new batch of lines, and, more crucially, a firm overall grasp of one's role throughout what may be several hours of screen time, so that a plausible character progression is evident in the final edited version. Few film or television projects have time or money for any rehearsal period worth the name: a couple of read-throughs, some notes from the director before each scene (usually more concerned with technique and positioning than with overall character considerations), and that's it. Actors have to come to their own decisions rather than working them out in company as part of a process of preparation. (Kenneth Branagh's approach as a screen director is an admirable exception to this state of affairs.) The difficulty is magnified by the fact that more often than not a screen drama will be shot out of chronological sequence, according to the resources and locations available at a given stage of filming, and slotted together in the editing suite. In such conditions, the final 'shape' of a character will always be something of a revelation even to the person who has been playing him or her.

It is not surprising that few film actors are equally at home onstage. Major names such as Al Pacino and Dustin Hoffman will make an occasional foray back into live theatre (Pacino in David Mamet's *American Buffalo*; Hoffman, surprisingly, as Shylock in Peter Hall's London production of *The Merchant of Venice* – not a role which lends itself to a Method approach, really), but will be judged by the audience at large, and certainly will sell tickets, on the strength of their screen reputation rather than reviews of that particular performance. Theatregoers will pay to collect the big-name 'scalp' rather than necessarily in the expectation of brilliance on that particular evening – not 'to be there' (in the words of the National Theatre's artistic director Richard Eyre), but 'to have been there'. Even British film actors are rarely seen on stage: Daniel Day-Lewis has not taken a theatrical part since his controversial and erratic Hamlet in the early 1990s; Hugh Grant (to the best of my knowledge) not at all since he became even a minor screen 'face'.

Television actors, for some reason, are more easily acceptable to a theatre audience. Despite the fundamental differences in the mechanics and scale of acting, the presence of the box in the corner of the room creates the illusion of greater familiarity, even intimacy, with small-screen actors; theatre punters know, or believe they know, what they will be getting when they see such figures. Brute economics also come into play, with screen appearances subsidising what actors may feel to be their 'real' work. When I asked one multi-award-winning actress, known for the extremity and rigour of her stage performances, why she had taken a role in a big-budget American movie aimed at the children's market, she replied candidly and succinctly, 'It's four years' pay.'

Crucially, few actors are of sufficient calibre to create a sizeable reputation through theatre alone. The screen, large or small, equals massive exposure. By the time of *Me and My Girl* Emma Thompson was known, though not yet famous, to a large number of people; she was to some extent a name, as (through the sitcom *Citizen Smith* in the late 1970s) was her co-star, Robert Lindsay. Stage appearances for her have been the exception rather than the rule: other than *Me and My Girl* and Kenneth Branagh's Renaissance productions, she has not appeared in a stage play since leaving university. In terms of her career as a whole it makes less sense to see *Tutti Frutti* as a televisual bolt from the blue than as the first discovery by someone who was already a screen performer of her particular *métier* within the medium. Impressive and relatively un-heralded by her comedy appearances as her Suzi Kettles was, it wasn't so much a fortuitous discovery as simply the break she had been waiting for.

Tutti Frutti was greatly lauded on its transmission. It brought John Byrne to wider attention, to the extent that *Slab Boys* is now something of a staple in fringe and repertory theatres (although his attempt to repeat his television success in 1990 with a series set on the Scottish Country and Western scene, *Your Cheatin' Heart*, proved much patchier), and was the first of two performances which would win Emma a British Academy of Film and Television Arts (BAFTA) Award the following year. Nevertheless, media-watchers were surprised when she was cast as the lead in Alan Plater's television adaptation of Olivia Manning's 'Balkan' and 'Levant' novel trilogies *Fortunes of War*.

The character of Harriet Pringle struggles to achieve personal and emotional autonomy in a staid, soporific mar-riage while the Europe and Middle East of the 1930s fissure all around her and her husband. With the benefit of hindsight, it's easy to say that the psychological heft of the part had Thompson written all over it; however, at the time, the only indication of her strengths as a dramatic actress was *Tutti Frutti*, which as far as any casting director was concerned could easily have been a flash in the pan. Furthermore, *Fortunes* director James Cellan Jones knew her only from *Me and My Girl*, and was taken aback when Emma arrived at his auditions 'with dyed orange hair [for her part as Suzi Kettles] which was monumentally disgusting'. Nonetheless, he opted to follow his instinct and offer her the part, knowing that there would be no middle ground – her Harriet would be either a triumph or a catastrophe. 'She's a woman of considerable intelligence,' he said later, 'and, with many actresses who are very intelligent and very educated, it gets in the way of instinct. It does not with her. She can shove all that intellect aside and react intuitively.'

But this was the meat with which Emma could prove once and for all that she could be more than funny and 'right-on', that *Tutti Frutti* had not simply been a serendipitous bit of casting. A nine-month shooting schedule traversed Yugoslavia, Greece and Egypt, so she'd damned well better get on with her screen husband. She did.

6

The Protestant Work Ethic

Julian Mitchell's play *Another Country* was a fictionalisation
of the schooldays of Guy Burgess, in which a homosexual love
story and the rigid authoritarianism of public-school life are
shown to lay the foundations for the protagonist's later
betrayal of his country in spying for the Soviet Union. Having
enjoyed great success in its original run at the Greenwich
Theatre in south-east London, it was set to transfer to the West
End in early 1982 pending the recasting of a few roles, for one
of which Ken had been invited to read.

His first audition, at Mitchell's London home in Knights-
bridge, began embarrassingly. The author made a passing joke
about the old striped blazer which Branagh had chosen to
wear in the hope of conjuring up the right atmosphere – a
throwaway remark, but enough to disconcert the hopeful
auditionee. His apprehension increased when he was asked to
drop the stiff-upper-lipped accent he had been affecting, but
his performance without vocal and sartorial accessories was
strong enough to persuade Mitchell and casting director
Celestia Fox to recall him. The second audition, in front of
director Stuart Burge and Fox's producer husband Robert (the
younger brother of actors James and Edward Fox), brought its
own upset: having been requested beforehand to look at the
role of Barclay, the head of house, Ken set foot on the stage of
the Whitehall Theatre to be asked to read as Tommy Judd, a

self-conscious lower-middle-class Marxist whose radicalism qualifies him for the role of gadfly in the circle of schoolfriends. Throughout the scene, opposite Rupert Everett (whose career also began in earnest with the play and the subsequent film version) as the Burgess character Guy Bennett, he flew by the seat of his pants. His quickness on the uptake and instinctive grasp of parts, so consistently praised by directors and actors he has worked with, saw him through. He was offered the part that afternoon.

As with so much of Ken's early career, events unfolded in the manner of a 'fortunately/unfortunately' storytelling game. Fortunately he hadn't screwed up the *Another Country* audition; unfortunately he now had to decide between playing Judd and signing on with the Royal Shakespeare Company, who had offered him a standard 'play as cast' contract for a season, on the strength of an audition the previous day. Equity had given a dispensation which had allowed him to appear in *Too Late to Talk to Billy*, but had insisted that such permission was strictly temporary. It had lapsed when he returned to RADA for the remaining three weeks of his term, and he still did not possess a full Equity card. The administrative machinery of the actors' union grinds slowly, and it was unlikely that the necessary card would be granted in the three weeks before Mitchell's play went into rehearsal. Unfortunately, the RSC would not wait that long for a response to their offer; fortunately, Robert Fox's representations to Equity (in a laudable display of brinkmanship which more or less boiled down to 'no Branagh, no production') succeeded in prising a card out of them.

The prospect of playing a public schoolboy brought out the familiar strain of insecurity in Ken, less about his nationality this time than his class; although he had suffered the experience of being uprooted from his homeland, the more middle-class English convention of childhood separation from family was alien to him. 'I have no idea what it's like to leave home as a child and live in a boarding school.' Then: 'I thought, come on, you *pretend* to be a public schoolboy; that's what actors do, for Heaven's sake!' Research was vital: he read what books he could find on the public school system and its psychological impact upon those who are put through it, and talked to everyone he could who had received a public-school education – including, conveniently, some other members of the cast. 'I wanted to know details like what it was like to sleep in a dormitory every night, and what they actually did in the evenings and at weekends.' But his starting point was more fundamental. By way of briefing on the underlying attitudes of the ruling class, he read the first great milestone in public-school literature, *Tom Brown's Schooldays*. From this foundation he fleshed out his knowledge of the public-school system, the ideological climate of the 1930s and the real-life models for the character of Judd, Esmond Romilly and the poet John Cornford, who died in the Spanish Civil War.

Rehearsals proved less daunting than the auditions. Rupert Everett, like Ken, was an instinctive actor, and the rapport and sympathy between Bennett and Judd in their many scenes together were mirrored by the actors' growing familiarity with one another – not least in the matter of corpsing. Another change of address, from Willesden to the much more run-down area of Harlesden further out in north-west London and a house let by a dodgy second-hand car salesman, was fitted in between rehearsals. (Like many of his addresses, it didn't last long: on this occasion he was shunted out by a team of thick-set decorators in the hire of the equally dodgy landlord.) Only when the play was put before an audience for several preview performances before the official 'opening night' attended by the press did Ken fully realise the humour of the script and of the character; rather than trying to play Judd for laughs, he infused a wry self-knowledge into his portrayal which pointed up the amusement without vulgarising it.

Too Late to Talk to Billy had been screened the week before *Another Country*'s official opening night and had been given a warm reception, and the eve of the press performance brought the news (announced to Ken by actor Albert Finney) that he had won RADA's Bancroft Gold Medal as the finest student of his year. More critical acclaim followed upon the play's formal opening – the Bancroft Medal was eclipsed by the *Plays & Players* Best Newcomer Award and the Society of West End Theatre Award for Most Promising Newcomer of 1982 – as did dinner at the Gay Hussar with writer Jessica Mitford, whose first husband had been Esmond Romilly, on whom Judd was partly based. 'She was fascinating,' said Branagh. 'I thought it might have been awkward because of her memories of Romilly, but she was so delightful and interesting – and promised that the next time she was over here she'd have me to dinner and cook me chicken in paprika herself.'

Faced with a run of six months, the young cast began fooling around to keep themselves fresh. The phenomenon is not uncommon even among more experienced actors, and is usually confined to Saturday matinée performances. To alleviate the tedium of delivering the same lines day in, day out, a company may for instance select a theme – say, kitchen utensils – which each actor has to work unobtrusively into his or her lines. The audience may hear only minor mispronunciations, while the cast are on tenterhooks waiting for the next secret reference. In the example cited – a genuine instance from the West End run of a comedy – the line 'I woke early' simply became 'I wok early.' Inevitably, such japes run the risk of producing giggles. In *Another Country*, matters progressed beyond mere word games to out-and-out practical jokes. With Branagh and Everett in the cast, the incidence of corpsing climbed steadily until one Wednesday afternoon they were confronted with the author's incandescent rage at their having just mutilated his play. Suitably chastened, the cast resumed normal service.

The other option to keep a role fresh during a long run is to re-examine it when one feels stagnation settling in. Ken, who was losing concentration on stage and, after drying one night, was even beginning to feel the icy hand of stage-fright, did precisely that, and felt his performance immensely improved and revived as a result. But it still wasn't enough. The company decided, simultaneously with the run of *Another*

Country, to stage another production at lunchtime at a fringe venue – Gogol's *The Gamblers*, with Julian Mitchell directing and providing a new translation.

At this point Ken's most significant meeting in the company of *Another Country* began to bear fruit. David Parfitt, a fellow cast member, was enlisted to handle financial matters on *The Gamblers* at the 103-seat Upstream Theatre Club in the Waterloo district just south of the Thames, near the Old Vic and Young Vic theatres. This was the first manifestation of what was to become Branagh's major business partnership in his stage and screen career to the present day. Little by little David Parfitt became his regular producer and to a large extent the business talent behind Renaissance's various incarnations, devoting his time to 'making Ken's mad schemes happen'.

The first of these schemes, however, had not yet occurred to Ken. Declining to sign on for a further six months in *Another Country*, he was almost immediately offered the chance of the title role in a production still in development, a four-part television mini-series for Channel 4 entitled *The Boy in the Bush*. Based on a story written in the early 1920s by D.H. Lawrence and Australian writer Mollie Skinner, it centres on teenager Jack Grant, expelled from a British public school and sent to Australia 'to build his character' by working on a farm. While the project was securing finance, he took the part of Charles Tansley in a BBC adaptation of Virginia Woolf's *To the Lighthouse*.

His big film break appeared to be on the horizon. Branagh was one of a number of young actors invited to read for the part of Mozart in Milos Forman's film version of Peter Shaffer's hit play *Amadeus*. The auditions were more protracted even than the Central School's selection process which had so irked him, but he hung on through two initial sessions and a further two screen tests over a period of several weeks, followed by a couple of months' limbo while Forman repeated the process with American actors. During this period he also shot *A Matter of Choice For Billy*, the first sequel to *Too Late to Talk to Billy*.

His stage and screen experience in the interim showed through, revealing a greater confidence in the camera's ability to convey subtleties of nuance. It was also clear that this was not a gratuitous sequel: family relationships continued to develop, and a third play was on the cards. When the news about *Amadeus* finally came through, it was bad – Forman had opted for American principal actors. Even Simon Callow, who had created the part of Salieri on the London stage, was given only a minor role as a consolation prize. For Ken there was nothing. After so many auditions, tests and changes of tone and accent, he was bitterly disappointed. Interestingly, he was to cast the American who beat him to the role, Tom Hulce, in *Mary Shelley's Frankenstein*, either to show that he bore no grudges or as a confirmation of his own power in the film world a decade later.

Within a short while, however, he had beaten Rupert Everett to the SWET Award for Best Newcomer, and had heard that *The Boy in the Bush* had finally been given the green light by Portman Productions. After two episodes as a 'guest nutter' in *Maybury*, a BBC television series starring Patrick Stewart as a psychiatrist (in the days before he became known as Captain Jean-Luc Picard in *Star Trek: The Next Generation*), and an uninspiring attempt to learn to ride a horse for the part of Jack Grant, he was off to Australia – but not before hatching the idea for a stage production of his own, to get back to basics after so much screen work. He had decided, after toying with the idea of a radio production of Tennyson's poem *Maud*, to stage a solo performance under its subtitle, *The Madness*, set in a padded cell. His Progress friend Colin Wakefield, who was now a professional actor, was enlisted as director before Ken flew to Sydney where the idea would gestate during the three-month shoot of *The Boy in the Bush*.

One of the major tasks that faced Branagh the urbanite was learning to ride a horse. His attempts in England had been slow, painful and too formal to be much use in the Australian 'cowboy' style of riding. Luckily he had a fine teacher in wrangler Graham Ware, and 'got on fine once I discovered that this great machine had a mind of its own and couldn't be "driven" like a car. But the horse was so well trained that it would buck or stop bucking on a word of command, so I didn't need a stuntman all the time' – not even in a spectacular scene where Jack Grant rides a wild horse.

This was the beginning of Ken's real education in screen acting. Onstage an actor can always pursue the line of a character from A to Z (unless a particularly adventurous writer has decided to muck about with chronology), but shooting for film or television obeys the dictates of a production schedule rather than a narrative through-line. This was not so much of a problem in the *Billy* plays and *To the Lighthouse*, in which the action took place over short spaces of time, but *The Boy in the Bush* dealt with Jack Grant's process of maturation over a far longer period. Branagh had to learn to switch over lunch from the tougher, weathered Jack of episode 4 to the callow youth of the first part as the schedule demanded. Appearing with more experienced screen actors was also instructive. He recalled that his leading lady, Australian star Sigrid Thornton, 'would do things in our scenes together that seemed strange to me as a screen actor, but when I saw the rushes I knew she had been right. She knew how to make an impact, how to attract the eye to herself. I watched her and learned.' He also struck up a warm friendship with cameraman Roger Lanser, another contact whom he would remember later in his career.

It seemed too good to be true, and inevitably it was. Director Ken Hannam showed a meticulous attention to detail and sensitivity of tone when shooting, but didn't do much for the production schedule and budget. He was unceremoniously replaced by a 'bash it down in one take' director, Rob 'Rocket' Stewart. Branagh protested fiercely, showing the producers a steely side no one, least of all him, had known was in his nature, but to no avail. As Stewart took the production in a crass direction at breakneck speed, blazing rows ensued, giving way to a grudging mutual respect – after all, following his ordeals at school in Reading and at RADA, this experience had at last taught Branagh how to stand up to intimidation.

The confusion over his national identity would sometimes crop up in the most unlikely places. When in Australia he met one of his early footballing idols, Belfast boy George Best, only to be greeted with the line, 'What the hell happened to your accent?' 'I felt so bad,' he said later. 'I'd met a hero and disappointed him – instant inferiority. Forgive me, George, forgive me.'

He returned from Australia in August 1983 to a bare week's rehearsals for *The Madness* before flying to Belfast to shoot *A Coming to Terms For Billy*, the third and probably the best of Graham Reid's plays, which culminates in a wonderful reconciliation between Billy and his father that is at once funny and very moving. He was filming during the week in Northern Ireland, and flying back to London for weekends of intensive rehearsal on *The Madness*, grappling at the same time with the character of Billy and the 1,400-odd lines of Tennyson's poem – not to mention doing his best in the few remaining spare moments to generate publicity that would bring sufficient audiences to the Upstream Theatre Club during the two-week run in September. David Parfitt, inevitably, lent general assistance on this truly mad scheme.

The first week's performances played to sparse houses, and spirits were low until a brace of reviews changed the production's fortunes literally overnight. The second week was a virtual sell-out, and Ken even agreed to slot in an 11 p.m. 'midnight matinée' so that actors in other productions could see it after their own shows. Celebrity punters included Alec McCowen, whose one-man version of *St Mark's Gospel* had been a source of theatrical inspiration to Ken, and Mary Wilson, the wife of the former Prime Minister. The profit-sharing production broke even, and Ken ended up owning the set, though what he did with the scaffolding poles afterwards remains a mystery.

From Waterloo to Rome and Assisi, where Ken combined a holiday with research for his next stage role: in Julian

Mitchell's new play *Francis*, he was to play the saint of that name at Greenwich. Francis's great blessing was to have been saintly without being ethereal – in the world and also, to an extent, of it, but with an unshakable devotion. The four weeks of rehearsals under David Williams (who had played the part of Vaughan Cunningham in *Another Country*) went well, and the company believed the play would be a success. The critics, who saw only the second public performance, thought otherwise, and Robert Fox felt unable to offer another West End transfer.

For a man who professed in his own memoir to feel desperation every time a job ended with nothing else in obvious immediate prospect, Branagh seemed to have little trouble in lining up employment. Of course, he was turned down on occasion – for a Terence Rattigan play in Manchester, for Hal in the *Henry IV* plays at Leicester, and after the protracted and tantalising *Amadeus* possibility – but in a climate in which the average actor works for only a quarter of the year (and, iniquitously, the average actress appreciably less), he was in considerable demand, given that he had come out of drama school only a year or two earlier.

Still it seems not to have been enough. *The Gamblers*, *The Madness*, even the English riding holiday spoke of a need for activity in order to give shape not simply to his life, but to his identity. Until he met Emma Thompson, his personal life always seemed to come a very poor second to his work. After *The Boy in the Bush* he had yielded to the inevitable and agreed with Katy Behean that they should separate. It is as if he were hoping that, through the accumulation of a professional history and a range of experiences undergone in the process, he might find that he had almost as a by-product assembled a self. If so, one can read more than mere career insecurity into his confession in 1989: 'There's an image of me as Mr Confidence. But that's nowhere near the truth. And I don't want sympathy. I don't want people to feel sorry for me. But I get terrified. And I suspect I'll get more terrified as the years go on.' He has indeed acquired a professional identity, but the drive to work persists;

the projects become fewer, bigger and of longer duration, but no less intensive. Speaking of the precept 'Know thyself', Goethe remarked, 'If I knew myself, I would run away.' Kenneth Branagh seems to run either to avoid himself or in the hope that the act of running might somehow come to define him. At any rate, whether or not such armchair psychology contains any truth, to continue the analogy, he was about to find himself running in his first national championship.

On-off negotiations with the RSC had been in train since before *The Boy in the Bush*. The company had gone so far as to ask Ken if there was a particular role he wanted to play, but his audacious suggestion of King Henry V had been met with laughter. However, RSC casting director Joyce Nettles had seen *The Madness*, and director Ron Daniels came to *Francis*. Shortly afterwards he met Ken to lend his support to the idea of *Henry V*, although he later pulled out in favour of directing *Hamlet* that same season. Nonetheless, an interview with Barry Kyle and Adrian Noble, and an impromptu audition on the Barbican stage, led at last to the RSC offer he couldn't refuse: Laertes in Daniels' *Hamlet* (Roger Rees, who had triumphantly played Nicholas Nickleby for the company a few years earlier, returned to play the Prince); the King of Navarre in *Love's Labour's Lost* and an Olympic athlete in Louise Page's new play *Golden Girls*, both directed by Kyle; and King Henry V under Noble. After finishing Edward Bond's play *Derek* for Thames Television, he began solo rehearsals and discussions with Noble about Henry before the company rehearsals began in Stratford.

His Henry was a deeply religious man, imbued with mediaeval morality which included a consciousness of the awaiting pains of hell should his actions be wrong and of the crimes by which his father Richard II had come to the throne, as well as a desire to atone for his riotous youth with the fat roisterer Sir John Falstaff. 'It's his faith which carries him through,' said Branagh, 'and the sense of sharing it, its commonness, so that he can open up other people's spirits. It seems to be a matter of realising what's important in life, for humanity, and that is the source of his response to people and theirs to him.' But in the crucial scene in which the King wanders disguised among his soldiers the night before the battle of Agincourt, 'he finds he has no friends, and that's when you have the most lonely and remote speech of the whole play. He is a haunted man until he meets Kate [Princess Katherine of France, whose marriage to him forms the non-territorial part of the peace settlement after the battle], and then we see the man who might be able to cope beautifully with the sadness he carries around with him.'

The story of the special consultant whose advice Ken sought on the particular burdens of royalty upon an individual has now passed into theatrical legend. Indeed, it is such a Branagh commonplace that differing versions have arisen. Some accounts ascribe the initial contact to the *chutzpah* of Ken's letter-writing habit; he himself recounts that the original suggestion came from a dinner-party host. Whichever version is more accurate (probably a combination of both), Lord Brabourne is believed to have acted as an intermediary in setting up an interview with His Royal Highness the Prince of Wales. Ken was invited to Kensington Palace for a private interview, in which the two discussed the isolation of royalty and the temperamental pressures which must be resisted by one in so prominent and visible a position. He left the meeting not simply better informed and more sensitive to the web of royal obligations and responsibilities, but with a deep and lasting admiration for Prince Charles. In addition, another useful bond was forged – as always, so Ken would have it, through sheer luck and the other party's generosity.

The *Henry V* company included a number of actors who were later to be employed by Branagh in his own dramatic enterprises. Andrew Jarvis (the Earl of Cambridge) would play Capulet in his pre-Renaissance production of *Romeo and Juliet*; Richard Easton (the Constable of France) reprised his role in the film version and appeared in the Renaissance stage productions of *As You Like It* and *Much Ado About Nothing*;

Harold Innocent and Stephen Simms, too, had to relearn their lines of four years earlier for the parts of the Duke of Burgundy and the conspirator Lord Scroop respectively in the film of *Henry V*. Above all, Brian Blessed as the King's uncle, the Duke of Exeter, would become not simply a Renaissance mainstay but a valued friend. Blessed – a huge, bearded figure with seemingly endless reserves of energy who had had a comfortable sideline in playing miscellaneous exotic and slightly barbarous figures given to crying 'Haagh!' in American films shot in Britain – gave physical advice to Ken for *Golden Girls* in the same RSC season and psychological support when the demands of his first film as director threatened to overcome him. Ken recounts how on numerous occasions a well-placed high-volume expletive from Blessed would defuse tension and calm nerves at a difficult moment. Declining to be interviewed for this book, Blessed stated that he had only a 'working relationship' with Branagh and Thompson; however, his 'supporting roles' off the stage and screen, including that of best man at the couple's wedding, give the lie to this modest claim.

Other members of the company testify that Ken's approach to the production was similar to Henry's relationship with his troops. Siôn Probert, who played the Welsh captain, Fluellen, remembers him as 'a very democratic, very unselfish actor; if you don't have that rapport the relationship between Hal and Fluellen will never work. We got on extremely well. He was very kind to me. My voice had diminished to a croak and after a few performances I wrote to Ken saying I thought I'd better leave. He wrote me a fabulous letter saying he didn't want anybody else to play it, that there wasn't a problem with my voice, and I think that was the best medication I've ever had. He's totally charming, and it's not calculated – he's just like that. I've never seen a horrible side to him.

'And laugh? Ken Branagh and Brian Blessed are the worst corpsers I've ever worked with. Brian is a total hooligan. There's one line where Exeter's having a conversation with the King and he has a line about the 'man that was his bedfellow'.

Brian couldn't remember the line and said, "Oh, you know, the bloke he used to sleep with!" They just *twinkle* at you. I don't corpse very often, but you get these little twinkling eyes looking at you and you think, oh no, not tonight!'

'I try to resist being in a position where I'm not allowed to make mistakes,' Branagh has said of his approach to work. When technical rehearsals fell behind schedule, he insisted on a full dress run prior to the first public performance. It meant a break of less than two hours between the afternoon's dress and the first preview that evening. During the performance proper, Probert recalls Branagh losing his composure completely. The night before the battle, Henry's incognito scene among his soldiers involves a quarrel to be settled the following day. So that the two parties may know one another, they exchange gloves; after the battle, the King presents the soldier Williams with his own gloves, revealing that he had been the man's mysterious opponent. A typical Shakespeare 'by their token shall ye know them' scene – except that, when the time came for the revelation of Henry's true identity, Ken's gloves were not in his belt as planned. In such a situation, the only option is to attempt to improvise in plausible Shakespearese to get out of it. Ken, frantically trying to stay in iambic pentameter verse, gabbled something about his gloves being elsewhere and ordered good Fluellen off to seek them thitherward, or words to that effect.

Ken's account of the incident in *Beginning* describes the gradual disintegration of the English Army until Probert returned with the only gloves he could find, only to discover that the King had just located his own gloves under the body of one of the English dead, and whispered an astonished 'Fuck me!' Probert, however, not only denies ever profaning the Stratford stage with a four-letter word – 'Shall we say [the story] has been *embellished*?' he remarks sardonically – but recounts that it wasn't only the soldiers who were falling into giggles. 'Ken was corpsing rotten because he knew that if the shit was going to hit the fan it would be all over me. So I was thinking, "Oh, my God, I've got to get a glove!" I ran into the wings to the stage manager, but nobody could find a glove. Eventually I got one from somebody who rode a motorbike. I came on and said, "Here are your gloves, my liege, I found them on yonder hill" or whatever, trying to make it scan, and Ken was creasing himself laughing because he'd already found his and could hear me pounding around backstage in these great big clumpy boots, all the leather and the armour, clank clank – and he just looked at me and *twinkled*. After the show somebody came up to him and said, "*Loved* the glove scene!" So ever after I used to nudge one of the boys, "Make sure he's got that glove on him, I'm not going to go through *that* again!" He's a wicked little pixie!

'I don't think he'll ever be cured of corpsing – it's a release, you're under a lot of pressure in a part like that. He relished the pressure. I remember once when I totally lost my voice my understudy had to go on for me. This poor boy couldn't do the Welsh accent, didn't know the lines and was trying to wing it, and they corpsed the whole way through. Ken and Brian Blessed were just up in the air. You can't really ad-lib Shakespeare, can you?' As Ken discovered.

The Prince and Princess of Wales had arranged with Ken that they would attend a performance of *Henry V*, but in order to maintain tight security he was unable to tell the company who the VIPs were for whom he had secured four tickets. It wasn't then known that the young actor had made contact with the heir to the throne for advice about playing royalty. When the news was revealed on the day, panic was rife at the theatre; the audience paid more attention to the guests than to the performance, and the whole event was an object demonstration of the tribulations about which Ken had consulted the Prince. 'They wanted to come round and meet the cast afterwards,' according to Siôn Probert, 'but for security reasons their minders wouldn't allow them, although they did manage to smuggle Ken out. They thoroughly enjoyed it and passed on their congratulations to the company. I think that's why they called their second son Harry.' On another occasion, a performance on the birthday of the recently deceased

Richard Burton was dedicated to his memory, and the great actor's family attended the show. 'Ken was delighted to do it, and in a way he was inviting comparisons,' says Probert, himself a friend of the Jenkins/Burton family, 'but he didn't think about it that way at all. "I'm not going to be Burton, I'm going to be me." Comparisons are odious, aren't they?'

At any rate, Ken had acquired an entirely different name within the company. A rash of camp nicknames had been bestowed by the actors upon one another, as Siôn Probert tells with glee. 'Brian Blessed, this huge man who later climbed Everest, was known as Wendy. Stephen Simms was Big Sylv, Harold Innocent was the Goodwife Innocent – it was all affectionate.' Given that Branagh was playing a monarch (and, as the season progressed, two – he was also the King of Navarre in *Love's Labour's Lost*), and given the general tenor of the soubriquets, it was unsurprising that the nicknamers should be reminded of the satirical magazine *Private Eye*'s term for Her Majesty the Queen. 'Ken was known as Brenda-Madge Branagh,' according to Probert, 'until he met the Waleses, when he became *Dame* Brenda-Madge. And he loved it.'

Not that Ken himself had any kind of camp reputation – another anonymous RSC actor remarked, 'He'd put his where you wouldn't put your umbrella, I tell you.' At this time he was romantically involved with actress Amanda Root, who was in the company of *Love's Labour's Lost* with him. But he wasn't short of admirers, as Siôn Probert discovered by accident. 'I used to get confused with Ken; a few times I'd come out of the stage door, and, "Ah, there he is. Can I have your autogra— oh no, you're not him, are you?"'

In the week and a half of free time given him after the opening of *Henry V*, Ken contrived to spend several days recovering in Australia with friends from his *Boy in the Bush* sojourn there before returning to begin rehearsals of *Golden Girls*. The play concerned a British women's relay team at the Olympics, and Ken's role as a 100-metre sprinter demanded a fitness programme. He and Jimmy Yuill (subsequently another

111

Renaissance regular, to whose son Calum Ken would stand as godfather) were put through gruelling exercise sessions and middle-distance runs by the indefatigable Brian Blessed until deciding, in the words of Laurence Olivier's advice to a Method-minded Dustin Hoffman on the set of *Marathon Man*, that they 'should try acting – it's much easier'. Not necessarily so in this case, with playwright Louise Page's rewrites and even the final scenes arriving piecemeal and the poor actors unable to build up a full mental picture of the play's progression until almost the eve of the first night. However, with the inexplicability of theatre the production, in the Stratford studio The Other Place (which, prior to the construction of a new venue in the early 1990s, had the atmosphere of a converted aluminium barn), went down a storm with audiences.

In preliminary discussions with Ron Daniels about *Hamlet*, the Blessed magic came into play once more. Sharing his thoughts about his role as Claudius, he explained with typical forthrightness – and much more colourful language than this indirect report – that in short the usurping King simply had the insatiable hots for Gertrude, who was only too happy to be getting some connubial jollies after years of unconsummation with old King Hamlet. There is a slim textual basis for this view – the Prince compares his dead father to Claudius as 'Hyperion to a satyr', and, well, satyriasis *is* the male equivalent of nymphomania – but it's unlikely that Blessed had this justification in mind. Astonishingly, rather than causing outrage this salty outburst broke the ice with Virginia McKenna, who was playing Gertrude. Ken had to find a similar key to the somewhat tangential part of Laertes. For a while he tried playing Ophelia's brother as mad, then as just plain stupid. The actors around him were kept on their toes, if nothing else.

However, before *Hamlet* even opened, to mixed reviews, rehearsals had begun for *Love's Labour's Lost*. Even for an actor without as yet a sizeable reputation, a four-play schedule for the season was excessive, and by this point members of the company were becoming exhausted and the tempers growing more volatile. Although *Love's Labour's Lost* drew a warm response, by now Ken was becoming quite frustrated by the labyrinthine nature of the RSC and the aloofness of its joint artistic director, Trevor Nunn, a feeling shared by many other actors. 'I saw Trev once, I think, at a party in somebody's garden,' recalls Siôn Probert acerbically. Indeed, a number of the company had recently demonstrated his inaccessibility by writing to the television programme *Jim'll Fix It* asking Jimmy Savile to fix it for them to meet their own boss. 'I went [to the RSC] expecting a family enterprise where you could always knock on someone's door,' said Ken. 'Well, you could knock on a door, but there wasn't usually anyone on the other side of it.'

He vented his frustration by organising productions on the fringe of the RSC. One such unofficial show appeared for one night in the 1984 Belfast Festival. Ken and Frances Tomelty (whose father, Joe, had so captivated Ken as Marley's ghost in *A Christmas Carol* all those years ago) had been musing on the possibility of doing some Northern Irish work. At that point *Henry V*'s assistant director, A.J. Quinn, mentioned that a friend from his days at Cambridge, David Grant, had assembled a collection of Ulster poetry, *Across the Roaring Hills*, for Cambridge Mummers to stage on that year's Edinburgh Fringe. Grant, then working for the Belfast Festival himself, was contacted and supplied the RSC actors with his script. Kenneth Branagh's first stage appearance in Northern Ireland took place not in a theatre, but in Queen's University's Whitla Hall, which had been temporarily converted for festival performances. By this stage the idea of forming his own theatre company was already germinating, and Grant recalls Branagh discussing his ambitions in this direction. 'At that time,' he says, 'all Ken knew for certain was that he wanted it to tour to Belfast and Reading.' David Grant subsequently became involved with the Ulster Youth Theatre, of which Branagh would later become a major benefactor.

For the company's 1985 fringe season in Newcastle, Ken had

written and directed a one-act musical satire entitled *Tell Me Honestly* which lampooned end-of-season interviews in order to bring to light the actors' grievances against the way the company operated – although the *Daily Telegraph* noted laconically, 'since one of the cast is required to swing upside-down with a carrot in her ear while singing a song, Branagh assured me that it could not possibly be seen as a direct reflection on his first season with the RSC.' The play transferred to London and on to the Donmar Warehouse, the only studio theatre in the West End. (Implausibly, it was also staged the following year in Oslo, in Norwegian.)

Furthermore, notwithstanding the deal he had struck with the company's directors regarding his roles, the young lead actor in his first season had been engaged on a standard 'play as cast' contract, and was consequently being paid less than some of his supporting cast. When he made an appeal against this iniquity, the RSC first threatened to remove *Henry V* from its repertoire. Branagh's retaliatory threat to resign set the company to investigating his contract, which they discovered was in his favour on the financial point. In the end the extra money was paid out of a trust fund by separate cheques, every pay packet reminding him how irritated the RSC was at his ingratitude. The pressures showed in increased corpsing, particularly in the London run of *Love's Labour's Lost*, and Ken was keenly conscious of letting down both the other actors and himself.

Having come to the conclusion that subsidised companies were now 'so large that the quality of work is affected – they're out of control,' Ken wanted to return to what he believed to have been the ethos of the RSC of old: more collaborative, but stopping short of direction by committee. 'I think a co-ordinator is necessary,' he said. 'I like to be told what to do.' This meant practical direction rather than abstract waffling such as he encountered in one of the RSC productions. 'There were thirty of us walking around the stage "feeling the space", and [the director] said, "What would be wonderful when the King and Queen come on is if you could embody the concept of honour and embody the concept of kingship and in a strange way absent yourself from yourself and give yourself to nationhood."

'And so I said, "You'd like us to bow?"

'"Yes."

'You try absenting yourself from yourself. That was when I thought, oh God, one of us is pulling somebody's leg here.'

Branagh had hatched a plan to direct and star in *Romeo and Juliet* with a company of his own choosing. Terry Hands, joint artistic director with Nunn, offered him the chance to do it within the RSC, but the offer was swiftly forgotten, and the play was produced by Kenneth Branagh Ltd in the studio theatre of the Lyric, Hammersmith, on a budget of £15,000. Planning the production spanned several months, during which the rising star took a clutch of screen engagements.

He returned to D.H. Lawrence territory, playing the writer himself in *Coming Through*, an Alan Plater-scripted film for Central Television covering his early life, with Helen Mirren as Frieda Weekley, with whom Lawrence eloped. It was followed by Ibsen's *Ghosts* for the BBC, with Michael Gambon, Judi Dench and Natasha Richardson. Ken played Osvald Alving, the protagonist's son and a second-generation syphilitic. It is one of Ibsen's bleakest plays, and unfortunately Dench and Gambon proved to be inveterate gigglers. A silent thirty-second dinner scene was to be interpolated into the film, during which the camera panned down the row of sombre faces at the table. Although music would be dubbed on top of the scene the actors had to extemporise banal dialogue so that they might be seen to be conducting stifled conversation. Ken, at the far end of the table, had the full benefit of seeing first Gambon then Dench dissolving in silent hysterics at the absurdity of the improvised lines. After several takes he was humiliatingly ordered out of the studio.

There followed *Lorna*, Graham Reid's coda to the *Billy* plays, in which Billy and Lorna finally step clear of the shadows of their family history to build adult lives for themselves. It was a muted ending to the sequence, but the group of plays remains one of the undisputed high points of BBC Northern Ireland's admirable drama output. Ken then attended a meeting with James Cellan Jones to discuss the part of Guy Pringle in *Fortunes of War*, having been recommended by its adapter, Alan Plater. He was pleasantly surprised to be offered the part on the spot. The five months before filming began in September 1986 were taken up co-producing (with David Parfitt) and directing *John Sessions at the Eleventh Hour* – the latter task was mostly a matter of questioning Sessions' more abstruse free associations – and a brace of films which would pay for the *Romeo and Juliet* he was determined to stage.

High Season was an undistinguished secret agent spoof filmed in Rhodes, directed by Bernardo Bertolucci's wife, Clare Peploe. An uninspiring tale of a group of foreigners wreaking touristic havoc upon an off-the-beaten-track Greek village, it is notable only for a *From Here to Eternity*-parody love scene in the surf between Branagh (implausibly replacing Jack Nicholson) as 'a sort of comic James Bond figure' and Jacqueline Bisset. 'That was a spectacular sight,' remarked Ken. 'The statuesque beauty and the nine-stone weakling!' His persistent guilt, however, precluded him from relaxing. 'It was April, the sun was shining, the place and the weather were beautiful, I had a pretty easy part, I had loads of time off, I was staying in a beautiful villa. And I just went bananas. It was almost a physical sensation, that I couldn't sit easy. I couldn't resolve for myself this thing of spending time doing nothing. I started planning and setting up my own production of *Romeo and Juliet* in London, a really difficult job, and then I felt much better.'

The problems of budgeting, finding a venue and scheduling a rehearsal period had been more or less sorted out during *High Season* – again, he was doing two things at once. Peter James had offered the Lyric Studio, David Parfitt had been engaged as producer and a recklessly tight rehearsal period of three and a half weeks had been allotted. In addition, Hugh Cruttwell had agreed to work as artistic consultant, and Dr Russell Jackson from the University of Birmingham's

Shakespeare Institute at Stratford came on board as text adviser (functions which both men have continued to fill in subsequent productions). Still concerned about money for the show, Ken agreed to take a role in Pat O'Connor's film *A Month in the Country* to subsidise the Shakespeare further. It also made for a schedule which was not just punishing, but blatantly masochistic. During the run of *Romeo and Juliet*, he would take a car at 6 a.m. to the film location, returning in the evening just in time for the performance.

A Month in the Country was a muted but haunting piece combining comment on the human legacy of the First World War with a mediaeval mystery and a love triangle. Branagh played Moon, an archaeologist working in a small country village just after the war and nursing a never explicitly stated homosexual infatuation with the other outsider and war veteran, Birkin (Colin Firth, who had played Ken's part of Judd in the film of *Another Country*). The film also starred Natasha Richardson as the parson's wife with whom Birkin falls in love.

The money-spinning screen work was 'fun, up to a point,' said Ken, 'but I don't like all the sitting around. I'm more of a doer. And the theatre is where I started and where I belong. In addition, I don't like feeling hemmed in.' Then, most tellingly, 'My definition of success is control.' *Romeo and Juliet* was his own project, and he therefore felt more at home with it. The play sold out, but it was never intended to recoup its budget, and Branagh lost £6,000 of his £15,000 over the run. Reviews were mixed, with a certain element of 'upstart' in the less tolerant ones. Satisfied with his achievement and the response it had drawn, and convinced that his money from *High Season* and *A Month in the Country* had been well spent, Ken realised that what he wanted was to form a permanent company of his own. 'Just the very act of doing it was helpful in establishing priorities. Whether one felt resentful at the end of it and thought, "Oh Christ, that's six grand that could have gone somewhere else," we got a lot of experience ... It was a bit raw but I think you're entitled to make a bit of a tit of yourself sometimes, and it was helpful in so many ways. It was definitely worth doing.'

He left for Ljubljana, the capital of what was then the federal Yugoslav republic of Slovenia (and standing in for Bucharest in *Fortunes*), having divided with David Parfitt the tasks involved in setting up the notional theatre company, and safe in the knowledge that between filming and preparatory administrative work, he would scarcely have time to breathe. Liaising by phone whenever possible during shooting with Parfitt in London, he was in prime frenzy mode, his head a jumble of possible financial arrangements, benefactors and repertoire for the company. In the event, he would find himself occupied by more than merely professional matters.

7

The Clash of Claws

Fortunes of War was one of those period dramatic adaptations at which the BBC sporadically excels, in which an entire world is recreated with just as much attention to detail as is given to the central plot. In the case of Olivia Manning's novel sequence, the world is that of Europe and the Middle East as they slide into war in the late 1930s and early 1940s. Guy Pringle, an English lecturer in Bucharest, is a man to whom ideals are often more important than the immediate lives of those closest to him – in this case, his new wife, Harriet. Whilst attempting to do what little he can both to help 'deserving cases' among his circle of acquaintances and to oppose the rising tide of Fascism in Romania, he neglects his obligations to the woman he has brought from London into the political cauldron of the Balkans. Matters grow no easier when they flee to Egypt; the story branches into two as the couple are separated, following the travails of each in turn until their ultimate reunion.

Emma had the onerous task of arousing viewer sympathy for Harriet Pringle, of trying to ensure that Harriet's constant exhortations to Guy to live his own life rather than seeking to be an all-purpose saviour were not seen as simple selfishness. Once again, she found a key to the part in Harriet's status as a woman who thinks as well as feels, resisting the almost automatic marginalisation which takes place simply because of her sex. 'I didn't have a very clear notion of Harriet from the start,' she said. 'People usually either hate Harriet or hate Guy. I didn't much like Harriet myself. She rather got up my nose. It was something I hadn't done before, playing someone not of my own time [needless to say, pointing to Sally in *Me and My Girl* does nothing effectively to rebut this assertion]. The situation for women was so different then. Harriet really couldn't be positive; she didn't have the language to protest. She was living at a time when it still wasn't possible for women to complain. She wanted to be a wife, to have status, purpose. It becomes clear to her that that purpose doesn't exist, that Guy doesn't need her.

'It was like playing somebody who finds that they are being slowly immured. But one of the things I enjoyed most about playing Harriet was her wit, her very powerful sense of irony that allows her to survive. I still think it's difficult for people to accept a woman who looks good and has a strong brain, which she uses. I've actually had very intelligent people saying to me, "It's wonderful that you can act and think." But in any branch of the arts there must be intelligence – that, surely, must be your starting point.' For her it was vital that her intelligence be seen as more than a media selling-point or fashion accessory.

If Emma Thompson the comedienne had occasionally felt obliged to be wacky for the press, the transition into straight drama offered by *Tutti Frutti* and *Fortunes* gave her greater freedom to speak what had been her mind all along. At a press photocall to publicise the BBC's 1987 autumn schedule, of which *Fortunes of War* was a centrepiece, the photographers were in their usual tabloid mood – 'Give us the leggies, darling. Go on, lift your skirt up a little bit.'

Emma bluntly replied, 'No.'

Hacks: 'Why not?'

Emma: 'Because it's demeaning and degrading and I wouldn't dream of doing it. You wouldn't ask your own daughter to do it, would you?'

120

One particularly thick snapper persisted: 'Do it for your Uncle Frank.'

Emma: 'We're not blood-related, are we? I hope not.'

She later fumed, 'What fussed me was that in order to protect me the press person – who was a woman, incidentally – said something like, "She's a serious actress now." And I thought, yup, all the same bullshit prevails, because the message was that it would all have been fine if I was doing comedy, and that makes me really cross.'

Fortunes was the first full-blooded manifestation of Emma's talent for creating a complete character out of silent reaction shots and minimal responses, showing someone who thinks before she speaks and often instead of speaking, and working by implication rather than explication. When Branagh's Guy fulminated against the evils loosed in the world, the camera would cut to Harriet for a wordless moment that was almost more eloquent. Alan Plater's script captured a relationship in which the personal is usually left unsaid or glibly dismissed; Ken's performance, too, made it clear that Guy is simply unable directly to address important areas of his life. 'I wasn't enamoured of him at first,' said the actor. 'I found it hard to imagine that anyone so intelligent and sensitive about many things could be so insensitive to his wife.' (After three years of marriage, though, Ken was to acknowledge similar traits in himself: 'Em sometimes calls me a walnut because that's how unemotional I could be.') Instead of devoting himself to the true priorities, Guy fights on the cultural front by presenting in Bucharest an English-language stage production of Shakespeare's *Troilus and Cressida*, even taking refuge in verse for his directorial pep-talks – 'Stiffen the sinews and summon up the blood,' he advises his cast in a moment of sly self-referentiality for those viewers who knew that Branagh's stage reputation was built on his performance as King Henry V. Character and actor overlapped, too, in another appropriate remark of Guy's: 'I'd be very angry if I died. I have all these shows to put on.' It's a line which is a godsend to anyone writing a retrospective of the speaker.

Guy and Harriet's relationship is perfectly crystallised in the understated final exchange of the series. Guy, having believed Harriet to be dead, is emotionally reunited with her, and atop one of the great pyramids at Giza asks her if she will ever leave him again. She replies thoughtfully, 'Don't know. Can't promise. Probably not.' Emma later sighed, 'I was up and down those blooming pyramids like a yo-yo. But at the end of filming I felt rejuvenated. The air there is so full of energy.'

Whether in Egypt, Yugoslavia, Greece or the BBC studios in Ealing, Ken's energy – or at any rate his drive – continued unabated. He maintained contact with David Parfitt concerning details of his company's first two-show 'season': John Sessions' one-man *The Life of Napoleon* and, he hoped, his own play *Public Enemy*, which he had drafted in late 1985 after his bout of television work on *Coming Through*, *Ghosts* and *Lorna*. Breaks between takes on *Fortunes* were occupied by the would-be actor-manager bouncing ideas for the company off anyone within earshot. On one day off, when a group of actors had crossed the border from Yugoslavia to Trieste in Italy, inspiration struck: wouldn't it be a great idea, said Ken, to put together a season of Shakespeare plays directed by great Shakespearean actors who would be directing for the first time? The notion, and Ken's enthusiasm, plainly appealed to his companion, Richard Clifford, who has subsequently become a company 'regular'. As the idea developed, Branagh wrote to Anthony Hopkins requesting a meeting about the possibility of Hopkins directing *Macbeth*. As usual, the letter was persuasive and Hopkins agreed to talk.

By the time he returned from Slovenia to London, three distinct phases of production were now in prospect for his company: the two opening shows in mid-1987, a four-play Shakespeare season in the spring of 1988, and between them a production of *Twelfth Night* which Ken himself would direct. The company also had a name: Ken claimed that, in the best tradition of out-of-the-blue inspiration, he awoke in the middle of the night in his Yugoslav hotel, scribbled it on a bedside notepad, and decided the following morning that it had all the right connotations for a young group aiming to revitalise theatre and especially the classics. David Parfitt's preferred name, Compendium, was superseded by Renaissance.

Before flying to Egypt at the beginning of 1987 for the 'Levant trilogy' episodes of *Fortunes*, he had held initial meetings with Hopkins, a terrified Judi Dench, his childhood acting hero Derek Jacobi and Hugh Cruttwell's wife Geraldine McEwan. A venue had been confirmed for *Public Enemy* – the main 500-plus-seat theatre space in the Lyric, Hammersmith – and a possible starting-point for the Shakespeare season had also materialised. John Adams, who had directed Ken at RADA, included the Renaissance plans as part of his application for the artistic directorship of Birmingham Repertory Theatre. If he got the job, Branagh, who had turned down Adams' initial proposal that he become an associate director, would have in the Rep studio a subsidised venue at which to rehearse and stage the first batch of performances.

Between the first and second Egyptian trips a London venue was confirmed for *The Life of Napoleon* and *Twelfth Night* in the form of the Riverside Studios, a converted television facility about ten minutes' walk from the Lyric in Hammersmith. A series of openings 'off-West End' would suit Renaissance very nicely, thank you; in fact, any openings would have suited them, but the Riverside option had the added marketing strength of giving some geographical cohesion to the first Renaissance outings. It also gave the company a chance to arrange a weekend festival of rehearsed readings of new writing, a mini-fringe season, which Ken was especially keen to fit in. Another former RADA director, Malcolm McKay, had been engaged to oversee *Public Enemy*, and had instructed Ken to rewrite the play whilst in Egypt. He also found time during this leg of filming to write a letter to Prince Charles, inviting him to become the company's patron.

The activity never stopped. Back in London from Egypt, Branagh and Parfitt approached the Arts Council for funding, but were told that without prior notice of Renaissance's plans the bureaucratic machinery could not change gears to accommodate them. The company would have to find its money elsewhere. Judi Dench had finally summoned up the confidence to give a firm agreement to direct; Derek Jacobi and Geraldine McEwan were also on board (the latter having agreed immediately and enthusiastically), leaving only Anthony Hopkins in doubt. In the course of the Greek leg of *Fortunes* filming and the final stint at Ealing, Renaissance acquired a logo, an administrator, a press agent and premises (the spare room in Ken's flat in Camberwell, south-east London) – and lost Anthony Hopkins, who finally felt unable to commit himself to such a fledgling enterprise. A press conference was held in April 1987 announcing the first eighteen months' activities of Renaissance including what would now be the three-show Shakespeare tour, and numerous prospectuses were mailed out to potential investors. General Branagh had crossed his theatrical Rubicon.

The birth of Renaissance, managed as it was in tandem with a filming schedule which took its progenitor across Europe and the Near East, bore witness to Ken's phenomenal drive and focus, and is a remarkable story in itself. But as far as this period of his life is concerned, it's only half the story.

Branagh the theatrical dynamo had reached the stage where he missed some kind of emotional stability. 'There have been sacrifices imposed by circumstances, or one's unwillingness to alter one's circumstances or ambition,' he said. 'I lived with a girl at drama school, but we split up five years ago and I haven't really been in a stable relationship since then. There has been a long-term one, yes, but stable is not the way to describe it. I'm always going away, and it's not easy having a relationship with someone who's always leaving. You need a cuddle of an evening, you need a friend, you need a bit of nookie.'

The not exactly stable relationship he refers to seems likely to have been with Joely Richardson, whom *Today* newspaper confused with Katy Behean as *Beginning*'s 'Wendy Seagram' during Ken's RADA days. By all accounts, his time with her was volatile; she reacted badly to their break-up around or shortly after the time of *Fortunes of War*, so much so that at one point the cast of a play in which Richardson appeared were asked to remove any posters of Ken that might go up in the theatre so that she would not have the anguish of seeing his name or likeness. Ken later dismissed these years of his personal life as 'my rogue phase ... Things tended to happen in quite pressurised and intense ways. One went through emotions and intensity in a different kind of way. I think working so hard gave one excuses to be more of a rogue than one would have wished to have been.' The verbal defence of using the pronoun 'one' instead of 'I' allowed him to get close to uttering a statement of candid self-criticism, a sentiment with which Joely Richardson might well agree.

He described his romantic taste as running towards 'women who are talented and attractive and intelligent, but my problem is that I can't accept they could possibly, willingly, put up with someone who is the way I am at the moment.' It is tempting to believe that as he gave this description he was thinking of Emma Thompson – tempting and probably true, as he was speaking just after the shoot of *Fortunes*. It's more prosaic simply to remark, as a friend did, that he tended to fall for his leading ladies – a tendency evident as early as his RADA relationship with Katy Behean, who had played opposite him in several scenes from *Richard III*.

At the time Ken would offer only professional praise of Emma as a 'maverick': 'I think she has a talent which will resist pigeonholes, rightly in my view. She's not going to give up the comedy but she will undoubtedly go on to Shakespeare. What she has is an ability, which isn't arrogance, [to] take on any new discipline if you approach it sensibly ... A comedian has a vulnerability and a natural self-questioning which are actually very useful in straight acting.' The Shakespeare prophecy, with hindsight, wouldn't have been difficult to make for a man who was planning several major projects in that area (although Emma played no part onstage in the first batch of

Renaissance stage productions, Branagh did include her sister Sophie in the company); as far as comedy was concerned, his forecast would be only partially correct.

As her co-star was lauding her abilities, so Emma praised his. 'Ken is such a prodigious talent that I was totally in awe of him before we met. I was scared, I thought I wouldn't be good enough. We became great friends – thank God.' In retrospect, these were the first hints that Guy and Harriet were not the only people discovering each other during *Fortunes of War*. Emma, too, spoke of the sort of people who attracted her: 'I've been rather eclectic in who I've been drawn to over the years but I suppose I like broad natures. I don't mean a physical type, but spiritually. I'm attracted to people who strike out in all directions, who see further than self and their own small concerns, natures with whom you can talk about anything, where there are no limits.'

As she intimated, she had had her share of relationships, believing it necessary that, when Mr Right comes along, one has to have a base of experience to which to compare him. She once put it succinctly, 'Marriage is an extremely dangerous step – don't take it until you have shagged everything with a pulse.' Speaking at greater length, she explained, 'Love is a killer; being in love is very difficult, terrifying and it's certainly hard work. I think the propinquity of actors and actresses, that nearness, is responsible for a lot of grave errors. When you work with somebody you often think you've fallen in love. One's watched countless pairings.'

The genesis of this particular pairing is known only sketchily; those accounts which have reached the public are vague and often contradictory. It was far from obvious on the shoot for *Fortunes of War* that anything was going on. 'They were obviously good mates, but I had no idea that they were going out with each other,' said producer Betty Willingale; co-star Robert Stephens 'was there for about twelve weeks and I didn't realise it at all'. Indeed, when Emma told actor Sam Dastor out of the blue, 'I'm very cold and hard, you know,' he realised that she thought he had been developing a crush on her; obviously, if she was in the throes of becoming attached to Ken, the last thing she needed was the spaniel-like devotion of someone else on set. Dastor in fact had no such feelings for her, nor did he spot the ulterior motive behind her remark: 'I wasn't aware of the romance with Kenneth – they played it cool,' he said.

Ken is reticent about the initial phase of their relationship in his autobiography *Beginning*: he mentions an early rapport, and twenty pages later they are a couple. As far as moments of truth go, the only interim mention of Emma outside the context of the drama doesn't exactly have the makings of an ardent courtship. The two of them, plus David Parfitt, were using the time between takes in romantic Ealing to stuff envelopes for a mail-shot to possible benefactors of his company. Emma found herself about to send off her own invitation, got up, walked out of the room, and came back a minute later with a cheque. As on other occasions, Branagh uses a story about his professional activities to sidestep having to give anything away about his personal life.

Emma has been a little more forthcoming on a few occasions, describing their courtship as 'like the mating dance of two lobsters. We clashed claws.' John Sessions also believed that 'They didn't get on so well at first... It was a little bit spiky.' The decisive moment, in Emma's account, took place while the two were resting under blankets between takes on a night location shoot: 'Ken started to sing, in a little falsetto, to kind of amuse me, and I burst into tears because he sounded exactly like my father singing on *The Magic Roundabout*. And it was most strange because it was, as it were, unsolicited.' Elsewhere she continued the Freudian link by musing that, like Eric Thompson, Ken has 'a hard sort of carapace of privacy and secrecy', not only towards the world at large but even in his personal life.

And yet their early days as a couple after *Fortunes of War* were anything but private and secret, despite Ken's protestations that he had no plans to marry anyone – 'I am as camp as a row of tents – and I intend to stay that way,' he claimed implausibly, adding elsewhere, 'As far as I am concerned, the nation can think I'm gay.' Emma, too, admitted at the time that she knew what it was like to be completely in love, but when asked whether it was with Ken, replied, 'Do you mind if I don't answer that? Just the question makes me palpitate' – a virtual confirmation without actually saying anything openly. She had, in fact, been smitten so thoroughly that she was beginning to reassess fundamental aspects of her life. 'I'd hate to think of myself as too violently independent. I'm a city person, live alone, I like it. But I'm beginning to think it wouldn't be difficult to share.'

Ken's public unveiling was in Emma's solo BBC television series *Thompson*. He appeared in a number of sketches as everything from a disgruntled Robin Hood to a mumbling, pencil-chewing floor manager on a television advertising shoot, and even danced on a gigantic record-player. 'The question, "What are you now – an actress or a comedienne?" wouldn't mean anything to me. I just want to do different things,' said Emma a few months before the series was transmitted. And, remembering her late father: 'One of the things he always used to say to me I've never forgotten was "Only be original." I suppose one of the reasons I got round to doing this series was a voice in my head saying "Be original."' She paid a discreet tribute to Eric Thompson by selecting as the theme tune to the series 'Unsquare Dance' by Dave Brubeck, 'one of my dad's favourite pieces and the music we played at his funeral. I've always wanted to use it.'

She had written the series herself, and insisted that it be shot without a studio audience and broadcast without a canned laugh track. 'I've been in absolute control,' she said. 'I wrote the whole thing myself and I suffered tremendous terror. I thought, "I've committed myself and everybody else to piles of rubbish." But if it's a desperate disaster I have done it. It is an achievement and a bit of me just feels very proud having got through it.' She described the series, in probably the most unselfconsciously 'luvvie' remark she's ever made on the record, as 'an allotment. I've got this little patch of ground.

And I've planted all these little seeds, and I've come up with a few carrots and a couple of mangy old onions and some potatoes and lots of different vegetables. They've got roots and they've come out of the ground and they were planted by me. Above the allotment is a massive, an incredibly beautiful oak tree, and that's Shakespeare. When you get very tired you take a deckchair and you go and sit under the oak tree.' The ghost of Juliana Talent in her Footlights sketch had not, it seems, been thoroughly laid to rest.

Emma's interviews at the time included frequent remarks about the terrors of writing an entire series: 'You end up lying in the bottom of the bath feeling like a deflated balloon, feeling incredibly heavy. That heaviness was what I started with. I had to kind of fill my own bath up.' She was open about the trepidation she felt, but in private she was much more fearful still. Her diary entries during the writing process reveal the terrors which led her to give the series the working title *A Big Mistake*. 20 August 1987: 'Somebody help me. Writing is the next miserable thing to . . .' She couldn't find anything worse. A month later: 'None of it's funny. None of it. I want to die.' These worries proved uncomfortably close to the mark.

Thompson was an oddly frustrating series to watch. Emma obviously had talent and intelligence, but seemed unable to focus them sufficiently. She could write amusing sketches and sharp punchlines, but rarely delivered both in the same piece. Some 'character' monologues elicit, rather than laughter, at best a sense of wary recognition and at worst plain discomfort: Phyllida Law as an eccentric woman living for years up a tree to avoid accidentally treading on and killing any of God's tinier creatures, for instance, provokes unsettled bemusement more than anything else. Musical numbers tended not to be integrated into larger routines, leaving them seeming to be largely gratuitous and included solely in a spirit of 'Look, I can do this as well.' A moving exception to this tendency consisted of a choral arrangement accompanied by shots of boiler-suited, hard-hatted women in an unspecified heavy industrial environment. As actress Josette Simon is seen tearing up what is

129

obviously a 'Dear Jane' letter in a locker-room, the number makes an implicit affirmation of women's strength in matters of relationships. The song is 'Sigh no more, ladies, sigh no more...' from *Much Ado About Nothing*, one of the Shakespeare plays which Renaissance were touring at around the same time, and in which her sister Sophie played the part of Hero's maid Margaret. The musical arrangement was not, however, Patrick Doyle's Renaissance version, but composed by Christopher Walker, *Thompson*'s musical director.

Topics covered in sketches included sexual harassment at work, the weight-loss industry and 'body fascism' in general, divorce, the vicissitudes of relationships and women's expected roles in all aspects of life. 'I tease my own sex,' she said, 'because that to me is more enjoyable than teasing the opposite sex... But I wrote the series for people. I didn't write it for women... I'm sure that somewhere or other I am exorcising demons... I do not know any woman who has not been on a diet or worried about what she ate.' Emma resolutely avoided the pits of tub-thumping earnestness, but she was nevertheless trying to be trenchant and funny at the same time, and unfortunately it simply didn't come off. In the midst of these subtextual comments, the straightforward wacky stuff also foundered as audiences wondered what else they might be missing in those pieces compared to the more 'messagey' material. *Thompson* is that rarity, a series which would actually have been improved by the addition of a laugh track signalling, not necessarily that laughter was expected, but that such a response was welcome.

Audience and critical responses were savage. 'I'd had all this success, unlooked for, as an actress, and suddenly, when I go back to my roots, I was somehow accused of cashing in on being a successful actress and trying to be a comedian,' she protested. 'I'd never wanted to be a successful actress – all I'd wanted was to be a comedian.' Since that series, although Emma has acted comic roles on screen, she has not done any sketch-based comedy work. Her image and career were already in transition by this time, and had been given added impetus by the British

Academy of Film and Television Arts' Award for Best
Television Actress, for both *Tutti Frutti* and *Fortunes*. 'It won't
happen again,' she said of her awards, showing either undue
modesty or an amazing lack of foresight, 'and I doubt I'll be as
busy as this in future so I might as well enjoy it.'

She was tipped in December 1987 to return to the stage in a
£2 million musical about King Edward VIII and Mrs Simpson,
appearing opposite Ian Charleson (star of *Chariots of Fire*),
with a book by Simon Raven, who had written the successful
television series based on the same story, and music and lyrics
by former Gary Glitter producer Mike Leander and Eddie
Seago (subsequently the team behind the musical biography of
El Cordobes, *Matador*). Although an album of songs from the
musical was predicted for early 1988, the project withered on
the vine. There was also talk of a television film with Judi
Dench based on novelist Elizabeth Taylor's book *Excursion
Source*. The reception given to *Thompson*, in contrast, persuaded her to go no further down that particular avenue, at
least for the foreseeable future. She claimed not to be taking
the criticism badly, 'because you think back, "I'm sure you're
right." I'm very keen to know how I could have done better.'
Nevertheless, she said, she would not do another comedy
series, although 'I hope the experience will have helped me for
the next task, hopefully a drama.'

The most significant by-product of the series took years to
emerge, and still has not come to full fruition. Its American
screening brought her to the attention of Sydney Pollack and
his colleague Lindsay Doran. Pollack had twenty years of film
direction behind him, including such titles as *They Shoot
Horses, Don't They?* and *Out of Africa*, and has also made
minor appearances in several films including Woody Allen's
Husbands and Wives and *Tootsie*, in which, in addition to
directing the movie, he played the part of Michael Dorsey,
Dustin Hoffman's theatrical agent. Pollack and Doran, now
setting up their own productions through their company
Mirage, subsequently became the executive team behind
Thompson's first major Hollywood film (and Branagh's first

Hollywood directing credit), *Dead Again*. Moreover, they were sufficiently interested by Emma's ability to delineate characters in her *Thompson* material that they suggested she turn her hand to screenwriting. Emma, with her abiding interest in the portrayal of women in the arts, began work on a screen adaptation of Jane Austen's *Sense and Sensibility*, a novel in which the undoubted native intelligence of the Dashwood sisters is given no other outlet by their society than in the complexities of genteel nineteenth-century courtship.

Personal matters, too, were about to take a dramatic turn, putting Branagh and Thompson into the public eye as a couple in a way which they had striven for many months to avoid. Ken, whilst giving nothing away about his relationship with Emma, had continued to bewail the emptiness of a life that was all work. 'It is lovely to work and to accomplish things. But [that] does not comfort you if you are alone in the wee small hours of the night. Work is not the be-all and the end-all for me. It does not replace all the other things.' He effectively admitted what was on his mind by adding, 'My parents' marriage was an inspiration to me and the right kind of marriage gives a centre to your life . . . more than a great list of achievements.'

When he did propose, it seems the circumstances could have been happier. Various accounts report that Ken popped the question at Shepperton Studios on *Henry V*, or that he flew Emma to New York on Concorde expressly to propose to her there. However, friends later recounted that Emma discovered a number of letters to Ken from a woman with whom he had had a brief affair whilst also involved with her. (The other woman is believed to have been an actress on the first Renaissance tour of three Shakespeare plays.) Thompson was allegedly ballistic with rage, declaring that she never wanted to see him again, and promptly left for New York – hoping, say the sources for this version of events, that Ken would follow her. When he did, it was to protest his commitment to her in the most demonstrative way possible, by asking for her hand.

Brian Blessed reckoned that 'Ken's efforts with Emma in those early days were comparable to Richard Harris in *A Man Called Horse*. He had to go through all those ceremonies to earn that lovely Indian girl. I think Ken had to earn Emma, and there's a lot to be said for that.' However, if this account is true, another cinematic parallel suggests itself – with Emma's then unreleased first feature film, *The Tall Guy*.

After months of press speculation, the couple finally announced in August 1989 that they would marry 'by the end of September. It can't be any sooner as we're in the middle of a run.' In fact it was much sooner – less than a week after the initial announcement. Although guests were not sent formal invitations in an effort to prevent leaks, a subsequent press release disclosed that on Sunday 20 August, beneath an ornamental rose garden gazebo at Viscount Astor's former home of Cliveden House, Berkshire (the scene, in the 1960s, of salacious goings-on which fuelled the Profumo scandal and, in the 1970s, of the teenaged Ken's portrayal of Cassio in the Berkshire Shakespeare Players' production of *Othello*), they were to take their vows in a short Church of England ceremony at which the Reverend Malcolm Johnson, Rector of St Botolph's in the City of London, would officiate.

In an attempt to defuse media prying, the release gave full details of the wedding breakfast (smoked salmon and roast lamb), the best man (Brian Blessed) and even the 'costumes': 'Branagh will be dressed in a hand-tailored, double-breasted, navy blue linen suit. But Emma's close friends, who have been sworn to secrecy over her wedding dress, will say only that she is not planning to wear white.' The press release constituted the 'carrot' of a two-pronged publicity approach to the event; the 'stick' to keep unwanted interlopers away was a full-scale private security operation, although this was stymied by the refusal of the National Trust (which leases Cliveden's grounds to a five-star hotel) to close the 375-acre estate to the public over the weekend.

The whole affair was shrouded in rumour and counterrumour. Branagh's relatives in Belfast denied any knowledge of the wedding. His grandmother claimed, 'I haven't heard anything yet except what we saw in the papers,' and cousin Joss Galloway was adamant that 'The papers have got it all wrong.' They hadn't; the ceremony went ahead as announced, with Judi Dench and Richard Briers giving readings from Samuel Pepys, Sir Philip Sidney and – naturally – Shakespeare. Ken opined that 'It was very nerve-racking and much worse than being onstage – but much more fun.' Emma, whose gown was revealed to be a multi-coloured pastel affair with a criss-cross pink lattice bodice and white veil, refused in theatrical terms to pose in Ken's arms – 'I don't want my husband to have a hernia on our first night.' The half-hour service was followed by a £30,000 party for the 200 guests, including an impromptu concert and a firework display. Any honeymoon was postponed; after a night in the hotel's honeymoon suite, it was back to the Lyric on Shaftesbury Avenue for the marital strife of *Look Back in Anger* the following night.

John Sessions later asserted that the wedding had been orchestrated not as a major 'luvvie' gathering but simply as 'a real humdinger. There weren't that many celebrity guests. Brian Blessed, Judi Dench and Michael Williams, Stephen Fry and Hugh Laurie, Richard Briers, myself and Ben Elton. After that it was mostly family and not-so-familiar actors.' The Rev. Johnson recalled Brian Blessed's speech at the dinner after the ceremony, which 'moved me almost as much as the service. He said that there were people who would want to pull down Emma and Kenneth, but the people in the room loved them and it was very important that we all kept in touch with them and surrounded them with a lot of love because there were a lot of people who would enjoy destroying them. I thought that was very telling.'

Ken rebutted allegations that the couple had in fact been married earlier in the week at a north London register office, saying, 'This was the real McCoy today. We got special dispensation for the legals.' Emma, too, confessed to enormous relief 'now it's all over'. Within forty-eight hours, however, came the news that it wasn't. The Rev. Johnson confirmed that the Cliveden ceremony had indeed been only a blessing, but one which in fact *preceded* the civil wedding. 'They hadn't realised that it was necessary beforehand,' he said. 'It doesn't matter that they just got it the wrong way round. It was genuine confusion. It wasn't a fake wedding. At the end of the ceremony I officiated at they weren't legally married, but they were married in the eyes of God and they were married in their eyes, because they told me that they regarded that as the wedding.' Suddenly the rash of 'next month, abroad' rumours were given a fresh lease of life, not least by Ken's apparent endorsement of them. The 'legals' actually took place five days later at the Register Office of Camden, the London borough in which they lived.

If the Belfast side of the Branagh family hadn't known about the Cliveden wedding at all, not even his parents had been told of its true nature. His father said in bewilderment, 'There were tears shed at that ceremony and I was one with tears. If it wasn't real, then that's news to me. I'm sure Kenneth would have confided in me.' Frances Branagh was even more distraught: 'As far as we were concerned, we were at our son's wedding and he became a legally married man.' Then, echoing her mother-in-law, 'The first I knew about all this was when I saw the papers. Of course I was shocked, but I'm not believing anything until I get it from the horse's mouth.' Ken's brother Bill junior speculated that the bride-groom had opted to hold back the nature of the ceremony from his traditionalist mother precisely because the know-ledge would upset her.

The whole experience reinforced Branagh's desire that his private life should be allowed to remain private. 'I've always made it plain that there are some things about which I do not want to talk, and that there are areas which I believe are totally personal. I found it offensive that Emma and I were chased all over the place before, during and after our wedding. We were both in the West End at the time, and we were followed – no, pursued – everywhere. Worse than that, they tried to get to my family and friends as well, by all sorts of devious means. They lied, they impersonated people. It's just not on, I'm afraid.' The great charmer now refused to give interviews to certain tabloid newspapers.

8

Only Themselves For Company

Renaissance activities were able to move into top gear after the shooting of *Fortunes of War* was completed. Emma had given the company a motto from Ovid: *Ingenuas didicisse fideliter artes emollit mores nec sinit esse feros* (To have conscientiously studied the liberal arts refines behaviour and does not allow it to be savage), and its first productions, Ken's play *Public Enemy* and John Sessions' one-man show *The Life of Napoleon*, were imminent.

Branagh clearly wanted to get away from the treadmill of appearing in other people's stage and screen projects. 'It's the best way for actors to have some control. I would much rather various people rang me up and said, "You're so wonderful, come and do this." But, sadly, it doesn't often happen like that.' And, despite his claim to the contrary, what he wanted most of all was to take the reins himself. Working as compulsively as he had done (and would continue to do), however, his motive was not so much impatience as a more general frustration. 'I wanted to create a bit of time to prepare the work that we do, to do work that was carefully thought out, to do plays that you want to do and not because they have come round again.' This aim would be borne out by the pace of the Shakespeare season, but sounds implausible in the light of the scuttling around which was taking place as Ken had been simultaneously setting up the company and shooting a television series.

The budget of *Public Enemy* had been set at £50,000, with costs and profits split between Renaissance and the Lyric, Hammersmith. Branagh and Parfitt had persuaded forty or so friends and colleagues to invest relatively small sums – between £100 and £500 or between £500 and £5000, the figures varied from report to report – in the play: 'It's not a bad investment if you are wanting a bit of a flutter and like the theatre, because we're not being ruthless and taking a huge rake-off. It really would give us great pleasure to return an investor's £500 or whatever with a bit on top.' In all, £40,000 was raised from private investors for the first two London shows.

Public Enemy, as its title suggests, was in part a homage to James Cagney, with Branagh's character a Cagney impersonator in pub talent contests who lives out an obsession with the actor, imagining himself as Cagney taking over Belfast Chicago-style and seeing everyone as a character in a gangster movie. Behind the antics, however, he was commenting on Belfast as a latter-day gangland, and on the convenient excuse furnished by the Troubles to allow mobsters to branch into organised crime, ostensibly to fund their 'armed struggles'.

Ken manifested a fiery determination that his playwriting debut proper should be well executed and publicised, although its director Malcolm McKay (who had directed him in *A Midsummer Night's Dream, No Orchids For Miss Blandish* and *Hamlet* several years earlier at RADA) thinks that his enthusiasm could have been more evenly distributed. 'He'd written a draft – it was fairly rough, but it was a good idea to try and connect Irish terrorism with gangsterism in that the people involved in each are essentially romantics. Probably the weakness of it was that Ken is also a romantic, so he wasn't quite hard enough with it. I think he really wanted at the time to be Jimmy Cagney, so he wrote it bearing in mind that he'd be playing that part. He writes very easy dialogue, it was a good idea; but when I first saw the script it was unformed. So I had a long session with him and told him what I felt about the play, and he wrote another draft which was much better, but I still felt there was quite a long way to go. But by this time he'd booked the Lyric and we were pretty well into rehearsals.

'We had one slight crisis about halfway through when I thought that there needed to be some fairly substantial rewrites, but by that point Ken had switched from being a writer to being an actor and wanted to get on and act it. There *were* holes in the play; the ideal would have been that after about two weeks' rehearsal we would have all packed up, Ken would have done another draft then we'd have come back and done it. But by then he was starting to work with John Sessions on *Napoleon*. As a kind of compromise solution I made him do *some* rewrites; he took a weekend and didn't really do it thoroughly.'

As against this reluctance to take time honing the script, Ken devoted himself fanatically to the preparation of the show. The opening scene, for instance, consisted of a re-creation of James Cagney's famous tap-dancing routine in *Yankee Doodle Dandy*. Even Cagney, who had begun his vaudeville career as a hoofer (and female impersonator!), had not performed the routine in a single take, but a stage production lacks the facility for such cheating. Ken had to practise until his feet ached. 'I remember him in *Public Enemy* doing that tap-dancing for an hour or two before every rehearsal and for a month or so beforehand,' says McKay. 'He's not a dancer, and he got away with it, all credit to him; he was determined to do it. And he's always been an incredibly astute publicist. Rehearsals stopped at five o'clock every day and he had a half-hour for interviews every day through the rehearsal period. That was part of the whole process.'

Once again – despite Ken's growing 'fan club' (McKay remembers that 'at the first night a hundred or so girls showed up, and there were huge whistles and applause as he came to take his bow') – *Public Enemy* was given a mixed reception. 'The play is not very good,' opined the *Financial Times* reviewer. 'But it does not exactly stink. The interest lies in Branagh exorcising his Cagney obsession, which you can easily read as

the reason he became an actor and star RADA graduate in the
first place, and in his relating this fad to his Ulster background.' Audiences tailed off, and once again Ken put the
critics' coolness down to his age. 'Some people thought I was
rather young to be writing my own play and appearing in it
myself.' The investors lost their money. Branagh had hopes of
recouping it with a screen version, or a triumphal return to
Belfast to the newly refurbished Grand Opera House, but none
of these dreams came to fruition. 'It had eight reviews,' recalls
McKay, 'three for, three against and two neutral. They weren't
powerful enough, and Ken wasn't big enough, to take it into
the West End. It's a shame if it's put him off writing, because
I'd like to see what he did as a writer, but what he's got to do is
concentrate a bit more. You have to sit at home and keep
cracking problems, going down one step and cracking them
again. On the other hand, he's unproven as a writer, and
maybe if he took off for a while and gave himself a long break
he might come up with something well worth it.' *Public Enemy*
was scheduled to be staged by local company Theatre Ulster in
autumn 1988, but the production was abandoned as not being
commercially 'safe' enough for a touring repertory company.
When Ken himself finally stood on the stage of his home town's
restored Victorian theatre, it was to be as part of Belfast's
Renaissance Week.

Concerned that the relative commercial failure of *Public
Enemy* endangered Renaissance's financial footing, he had
taken a couple more television roles, shooting Eugene O'Neill's
Strange Interlude with Glenda Jackson while the play was
still running at the Lyric and agreeing to appear in Christopher
Fry's *The Lady's Not For Burning* after *Napoleon* was up and
running. Not surprisingly, he was falling into poor shape both
physically and mentally as he tried to hold his several performing, directorial and administrative schedules together.
The man regularly spoken of by colleagues as a fine 'team
player' lost sight of everyone but himself, going absent when
fatigue struck and then lying to justify himself. The publicity
for *Napoleon* coincided with that for *A Month in the Country*

and pre-publicity for the autumn broadcast of *Fortunes of War*, and Ken the astute publicist found himself on another clutch of treadmills.

Thankfully, *The Life of Napoleon* fared better than *Public Enemy* down the road at the Riverside, a pair of former television studios converted into theatrical spaces with a cinema and art gallery attached. John Sessions had first come to public attention after RADA as one of the regulars on the radio and (subsequently) television series *Whose Line is it Anyway?*, in which performers improvise comedy sketches from random props or suggestions given by the audience, and he has since made a number of solo television series out of surreal half-hour multi-character rambles based on the same principle. His particular forte is in blending pop-culture references with abstruse historical material which could perhaps best be described as Robin Williams with a PhD in English Literature. His improvisations rapidly gather a juggernaut momentum which once led another *Whose Line* contestant, Jonathan Pryce, to lunge for Sessions' throat in a desperate attempt to get a word in edgeways. On another occasion, a round of the game show consisted of imagining the world's worst person with whom to be stuck in a lift. Straight off the mark came comedian Paul Merton with, 'Hello, my name's John Sessions.'

Napoleon, however, required much more forethought and restraint. Sessions aimed to tell Bonaparte's story with historical accuracy, but personifying the dozens of eighteenth- and nineteenth-century characters of his life through the voices and mannerisms of recognisable contemporary political, artistic and media figures. It was wildly ambitious, and rehearsals with Branagh largely consisted of the pair evaluating, say, which theatrical knight most appropriately represented which French Revolution lynchpin. Technical preparation was another ball game entirely: with some 150 sound and lighting cues, the show was as complex for the tech team and stage manager as for Sessions, and sure enough the first preview was so jinxed that Branagh cancelled the second to work on perfecting that side of the show. However, when it hit cruising speed it was truly a tour de force, and for once Ken didn't need to dismiss any snobbish bad reviews. Although *Napoleon* never made a profit, it transferred to the West End and confirmed Sessions' growing reputation as a fearsomely intelligent maniac.

The Olivier comparisons continued to dog Branagh in his role as actor-manager, and for once he didn't deny them outright: 'There's a story that, when Olivier was doing *Antony and Cleopatra* with his own company at the St James Theatre, he and Vivien Leigh each Friday would sit at a table at the edge of the stage handing out the actors' wages. I rather like that.'

He also claimed a great awareness of the tradition in which Renaissance would operate: 'I love that sense of theatre being handed down, through the generations, from Irving, who was seen by Olivier, who was seen by Hopkins, who was seen by me.' The role of the actor-manager was clearly not quite dead yet: 'I do want to break down the idea that, if you happen to be an actor, anything else you do you'll necessarily do less well.' But, he added, 'I'm more of a tortured nutcase than a tortured genius – I hope I'll stay on the right side of megalomania.' At one point, however, the pressures of organising the company simply became too much; he fled overnight to a friend's clifftop cottage at Dover where for a week he kept in contact with the Renaissance office only through daily phone calls to deal with the most urgent matters. 'Nobody knew where I was. It was bliss.' The books he had taken with him remained unread, as he spent his time sleeping and watching television. Ken the ordinary, boring bloke confessed to being a soap addict: 'I watch all that stuff – *Dallas, The Colbys* ... I got very excited the other day. I was rehearsing and Kate O'Mara was stuck in the revolving door and I carried her bags. I was very thrilled because I'd seen her as Caresse [Carrington, in *Dynasty*] only the week before.' Testimony yet again to Branagh possessing 'the sunny, uncomplicated personality of a club tennis coach', as the *Observer* described him, although it might have helped

that O'Mara, too, had once tried to establish her own privately
funded touring theatre company.

After the poor critical showing of *Public Enemy* and the
more positive reception given to *Napoleon*, *Twelfth Night* drew
nothing but admiration from reviewers. Branagh spoke in a
1988 television programme about Renaissance of having
played Orsino (badly) in a radio production and feeling a
strong desire to revisit the play, 'a sort of gut feeling, like a
favourite novel that you finish and you want to be involved in
... I ended up not acting in [the stage production] because I
wanted so strongly to have a hand in directing it.' He had
succeeded in talking Richard Briers, best known for television
sitcoms, into playing Malvolio – Briers' initial response had
been, 'Blimey! You serious?' His commitment had in turn
persuaded a number of other actors of quality to join the cast:
Anton Lesser, who had the previous year played opposite
Juliet Stevenson in the RSC's *Troilus and Cressida*, took the
role of Feste the jester; Caroline Langrishe (whom Ken had
met on *Fortunes of War*) played Olivia and Frances Barber (his
stage sister Ophelia in the 1984 RSC *Hamlet*) was Viola. The
biggest name, however, was that of Paul McCartney, who
permitted his song 'Once Upon a Long Ago' to be adapted for
the melody of Feste's song 'Come away, death...' The rest of
the stage score was written by Patrick Doyle who progressed
from playing a recording engineer in *Tutti Frutti* to regular
involvement as composer (and occasionally actor as well) in
all of Branagh's subsequent stage and film projects. The play's
stage manager, Tamar Thomas, is now Ken's permanent
personal assistant.

While Emma was appearing in *Saturday Night Fry*, Stephen
Fry's BBC radio comedy series with his frequent comic
partner, her former boyfriend Hugh Laurie, Ken was directing
Renaissance's third production, and the first to indicate the
extent to which his primary aim for the company – revitalising
the classics, and especially Shakespeare – was likely to
succeed.

Ken had announced beforehand that his production was

143

'going to be really Christmassy with snowmen, pressies, trees and Victorian costumes', but this mischievous remark was deliberately misleading in terms of his vision of the play itself. Modern views of *Twelfth Night* – one of Shakespeare's so-called 'festive' comedies – find it difficult to accept as simple amusement the subplot, in which the hangers-on in the lady Olivia's household trick her officious steward Malvolio into wild misbehaviour and have him imprisoned as a madman. On the discovery of the stratagem, the freed Malvolio's final line of the play – 'I'll be revenged on the whole pack of you!' – casts a pall over an otherwise straightforward resolution in which order is happily restored, with a couple of marriages into the bargain.

Branagh had determined to highlight these shadows, and also to draw out the full darkness of the main plot's secondary elements of exploitation (as ageing debauchee Sir Toby Belch lives off the purse of the hapless Sir Andrew Aguecheek), and the confusion and unwitting betrayals resulting from the main plot device of identical twins living, unknown to each other, in the same city. With snow falling on a set which included a family tomb, bare trees in the background and washes of blue, wintry light only partially illuminating the action, the audience was in no doubt that this was not a standard festive reading of the play, that their laughter was to be rationed and that the denouement of Act 5 did not herald a golden New Year in Illyria after the final curtain fell on the action. Controversially, director Ken even elected to transpose the two opening scenes, so that the first line heard by the audience was not Orsino's lyrical 'If music be the food of love, play on' but the shipwrecked Viola's bewildered 'What country, friend, is this?'

Richard Briers was magnificently sour-faced as the 'proper', humourless Malvolio; the spectacle of his ragged, shambling but still dignified figure on his release from durance in the final scene was striking, and chuckles died in the audience's throats. But the tone of the production was more completely personified in Feste the jester. The character is given a number of cynical lines, climaxing with a malicious glee when he announces to Malvolio his part in the trickery, and his motive of revenge upon the steward for earlier slighting remarks. Anton Lesser's powerful, icy performance drew on these elements to create the most sinister representation of a Shakespearean jester, more so even than the Fool in *King Lear*: a surreptitious alcoholic and a scabrous misanthrope whose witticisms were simply part of a job he did not relish. The final line of Feste's closing song, 'And we'll strive to please you every day' – inviting audience forgiveness and approval – had seldom rung more chillingly hollow.

The press performance, given when many of the company (Ken included) were nursing hangovers from a royal gala and party the previous night, was smooth and assured, and the critics raved. Thames Television filmed the play (Paul Kafno's TV version was screened by Channel 4 the following Christmas – although, because of festive-season scheduling, it went out on the sixth rather than the twelfth night of Christmas), and future Renaissance projects were keenly awaited. In the meantime, its success made it easier to raise the £250,000 pounds needed to finance the three Shakespeare plays due to go into rehearsal in February 1988.

Ken had somehow put together the first major season of the Renaissance Theatre Company in between globetrotting *Fortunes of War* commitments: *Much Ado About Nothing*, directed by Judi Dench; *As You Like It*, directed by Geraldine McEwan, and Derek Jacobi directing him in *Hamlet*. Once again, his charm and the passion with which he conveyed his ideas for the company won over all his intended directors, just as he had earlier persuaded Richard Briers to play the classics for an untried company. Even Judi Dench, who had never directed before and professed herself horribly frightened at the prospect, was finally persuaded; only Anthony Hopkins, wary of directing *Macbeth* in such an untried set-up, had slipped through his grasp. One critic described Branagh's talent for the politics of self-effacement as being 'the knack of modestly backing to centre stage and reluctantly taking the limelight, thank you.'

The season would open at Birmingham Rep's 140-seat studio theatre, which had agreed to give Renaissance space and facilities for twelve weeks in return for a share of the box-office take. It would then tour to Belfast, Dublin, Bath, Brighton, Manchester, Newcastle and Leeds (though, despite Ken's early remarks to David Grant in 1984 regarding his intentions for a then hypothetical company of his own, not Reading) before coming 'into town'. He explained the reasoning behind the decision to begin away from London: 'I wanted to do this in the regions because the audience is different. What we are trying to do is new and raw and I think it will go down very well there. My experience last year [with *Romeo and Juliet*] was that there was an element of the London audience that thought what we were doing was a little unsophisticated.' Once again, he showed a characteristic blend of commitment to his aims of accessibility and freshness with a desire to defend himself even before any accusations might be made – if some of the London crowd didn't like what he was doing, he would take it to people who would. Success equalled control, not just of what he was doing but as far as possible of how it was received.

Although the £250,000 budget for the season and the £60,000 for *Twelfth Night* were raised entirely through a combination of private investment and box-office income (the three-play tour was budgeted to be self-financing once it hit the road, but the rehearsal period and initial performances in Birmingham demanded resources of £80,000 up front), Branagh felt neither pride nor enthusiasm that Renaissance might be cited by the government as a shining exemplar of succeeding without subsidy. 'I hate doing it,' he said at the time of *Public Enemy*. 'I hate the enforced Thatcherism of it. The re-election of this government [two months earlier, for a third term] is the biggest disaster for the arts this century, and the more we make it work in this climate the more in trouble we are. The idea that we might be held up as an example of good Thatcherist practice is appalling.' He mused, 'I don't know what [the government and the Arts Council] think people would do – whether they think that if all artistic directors of theatres were given the kind of budgets they want they would all immediately have villas in Spain or whether they'd only do plays with £1 million budgets about left-wing one-legged black lesbian single parents or something. It's a symptom of a wider disease in our society.' While Emma Thompson was putting her growing weight as a performer behind numerous quasi-political causes, Ken remained primarily exercised by the effects of the political climate within the arts – a perspective which would later broaden, in no small part due to Emma's influence.

At the time, his own focus on Renaissance funding was more personal. 'It costs £38,000 a year to keep the company going whether or not we stage any plays. At the moment, we seem to have the money coming in, but if it doesn't I'd have no qualms about selling the flat ... The advantage of being an actor is that you have to be used to an itinerant life, and a bit of me wouldn't mind the prospect of living in one room in someone else's flat... Happy and comfortable as I am in my own home, despite the fact I have a sentimental attachment to it, it's less important to me than the theatre company' – which was run at the time from the flat's spare room. However, when the time did come for him to sell the Camberwell flat and move to West Hampstead with Emma, continuing uncertainty surrounding the route of the proposed Channel Tunnel rail link through London meant that he had to drop the asking price by £20,000 before he could find a buyer. Branagh and Parfitt, whose house was marked for demolition, formed a local action group, PEARL – Peckham and Environs Against the Rail Link. Its success in the face of the government's chronic dithering on the issue is not recorded; in any case, the final decision on the route was not taken until years later.

Once again, Ken was enthusiastic about the notion of Renaissance carrying on a tradition in theatre passed down through generations of practitioners. 'When you have someone like Judi Dench directing, instead of giving academic lectures on the text, she passes down lessons that were given by

William Poel to Edith Evans; Edith told George Rylands, he told Peter Hall who told Trevor Nunn who told Judi. That's a direct line of experience which seems to me very important.'

Geraldine McEwan's direction of *As You Like It* concentrated on the pastoral exuberance of the comedy in the Forest of Arden, where the exiled members of the ducal court dabble enthusiastically in the rural life until Act 5 restores them to their fortunes. The exception to this sylvan slumming was Touchstone, the Fool. As with virtually all of Shakespeare's low comedy, the passing of four centuries has not been kind to Touchstone's witticisms, and actors who take on the now thankless role have to grapple with the demands of what has become one of the Bard's great unfunny clowns; they have to create comedy in their characterisation to make up for what has evaporated over the years from his lines. Branagh chose to play him as a music-hall comic: loud red and mustard checked suit, hair slicked back and his patter likewise well greased. The portrayal was variously compared with Benny Hill, Eric Idle, Max Miller and most frequently Archie Rice, the fading protagonist of John Osborne's *The Entertainer* and the part in which Laurence Olivier reinvented himself in the late 1950s – try as he might, poor Ken just couldn't get away from those hated comparisons.

His main acting role on the tour was, of course, Prince Hamlet. Derek Jacobi had originally been approached to direct *Richard II* (the title role of which he had played as part of the BBC project to televise every one of Shakespeare's plays) with another actor in the lead – Branagh was keen to ensure that Renaissance was seen as more than simply a vehicle for himself. Jacobi, however, was less enthusiastic, and instead suggested directing Ken in *Hamlet*. In a television interview during the tour, Jacobi recalled that the original idea for the project 'came out of a discussion about "where do classical actors come from these days?"' and that its aim was 'to pick the brains of actors who have had the experience and can pass on their expertise, tricks, whatever, to another generation.' He admitted that, like Judi Dench and (to a lesser extent)

Geraldine McEwan, he felt trepidation about directing for the first time, but was largely persuaded by the fact that, during a discussion over dinner about approaches to roles and staging, Ken pointed out that what Jacobi was doing at that moment was effectively directing, in his head at least. He then consulted other directors on how actually to go about the business, and was told, 'It's like directing traffic: get 'em on, get 'em off, try to make sure they don't bump into each other.' Thus reassured, he committed to the Renaissance *Hamlet*.

Branagh has noted that '[The role of the Prince] has been called "a hoop through which every serious actor must sooner or later jump". I had a feeling that it would be later if this particular serious actor were required to jump at all.' This is disingenuous: he had already played Hamlet at RADA and had had to suppress his natural urge to petition for the part in the RSC production in which he played Laertes – of course he wanted to play the part again. He simply hadn't dared to think the opportunity would arise so quickly. Furthermore, he was daunted by the prospect of being directed by the man whose performance as Hamlet had been one of the original inspirations for him to pursue a career in acting. Inevitably, though, Jacobi's proposal was too tempting for Ken to pass up.

Nevertheless, there proved to be an initial hesitancy – 'a couple of days of bristling,' in Branagh's words, with him 'terrified of simply copying Derek and being shirty as a result.' Jacobi, too, admitted to 'enormous' fear in taking on the play: 'Would I have the generosity to give away to Kenneth what were ideas and instincts for myself? Would he receive them?' The first few days were to be a crash course in directorial diplomacy. 'Note sessions were scary at first; some [actors] took them as criticism, something to be slightly upset by and wary of, others as useful and meaningful hints. Ken reacted both ways, but mainly the latter, allowing me a sigh of relief.' Once a proper relationship was established, the two worked hand in glove on the role, paying minute attention to the various acting devices which could be used to elicit a particular effect at a given moment. The fact that Jacobi had

149

played the part gave him an innate understanding not just of its psychological convolutions but of the practical techniques which an actor needs to use to convey them. 'Actors understand the difficulties of creating a role better than non-actors can,' explained Ken. 'Between actors a sort of shorthand develops. I would know what Derek meant before he finished giving me a note. Instead of explaining an effect, he would talk about the means of getting it.'

The result was strong, vigorous and intelligent, but a little transparently technical: 'We can understand [Branagh's] Hamlet,' said one critic, 'but we seldom feel for him.' With uncanny prescience, Milton Shulman of the London *Evening Standard* judged the performance 'an interesting Hamlet with the promise of a better one next time he runs the course' – as he would four years later, rejoining the Royal Shakespeare Company for that single role. The part of Ophelia was mistakenly seen as an early break for Emma's younger sister Sophie Thompson, who had in fact been acting since the age of fifteen. Sophie denied any element of nepotism: 'Of course, people think I just schlepped in because of them but I had to audition just like everyone else. The company even turned me down for a couple of roles at first.'

If *Hamlet* received only qualified approval, on Judi Dench's *Much Ado About Nothing* opinions were unanimous. The terrified debutante director had been sensitive and in control throughout rehearsals, but was immensely rocked by the first preview. Putting a play in front of an audience for the first time is always a learning experience for the actors themselves, who discover with shocking suddenness that an audience never responds quite as expected and have to alter their performances to meet that climate. For an actor who is directing for the first time, the feeling of impotence can be cataclysmic. But, apart from the usual first-night notes, her worries proved unfounded. She had elected to dress the cast in vaguely Edwardian costumes, reportedly because she considered the sight of young men in tights too distracting for an audience. This decision allowed her simultaneously to express the formal strictures of nobility and its codes of conduct and the disruption caused by their breakdown in both the villainous plots of Shaun Prendergast's Napoleonic Don John and the romances of Claudio and Hero and of the hitherto confirmed bachelor and spinster Benedick and Beatrice. From the cast she drew a range of comic and tragic moments with subtlety and delicacy, serving the text rather than trying to bend it to a scheme of her own.

The *Daily Mail*'s Jack Tinker spoke for the vast majority of critics when he hailed the production: 'as triumphant a celebration of the Bard's most complex piece of courting as ever roused an audience to roar its approval'. As Benedick, he said, Branagh 'offers the words as if they had just tumbled into his consciousness; lifts phrases with the bafflement of a nimble wit suddenly out of its own depth. In short, is wildly funny and unexpectedly touching.' As Beatrice (and in the smaller part of Phebe the shepherdess in *As You Like It*), Samantha Bond was hailed as a name to watch for in years to come.

During the Birmingham run the royal patron of Renaissance had asked the company to provide a Shakespearean entertainment for a party at Windsor. Ken directed Judi Dench, Derek Jacobi and one non-member of the company, Emma Thompson, in a fifty-minute programme before the rest of them left Birmingham for the first venue of the tour proper. That venue had provided the occasion, at long last, for Ken to act on a Belfast stage for the first time. Renaissance played for a week at the Grand Opera House, with a full programme of talks and workshops. The return of the native gave Branagh an opportunity to stress how close his ties still were with the city, where he was of course received with open arms by local press, public and extended family alike.

Another highlight of the itinerary was the two-week residency of *Hamlet* at the Danish castle of Krönborg at Elsinore. The notion of performing the play in its actual historical setting was first realised in modern times in 1937 by – yes – Laurence Olivier, although the castle records hint that Shakespeare's own company may well have performed there. Branagh, however, was to be the youngest recorded Hamlet at Elsinore; at twenty-seven he reversed the usual state of affairs by being younger than his thirty-year-old character (most actors are several years older by the time they have acquired the range and experience necessary to portray the Prince in a major production). Nor was he fazed by the prospect of encountering the most rigorous critic of all – the castle's ghost, notorious for causing rattling doors and windows, flickering lights and even, so the legend runs, bad weather for those he dislikes. 'There's a great shiver-down-the-spine atmosphere at the castle, and a real ghost would be quite handy,' Ken remarked. 'I defy him not to turn up – he won't even need an Equity card.'

During rehearsals it rather seemed as if Ken had displeased the royal spook. The heavens had opened, and the malcontent Prince was to be seen the afternoon before the first performance going through his moves on the open-air stage in a waterproof cycling cape. Things were 'beginning to look distinctly hairy', he said, and makeshift arrangements were made for an indoor production if the weather didn't let up. But, whether due to meteorological coincidence or to Branagh's charm and negotiating skill succeeding even beyond the veil, the skies cleared by evening and the performance went ahead as planned in front of the castle to an audience of 1,300 including the Queen and Queen Mother of Denmark and Renaissance's patron, Prince Charles. Before His Royal Highness went backstage to offer his congratulations, the company asked Ken how he should be addressed. 'You call him sir,' he told them, 'just like me.' Collapse of stout party.

The bulk of Channel 4's *Caught in the Act* documentary was filmed at Elsinore, with additional footage shot in rehearsals for the three plays. The company came across as intimate and at ease with one another – truly like a family, as Samantha Bond pointed out, in that living in one another's pockets for months on end had given them the freedom to blow up in rage at each other, 'although we are getting better at saying sorry'. Little impression was given of Ken as an Olympian leader;

'There's [sic] a lot of jokes about management; it's not as if everybody's sitting around being loyal all the time,' he noted. The point was ably demonstrated by a cut to Patrick Doyle mercilessly taking off some of Branagh's acting mannerisms and David Parfitt's 'kangaroo walk'. Ken also took the opportunity to repudiate the point that, despite some rather sour innuendos elsewhere in the programme from Terry Hands of the RSC, he was not interested in being an old-school actor-manager, 'hanging on to the curtain and saying, "To the people of Leeds, I thank you for the warmth of your reception" like Donald Wolfit.' Renaissance, he maintained, was 'not a novelty; it's committed . . . and it's hard bloody work'.

Most importantly, the programme made it obvious that Renaissance was not Ken's pigeon alone, but that David Parfitt was an equal partner in management duties and in his vision of the company. As Branagh has grown as an icon, so Parfitt has moved into eclipse in terms of media coverage, not least because of his natural move towards back-room activities. As he pointed out, given Ken's commitments to acting in all three plays, it was natural that more of the administrative tasks – National Insurance contributions for the company, VAT calculations and the like – would be taken on by the other partner, but 'I'm getting quite into that now, and enjoying it.' The precise terms of Parfitt's credits on Branagh's films have varied ('associate producer' on *Henry V*, 'line producer' on *Peter's Friends*, plain 'producer' along with Branagh and Stephen Evans on *Much Ado About Nothing* and now 'co-producer' with Branagh on *Frankenstein*), but his role has consistently been that of Ken's administrative 'other half', the person on whom he relies to share ideas with and to work behind the scenes so that they may be realised, whether on a $45 million Hollywood film production or when his partner is performing in the teeth of a gale outside the battlements of a Danish royal castle.

Olivier's Ophelia had been Vivien Leigh; Branagh's was Sophie Thompson. But at this time he was still fielding questions about the now-general rumours concerning his

153

relationship with her sister Emma: 'Emma and I are terrific mates, but she is also a great maverick. [We] can talk to each other, but she is very wise as well, and we both go our own way ... She also has her own circle of friends, who are a comfort. And you need that, but a lot of the time you are on your own and you do miss a cuddle. A hug is great.' The pressure and loneliness of actor-management were evidently making themselves felt. 'Now and then you need a shoulder to cry on or someone to turn to for a cuddle. Whose shoulder do I cry on? Sometimes you don't. You have to take a deep breath and cope with it yourself.' He managed to put the loneliness on hold to be best man when David Parfitt married costume designer Susan Coates between performances at Elsinore. Coates had proposed to Parfitt on Leap Day 1988, with Ken as witness 'so David couldn't wriggle out of it', in Susan's words.

Ken had spoken of plans, after the tour – which won Renaissance the British Theatre Association's *Drama* magazine Special Award for 1988 and also earned Branagh and Parfitt a *Time Out/01 For London* award for establishing the company – to work on a screenplay before finally taking a year's sabbatical to write a 'warts and all' novel about the RSC and simply spend his time 'having lunches, dinners, cooking for friends.' With hindsight, this sounds implausible. Even before *Twelfth Night* he had already floated the idea of making the next career step, into film – and, once again, making it on his own terms by adapting, directing and starring in *Henry V*.

9

The Action of the Tiger

A first draft of the film script of *Henry V* had been all but completed when rehearsals for the stage production of *Much Ado About Nothing* began, and Ken had already determined that the film should begin shooting directly the Renaissance Shakespeare tour ended in autumn 1988. With such a schedule, he had once again boxed himself into a round of meetings for budgeting, finance and artistic preparations for the film – not to mention the inevitable interviews to give publicity to the three plays, which had been budgeted with very little room for manoeuvre if audiences were not absolutely solid.

Yet Renaissance would scarcely have been seen on stage in the first place if there had not appeared Stephen Evans. Evans, who worked for the UK broking arm of Jardine Matheson and described himself as an 'armchair theatre critic', contacted Branagh after reading a magazine article about Renaissance. 'It caught my imagination and I thought it would be nice to help him. I was used to raising money for industry, so why not try the arts?' After presenting himself to Branagh during rehearsals for *Napoleon* (popping up, according to Branagh, more or less out of thin air), he agreed to find the £60,000 necessary for the following production, *Twelfth Night*. Along with West End theatre producer Howard Panter (who had transferred *The Life of Napoleon* to the West End), Evans oversaw the £250,000 financing of the Shakespeare season, and became the sharp-end financier on all subsequent Renaissance projects, forming a triumvirate with Branagh and Parfitt. He went on to set up his own film production company, Bridgewater, which folded in 1994 following the collapse of its Henry James film venture *The Wings of a Dove*.

On the *Henry V* project, it was Evans who lined up Elstree Studios for the filming and, when Elstree was suddenly sold from under their feet, discovered the possibility of shooting at Shepperton if, as looked likely, another film cancelled. Producer Bruce Sharman had costed the picture at £4.5 million, nearly twice Branagh's original off-the-cuff estimate (although subsequent reports put the figure as high as £5.3 million), and Evans put the director in contact with Completion Guarantors, who agreed to guarantee any excess spending beyond the £4.5 million that might become necessary during production if the basic sum could first be raised. Branagh was spending every Monday off from tour rehearsals in Birmingham by travelling to London to pitch the film project to whomever Evans could interest in putting money into the enterprise. Affairs were scarcely less frenetic once the plays were up and running: there were script rewrites, designs to finalise and always more money to raise. Evans doubted that Ken could find the time or energy that the film project demanded, but the latter was convinced that if the picture were to go ahead at all it had to come in on the back of the interest which the tour was generating.

The government's Business Expansion Scheme helped matters at an early stage. The scheme allowed for modest tax breaks of around 20 per cent on moderate-sized investments in commercial ventures made under a five-year deal. Evans pieced together a BES package to attract development finance in units as small as £500. It was hoped to raise as much as £1.5 million this way, and in fact the scheme raised around £1 million. At this point legend begins to edge reality out of the picture when *Henry V* is discussed. The film is often spoken of as one of the great successes of the BES as applied to film financing, as if it had been largely bankrolled by small donations through the Evans-formulated scheme. In fact, although a few British films have obtained funding in this manner (notably *Leon the Pig Farmer* and *Beyond Bedlam*), *Henry V* used the BES only to raise money for the project's development stage, its pre-production. The bulk of the actual production budget came from what the film industry refers to as 'pre-sales', selling screening rights in advance to film distributors and broadcasters. The first cards of the film's opening credits reveal the primary sources of finance – it is presented by Renaissance Films plc 'in association with the BBC and Curzon Film Distributors Ltd', who had bought in advance the television and 'theatrical exhibition' rights respectively.

But before these final deals had been put into place, and with £2 million still to raise, David Puttnam, whose name continued to command almost automatic attention in the film world despite a brief and turbulent period running one of the major studios in Hollywood, had suggested that he approach his own Enigma company's American distributors, Warner Brothers, with a view to pre-selling the American cinematic rights. Warners prevaricated (during which time the BBC bought into the picture), and Puttnam agreed to join the project as executive producer in the hope of giving it the clout to find the remaining money elsewhere. He visited Ken during the Elsinore run of *Hamlet*, but back in London he withdrew, stating that he simply couldn't see how the picture would be completed and certainly not according to the original proposal. Nik Powell and Steve Woolley, then of Palace Pictures, were also initially interested parties who subsequently backed out.

Branagh's last set of meetings with prospective actors Ian Holm (who had been asked to play Fluellen) and Paul Scofield (the King of France) was conducted in a state of agonised uncertainty about whether the last million (as it now was) would materialise. By now, though, Evans could see light at the end of the tunnel; by calling upon his own financial contacts which were outside the film world, he had access to people who, lacking an intimacy with the ins and outs of film finance and production, lacked also the jaded caution of those in the industry. With barely a month to go the finance was finally in place and the seven-week shoot could begin as planned on Hallowe'en. The cast would include his three Shakespearean directors (Judi Dench as Mistress Quickly, Geraldine McEwan as Princess Katherine's companion, Alice, and Derek Jacobi as the Chorus), Scofield, Holm, Brian Blessed, Richard Briers, Charles Kay (from *Fortunes of War*), John Sessions, Robbie Coltrane as Falstaff (in a number of interpolated flashback scenes), a number of previous acquaintances, and of course Emma – straight from filming *Camden Town Boy* (released in 1989 as *The Tall Guy*) with Jeff Goldblum – as Princess Katherine of France. 'I told him to cast someone French,' she said later. 'He said, "No, I want it to be played this way, and you'll do it the way I want it." We love working together. I'm surprised at the old-fashionedness of the reaction to the old husband and wife thing.' Even David Parfitt played a minor role as a messenger.

Unusually among film directors, Branagh believes that rehearsing before the shoot is more than worth the time, since it can sort out knotty points in advance rather than making it necessary to perfect them over several expensive takes. 'Rehearsals break down everyone's nervousness,' he has said. 'It is a place to establish a trust and rhythm with the actors. You can settle all the arguments over interpretation and character before the cameras ever start rolling. For me, it is like putting a flame under things to get them hot, but not quite to the boiling point.' *Henry V* could afford only two weeks of such rehearsals, but they proved to be of great value. 'People were very patient,' he said, before digressing into an anecdote which implicitly paid tribute to his own achievement in assembling such an illustrious cast: 'With the English army there's usually a bonding moment – you walk past this knot of people and there's Robert Stephens [who played Pistol] going, "...and then Larry said...", and you think, "Christ, there's five Henry Vs here, seven Hamlets!"' Then a brief test shoot a week before production proper began – significantly, 'upon Saint Crispin's Day', the anniversary of the Battle of Agincourt – reminded him embarrassingly that in order for things to happen in front of the camera he had to shout 'Action.' Now, with Hugh Cruttwell once again on hand to advise Ken on his own and others' performances, the real action began.

For an actor constantly dogged by unwanted comparisons, choosing *Henry V* as a cinematic directorial debut was both an extraordinarily brave and a remarkably foolhardy decision. Laurence Olivier's classic film version, conceived as a propaganda exercise during the darkest days of the Second World War and released just as the tide of combat was turning in the Allies' favour in 1944, occupies a cherished place in both the history and the mythology of British film-making – 'an amazingly enduring film', in David Parfitt's words. Ken later described the genesis of his version as 'a mad feeling growing several years after [the RSC stage production] that the play was full of images that would be brilliantly served by the cinema camera', and also, naturally, the belief that a film version would give many more people access to the play than would be able to see any stage production. He admitted in 1994 to being flattered that some schools screen scenes of the Olivier film side by side with excerpts from his version to increase pupils' acquaintance both with Shakespeare and with the 'language' of film.

In the wake of what had been dubbed the 'post-Falklands' production at the RSC, Branagh felt that a cinematic reassessment of the play was possible. 'The play is about a young monarch achieving maturity but at some cost to himself. We are addicted today to the media images of people who make decisions that affect hundreds of thousands of lives. The Olivier film didn't touch on this because it was not what the English public wanted to see at the time. In fact, Churchill asked Olivier to cut certain bits – the conspiracy scene, the speech to the Governor of Harfleur about putting children on spikes – so as not to undermine morale. Now is the right time to explore the paradoxical aspect of Henry's character.'

Once again, the watchword of *Henry V* was to be accessibility. 'When you have control you can say, "What would make my eighteen-year-old sister see this?"' explained Branagh (whose sister Joyce was that age herself) shortly before the film's release. 'It's the first exposure to Shakespeare for a lot of kids at that tender age when they're usually put off. You have to remember they've been watching *Neighbours* the night before, and want something that comes from the same world. I've tried to make it punchy, accessible and to maximise a good yarn. You don't need a degree in English to understand it.' Five years later, he said that his aim had been 'to bring out as much as my experience of doing the play had revealed: that it wasn't fun going off to fight; that political power could be very difficult to wield for one person and very easy for another, and sometimes in the same person; and that this was a thing which changed people's lives.' In particular, he said, the 'Saint Crispin's Day' speech with which the King rallies his smaller army before joining battle was 'a moment where people are ennobled, their lives are enlarged, but perhaps what led to them being there need never have happened'.

And again, the patronage and advice of the Prince of Wales gave them valuable support. Hearing of the difficulties of getting a budget and production together, Prince Charles offered Branagh special dispensation to film the Battle of Agincourt scenes on Duchy of Cornwall land at Bodmin Moor. In the end, the dubious luxury of location shooting in Cornwall was forgone for budgetary and scheduling reasons – the production had neither the time nor the money to go anywhere – and the battle was shot on meadows near Shepperton Studios.

As the emotional climax of the Agincourt sequence, Branagh thought that the bleakness of victory would be feelingly conveyed if, as Henry, he were to carry the corpse of a young English soldier (played by Christian Bale, who would later star in the film *Swing Kids*) across the battlefield in a four-minute tracking shot, while the hymn *'Non nobis, Domine'* swells on the soundtrack. All well and good in theory.

However, although always keen on sport, Ken would be the last to claim that he was cast in the Schwarzenegger mould, either in terms of his frame or his musculature. The camera had an easier time traversing the quaggy 'battlefield' than the staggering King, who ended up sinking to his knees in a puddle and dropping Bale face-first into the authentic Agincourt/Shepperton mud. The first take was crowned – in every sense – when a nearby horse decided to answer the call of nature on Branagh's head. Hampered also by poor video playback facilities on location, he had to go through the shot several times to ensure that a good-quality take would be available. Returning home at the end of the day, he wept with relief and exhaustion. The shoot as a whole was marked by tempestuous human-equine relationships. Ken also revealed that the end of the 'Once more unto the breach' speech didn't quite go as planned: 'The horse, who could rear at a signal from his master, received that signal from me by accident, so that is me rearing on the film . . . which was rather a surprise!'

The pressure of Ken's workaholism had been taking a serious toll. Guilt and anxiety manifested themselves in an increasing tetchiness; the charm which had seen him through so many deals had evaporated. According to one friend, 'He was appalling . . . completely exhausted. He became a monster – especially to those closest to him – treating them totally thoughtlessly, almost cruelly.' Ken himself recalled ruefully, 'I was pretty close to a total breakdown. It was ongoing, deep, deep thoughtlessness to the people around me, which was very wounding to them. Emma, particularly, suffered at the hands of it.' She later remembered that 'Ken was so exhausted and stressed out I had to cradle him in my arms after the day's filming.' Still, however, he would frequently bite the hand that soothed him.

'All my friends helped me through,' he explained gratefully. 'Brian [Blessed], who is mad as a hatter, used to take me for long walks around his home in Bagshot and tell me to look at the world all around us and work out what was important. But it was Emma who brought wisdom and understanding and

161

peace and love and became the centre of my life.' In another friend's words, 'It was at its worst just before and during the filming of *Henry V*, when he really was working to the limit of human endurance. Emma showed him the value of the simple things like putting your feet up together in front of the telly and having Sunday lunch and just spending time together.'

Several years later, on the crest of the wave of *Much Ado About Nothing*'s screen success, Ken spoke again of his constant lack of self-confidence. 'I wouldn't describe it as neurosis, but I do get really black spells; that is why I'm so obsessed with *Hamlet*... but I don't care to talk about it because people don't care to believe it. And why should people have to know about my depression after a performance or whatever? That's boring. It's not a sign of a great actor.' It was as if, even in that moment of candour, he was concerned to live up to the image of greatness rather than allowing himself fuller expression.

Henry V was completed ahead of schedule and under its £4.5 million budget which, with the passage of time and the accretion of interest, had swollen to £5 million by the time the press reported in early 1994 the winding up of the Renaissance theatre and film companies. The film acquitted itself respectably of the Olivier comparisons, infusing more grit into the scenes than the jingoistic opulence of the 1944 version had permitted – 'The Battle of Agincourt *was* fought in the mud,' as Parfitt matter-of-factly pointed out. Branagh didn't try to deny a certain amount of influence: 'You may or may not spot the various nicks that are in my film from his film ... I hope you don't.' It was also the most complete assembly yet of the Branagh Rep Company – an all-star cast composed, virtually without exception, of professional friends of the couple. The wooing of Princess Katherine of France by Henry furnished the audience with a rose-tinted window on to what was then the continuing courtship of Ken and Em, albeit a window with a view heavily filtered through both the Shakespearean context and the complexities of international dynastic alliances. In fact, they have never portrayed an uncomplicated, unambiguously

(Above) No. 30 is probably the only house in West Hampstead with an Oscar in the downstairs loo *(Rex Features)* (Below) As Roman and Margaret Strauss, one of the two central couples in *Dead Again*. Ken's goatee now looks more plausible than his teenage bum-fluff *(Paramount)*

Tired but triumphant: flying into Heathrow after completing *Dead Again* *(Camera Press)*

Ken with Pauline Gray, membership secretary of Reading's Progress Theatre for which he arranged a benefit preview of *Dead Again* *(Reading Newspaper Co)*

A haggard Emma at a CND anti-Gulf War protest *(Camera Press)*

Judi Dench's production of *Coriolanus* led critics to draw more than stage blood from Ken *(Camera Press)*

Emma with Anthony Hopkins in their first Merchant Ivory film together, *Howards End (Camera Press)*

Emma with her mother Phyllida Law arriving at the sixty-fifth Academy Awards ceremony *(Popperfoto)*

A victorious Emma receiving her Best Actress Oscar from Anthony Hopkins for *Howards End (Universal Pictorial Press; Popperfoto)*

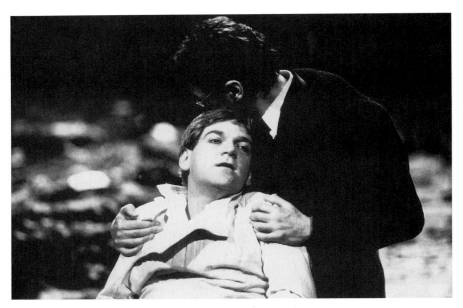

Ken, meanwhile, was giving the Hamlet of his life with the Royal Shakespeare Company *(Camera Press)*

Beatrice and Benedick in *Much Ado About Nothing (Kobal Collection)*

The stars of *Much Ado* . . . at the Cannes film festival: Denzel Washington, Robert Sean Leonard, Keanu Reeves and the other two *(Mirror Syndication International)*

Ken still makes a point of visiting his granny Elizabeth Branagh whenever he is in Belfast *(Belfast Telegraph)*

Ken and Helena Bonham Carter in a scene from *Frankenstein*
(David Appleby/Tristar Pictures)

Branagh looks set to spend more and more time behind the camera
(Popperfoto)

positive relationship on stage or screen. Those don't make for good drama, of course, irrespective of considerations regarding their individual careers. At any rate, this was to be the first manifestation of the couple's professional collaboration as a couple, which would on occasion prove, in the eyes of many, catastrophically self-obsessed.

A screening in competition at the 1989 Cannes Film Festival would have been the perfect showcase for the film, but in the year that France celebrated the bicentenary of the Revolution, festival director Gilles Jacob decreed that an account of an English victory over the French would not be appropriate for the competition. The picture was screened at Cannes during the festival season, but was not eligible for any of the main jury awards.

Almost immediately upon the completion of *Henry V*, Branagh was hailed as the latest saviour of the British film industry. The label tends to be over-enthusiastically hung upon any and every British director who makes a British-funded feature in the UK, but Ken seemed more likely than most to fit the bill, and his reputation has grown with subsequent projects. However, it misrepresents both the nature of his work as a director and the industry itself.

It is generally known that the British film industry has greatly diminished in size and power since the days of Alexander Korda, the Ealing Studios, Powell and Pressburger and numerous others. The patriotic feeling persists that somehow or other these glories can be re-attained, but such efforts are fundamentally misplaced. Nik Powell, joint managing director of Scala Productions (whose most recent success is *Backbeat*) and formerly of its predecessor Palace (*The Company of Wolves, The Crying Game*), has made the point that the UK now has essentially a 'cottage' film industry; that within those terms it has been remarkably successful, but ultimately it should not be preoccupied with attempting to play by Hollywood's rules.

The last twenty years have been marked by a succession of British failures to develop a Hollywood-like studio or a steady stream of Hollywood-style product. In the 1970s and early 1980s EMI assembled a slate of big-budget, ambitious movies (many of which were in fact shot in the USA, although financed by British money), which culminated in Michael Cimino's *The Deer Hunter* in 1978. However, their strategy came spectacularly asunder with John Schlesinger's expensive and disastrous 1981 comedy *Honky Tonk Freeway*. EMI has now largely pulled out of film production. A few years later Lord Lew Grade's company ITC tried a similar strategy; after success with medium-to-large-budget films such as *Capricorn One* (1977) and in 1979 *The Muppet Movie* (a UK failure but an American smash hit) came a string of spectacular failures: *Saturn 3*, in which even then journeyman actor Harvey Keitel insisted that his dialogue be dubbed by another actor (Roy Dotrice!), *Green Ice* and the now-notorious *Raise The Titanic!*, which generated far too many obvious jokes to repeat here.

The reasons for these failures are twofold. Firstly, the companies were lured into the perilous trap of mid-Atlanticism, a snare which subsequent companies' campaigns have largely avoided. However, it remains the case that any non-American company trying to compete with Hollywood seldom gets first access to the best scripts and consequently fails to attract the best actors: *Green Ice* starred a past-sell-by-date Ryan O'Neal, and *Honky Tonk Freeway*'s biggest talent was William Devane – a familiar face, but not a 'bums on seats' name by any stretch of the imagination.

Furthermore, while ITC and EMI were trying to develop powerful production enterprises, they did not always elect to shoot in the UK, so that the side benefits were not necessarily reaped by local infrastructure or talent. It is estimated that for every £1 of a film's budget, an overall contribution of £7 accrues to the economy of the country or region in which it is shot. Conversely, American productions *were* utilising the services sector of the British industry: Steven Spielberg on the *Indiana Jones* movies and 20th Century Fox in its *Alien(s)* sequence, for instance. Consequently, the ancillary side of the industry in the UK remained relatively healthy and facilities for big-budget projects continued to be available despite the international failures of local producers – hence the situation where it was possible, several years later, to shoot a film such as *Mary Shelley's Frankenstein* at Shepperton for an American major.

Despite these crucial errors of judgement, by the early to mid-1980s *Chariots of Fire* screenwriter Colin Welland's cry at the Oscar ceremony, 'The British are coming!', sounded far from ludicrous. A trio of companies had arisen which, in their early days at least, bore out Nik Powell's 'cottage industry' remark: Palace Pictures, Goldcrest and Channel 4.

The first production from Palace, run by Nik Powell and Steve Woolley, was *The Company of Wolves* in 1984. An object testimony to the potential of this approach, it was made on a relatively low budget, but by using the UK's wide access to acting talent – and, more importantly, world-class technicians – it looked much more expensive. Palace were to repeat this formula with *Scandal* and *The Crying Game*. The company's ultimate collapse, often simplistically attributed to its involvement in the spectacular flop musical *Absolute Beginners*, was more directly a result of over-diversifying from its production and distribution core into areas such as retailing, which weighed down what was, by British industry standards, an essentially sound business. This view is supported by the fact that Powell and Woolley's new company, Scala, unencumbered by the various add-ons that crippled Palace, continues to make movies and to strike deals with film investors from the United States, Europe and even the UK.

David Puttnam's company Goldcrest worked in similar medium-budget terms in its early days. Films such as *Chariots of Fire*, *Local Hero*, *The Dresser* and the screen version of *Another Country* both won awards and made money. Under the managerial stewardship of Jake Eberts, Goldcrest's shareholders were happy to leave the company to its own devices. It did not over-expose itself financially, tying up production deals either through pre-sales to a number of international distributors (in the days when such contracts were easier to secure) or with the American majors. Then Goldcrest succumbed to the siren song of big-budget Hollywood-style movies: Roland Joffe's *The Mission*, Hugh Hudson's *Revolution* and, once again, *Absolute Beginners*. None succeeded commercially, even though *The Mission* won the Palme d'Or at Cannes in 1986, and by the time the company's major shareholder, media conglomerate Pearson (owner of the *Financial Times* and joint owner of the disastrous dish-TV enterprise British Satellite Broadcasting), tried to rein things in it was already too late.

Goldcrest, EMI, ITC, and even, for a brief period in the early 1970s, Rank all came unstuck by attempting to produce slates of almost exclusively major releases. In contrast, US studios can counterbalance the potential success or failure of their big movies by also being able to produce a number of low- and medium-budget pictures, some of which break even, some of which do not, but which do not damage the company's overall financial standing if they do fail, and which can help it immeasurably if they turn out to be 'sleeper' successes. For example, Arnold Schwarzenegger's *Last Action Hero* is now believed to be the biggest flop in cinema history, losing Columbia/TriStar a staggering $120 million; yet in the year of that disaster, 1993, the same studio enjoyed more than comfortable successes with *Sleepless in Seattle* and Clint Eastwood's *In the Line of Fire*, neither of which had been made on such an astronomical budget as the Schwarzenegger picture. Such a volume of production also ensures that American companies have a cashflow to keep creditors at bay. The British companies lacked the resources to generate such a volume of production but, flushed with the initial success of their more modest productions, decided to gamble their all, such as it was, on a few titles.

Channel 4, also a major financier of British film production, is a case apart. Its resources are limited by statute to lower-budget productions by virtue of its remit to cater for minority audiences, and as a broadcaster it needs to spread the money it does have across a number of television slots each year rather than concentrating on two or three cinematic releases. Pictures produced with Channel 4's financial involvement have generally been steady earners, and the television link gives them something of a right to fail. The company's difficulty has been that the 'minority' label has tended to steer the subject matter of its films away from the mainstream (aside from the conspicuous, but exceptional, success of *Four Weddings and a Funeral* (1994) – for a more typical Channel 4 film, consider Mike Leigh's *Naked*: critically acclaimed, but dead at the box office), thus in a sense depriving Britain of much of the potential success of its own productions. This is not to belittle Channel 4's importance and success in providing funding and employment for numerous projects – it is no coincidence that the company's remit happens to dovetail neatly with the scale of production which, as Nik Powell points out, is now the UK industry's true strength.

The most consistently successful company in terms of matching quality and audiences has been Merchant Ivory, who simply understand how to play the game. The company makes only one film a year, aimed at an audience with which they are fully familiar, and with production values far above the actual cost. Says a UK film industry source, 'Ismail Merchant is a complete genius at making $10 million movies look like $30 million movies.' Like the BBC, Merchant Ivory's reputation for quality means that they can attract the best talent at the lowest cost. The company's thirty years in business have indeed been glorious ones.

The only way to explain how Kenneth Branagh fits into this picture is to leap ahead of strict biographical chronology and consider his directorial and production output as a whole.

There is little doubt that Renaissance did not expect to make money on its first film venture. *Henry V* was, if anything, a 137-minute cinematic calling card: Branagh had attracted much of the money from the BBC, was sticking to an area he knew – Shakespeare – and, as he admitted, was learning how to make movies while on the job. 'Once he had had an experience of the UK business,' according to the same industry source, 'to be quite frank, he ankled quick; off he went to Paramount to shoot *Dead Again* in the States.' All his subsequent films, whether Renaissance or not, whether shot in the UK or abroad, have been largely funded through the United States: *Peter's Friends* and *Much Ado About Nothing* through Renaissance for the Samuel Goldwyn Company, *Mary Shelley's Frankenstein* for Columbia's sister production outfit TriStar and Francis Coppola's Zoetrope.

Branagh has been careful not to get excessively involved with financing films through the British industry (even, as detailed earlier in this chapter, using the Business Expansion Scheme only in the development stage of *Henry V*), while remembering that it contains the skills and acting base to make good popular films. The industry 'mole' again: 'He's a Good Thing, but he uses the British film services industry, not the British film production industry. To that extent he's very clever, and he's wised up to what the Puttnams and Nik Powells have known for years – that you follow the money.'

The conspicuous absence from the list of Goldcrest's successes mentioned earlier, *Gandhi*, was left out for two reasons. Firstly, it was a deeply personal project which director Richard Attenborough had been trying to fund for twenty years before it finally entered production – it would be more apposite to cite the difficulties Attenborough had to go through to get the film made as an example of the British film industry's problems than to point to the fact that it *did* get made as one of the industry's triumphs. More immediately relevant, however, is the fact that Attenborough is not a 'British' director-producer, as the industry sees it: he is an international figure who just happens to be British. Films such as *A Bridge Too Far, Oh! What a Lovely War* and *Young Winston* had already shown that he was capable of handling big-budget films; he could thus draw international talent to the *Gandhi* project, which in turn made it possible to raise international funds. Most British companies or producers cannot gain access to talent or finance this way. The indications, however, are that Kenneth Branagh is about to join the exclusive club of those who can.

10

Stars of Stage and Screen

After *Henry V*, Ken and Emma's next joint appearance in a dramatic project was preceded by the release in early 1989 of *The Tall Guy*, comedian Mel Smith's first film as director, which starred Emma and Jeff Goldblum. Written by comedian Rowan Atkinson's former stooge Richard Curtis, who more recently scripted *Four Weddings and Funeral*, its protagonist Dexter (Goldblum) makes a living in London being abused onstage by comedian Ron Anderson (Atkinson playing a nightmare version of himself). Thompson is Kate Lemon, a brisk, straightforward nurse with whom Dexter embarks on a course of fearsome immunisation injections in order to see her frequently while he tries to work up the courage to ask her out.

This role reversal – dithering American man, strong, no-nonsense Englishwoman – is at the heart of the film. When Kate leaves Dexter after realising he has cheated on her, the scene is refreshingly devoid of melodrama. 'Kate is just the most wonderful role,' explained Emma, 'because she is exactly that woman who says the thing you wish you had said at the time. She knows what she wants but she's not callous. She's just very practical. He is the one who cries because he is the one who has hurt himself. It's so accurate. You know she's upset but she's holding it in ... so off she goes and you never see her crying, which is great because normally what you see is man is vile to woman, woman goes away and dies the death. It's lovely to see the other side of it. Man hurts woman and in doing so hurts self badly.'

The film also marked Thompson's first screen sex scene, an energetically parodic episode in which the rutting couple demolish Kate's flat in their fervour. 'I love that scene,' she said. 'If I never do another sex scene, I'll be happy. It was terrifying at first but' – in contrast to the vigorous interior redecoration seen on the screen – 'the atmosphere on the set for those two days became very compassionate and kind. People talked in slightly lower voices and behaved terribly well. The main thing you notice is that everyone in the room stares you right in the eye all the time. Even when they've made you a cup of tea the crew are terrified to look at you below the neck, which is actually a bit unnatural!' Then, teasingly, 'We might even have carried on kissing for a while but we kept hearing muffled giggling.'

In fact, Emma has to date appeared in only two other sequences which could remotely be called 'sex scenes', both brief: a quick bodice-ripping ravishment in *Impromptu* and equally fleetingly being discovered mid-bonk with young Alex Lowe, playing a sixteen-year-old, in *Peter's Friends*. All three are heavily comic. The net effect of this sly ridicule is twofold: on the one hand it asserts her refusal to play the movie-formula sex game and keeps things in perspective, but it is also another suggestion of an underlying discomfort with her sexuality. Comparing herself with major contemporary screen goddesses, Thompson said, 'As far as I could see from Sharon Stone's love scenes in *Basic Instinct*, they'd moulded her body out of plasticine. None of it *moved*. I thought, "What have they done, *coated* her with something?" Had that been me, there would have been things flying around the place and hitting me in the eye.' It is as if her persistent worries about being 'a great, hulking ex-Footlights turn', too 'meaty' to be truly desirable, lead her to believe that she can best get away with sex scenes if they are mickey-takes. This insecurity would make her insist on the removal of all references to her two characters' beauty in the script of *Dead Again* the following year.

The final reel of *The Tall Guy* bears a startling resemblance to the most sensational version of Ken's proposal to Emma herself. In the film, after Kate walks out on Dexter, he goes absent without leave from his current stage engagement (in the lead role of *Elephant!*, a musical based on the life of John Merrick, the Elephant Man) and dashes across town late at night to admit his perfidy, swear that he doesn't want to lose her and beg for a reconciliation. If the account of Ken's on-the-road affair and Emma's departure in high dudgeon to New York is true, art imitated life quite as uncomfortably as it had with Ken's 'breaking up' improvisation opposite Katy Behean at RADA.

Shortly after the film's release Emma made her first major television appearance since *Thompson*. In a production of Terence Rattigan's *The Winslow Boy* for BBC2's *Theatre Night* strand, she played Kate Winslow. Rattigan's 1945 play, dedicated to the young Paul Channon, with whose Tory minister father 'Chips' Channon the author had a relationship, and who occupied ministerial positions himself in the Thatcher government, was based on the real-life Archer-Shee case some thirty years earlier in which Parliament was suspended to consider the case of a Royal Naval cadet falsely accused of stealing a postal order. The play was intended as an early cry for the upholding of democratic process in the face of burgeoning faceless bureaucracy. By focusing on the Winslow family's gruelling two-year struggle to clear their younger son's name, Rattigan painted a picture of the human cost of resisting vast and inhuman administrative machinery.

Today Rattigan is seldom given his due as a dramatic subversive. His well-made plays were easily palatable to the middle-class audiences of his day, yet gently questioned and broadened their perspectives on general social matters. At the core of the Winslow family is daughter Kate, a campaigner for women's suffrage who sacrifices her engagement so that the family might pursue their case, and who comes to realise that occasionally noble motives may transcend party political

171

boundaries. Her forthright blend of intelligence and passion makes her a confidante even to her ramrod-backed, authoritarian *paterfamilias* father (played by Gordon Jackson) – 'my only ally', as he calls her.

Kate is, in short, another role which had been waiting to be played by Emma Thompson. The actor's sympathies and temperament were in smooth alignment with those of her character, and once again she turned a central part from the pillar supporting the family into its beating heart. By now some of Thompson's screen acting trademarks were becoming apparent, such as a weak smile combining with a momentary downcast break from looking her interlocutor in the eye to indicate slight, never verbally expressed sadness and disappointment. Whilst Emma does not by any means 'act by numbers', certain expressions become a little familiar among her favoured character types. Nevertheless, her performances as Kate Winslow and, the following week, in *Knuckle* in the same BBC2 strand, were timely reminders of her dramatic strengths. Combined with *The Tall Guy*'s demonstration of her comic prowess, they served to push *Thompson* into the background as no more than a skeleton to be rattled periodically in subsequent journalistic pieces written about her.

Early in 1989, Emma undertook a role which is known to have been intensely personal to her. Paul Murton, whom she had known from her childhood holidays at Ardentinny, was writing, producing and directing his graduation film at the National Film and Television School. *Tin Fish* tells of a ten-year-old boy living near a Scottish nuclear submarine base who is diagnosed as suffering from leukaemia. It is based closely upon the true story of Murton's elder brother, Gerry, who died when Emma was fourteen. Mary Murton, on whom Emma's character was based, remembered the girl consoling her at the time of her son's death with the words, 'Well, at least you have God, Mrs M.'. When Paul approached Thompson to play the part of the dying boy's mother in the fifty-minute film, 'I thought she'd be far too busy. Emma was this famous actress and I was a film student. But she said yes. She was so desperate to be involved she squeezed in five days between major film parts.' The project proved compelling, combining as it did an appeal to her campaigning instincts (with its comments upon the dangers posed by nuclear facilities to families, and especially children, living near them) and the strong emotional pull of being based upon people whom she had known herself as a child. Once Emma came on board, the production had markedly less difficulty raising its £40,000 budget. She herself worked for nothing, even donating her *per diem* expenses towards the cast party. *Tin Fish* was screened in the 1990 Edinburgh Film Festival and on BBC2 that year.

After *Henry V* Ken and Emma returned to the stage to portray one of the least ideal couples in twentieth-century drama. Theatre myth now includes the account of the woman who stormed out of Renaissance's *Look Back in Anger* in 1989, raging, 'Dreadful! Dreadful! Absolutely the worst performance I have ever seen!' She fortuitously chose to depart at the moment when Branagh's Jimmy Porter, the original angry young man, launched into a scathing attack on everything 'female!', spitting the word and a string of vituperation at the vacant seat. A great moment, and certainly not prearranged, it summed up the main problem with Judi Dench's production: that Jimmy's anger flapped about aimlessly without an object close at hand in the world outside the play on to which it could be guyed.

Jimmy's long-suffering wife Alison was played, of course, by Emma. If Kate of France was a charming cameo, Alison is a thankless role, a martyr who quietly either endures Jimmy's fulminations or indicts his petty atrocities, a mere dramatic device to cue and link his set-piece rants. Emma did say that if she met Jimmy Porter in real life 'I'd lay him out cold,' and confessed, 'When I read the play I did think, I can't do this. It's so depressing and misogynistic. But I think it is saved by the quality of the writing.' Perhaps, but not wholly saved as far as the role of Alison is concerned. However much bruised integrity any actor brings to the part, she cannot hope to counterbalance the centripetal force of Jimmy himself, the first modern anti-hero.

'I think the play has sloughed off its first skin,' continued Emma, perhaps needing also to justify her participation to herself. 'Men are much less willing to identify with the character of Jimmy than they once were. It has become about how hate occurs and how people invite it. About fear of women. About the way people persuade themselves that other people aren't actually human and that you can do what you like to them.' She even went so far as to describe it as 'Sartre's vision of hell – three people in a room.' But although Jimmy no longer embodied the feelings of any men beyond a sad and vitriolic handful, the burden of history still sat heavily upon the piece.

John Osborne's play had gone down in history as one of the twin theatrical watersheds of the 1950s (the other being Samuel Beckett's *Waiting For Godot*). The press latched on to the figure of the Angry Young Man, railing against both the iniquities of society and a stifling middle-class morality. Osborne himself, along with such unlikely bedfellows as novelist Kingsley Amis and even poet Philip Larkin, were painted as the standard-bearers of a new wave of cultural malcontents. But the playwright believed that *Look Back* was always more successful when treated as a comedy, and wrote to Judi Dench asking her not to play it as heavy drama.

The advice turned out to be a mixed blessing: downplaying the gravity of Jimmy's vitriol (the sincerity of which is hard to doubt in the light of Osborne's autobiographical writing and of his atrocious 1992 sequel *Déjàvu*) left many wondering how he could ever have been perceived as a spokesman for his generation. One of Branagh's former directors also believes that he simply lacks an instinctive sympathy with Jimmy Porter: 'John Osborne is unhappily and truly a very angry man. Ken isn't – he might be deep down, but it doesn't come out. So you have an extremely good actor quite superbly delivering Osborne's words but not, in the end, keying into the anger that produced [them].' Judi Dench later agreed that 'he wasn't the bastard that perhaps Jimmy Porter should have been. Porter should be more ruthless, and Kenny is not ruthless.'

Acquiring permission to stage the work in the first place had been a problem since the rights were held by the Royal National Theatre. Not to be put off, Ken met with the RNT's artistic director, Richard Eyre, who gave the go-ahead for the Renaissance production. Osborne, however, gave permission for only one London performance, at the London Coliseum on Sunday 11 June 1989 – 'He's a bit of a law unto himself,' said Ken. Indeed, after seeing the Coliseum show Osborne relented, opining that Branagh's Jimmy was the finest since Peter O'Toole and authorising a four-week run at the Lyric Theatre on Shaftesbury Avenue in August and September. It was also filmed by Thames Television, and broadcast during the West End run. Branagh denied that the production had reached the stage after only seven days' rehearsal. 'Not quite true – it was seven and a half days. We were all reeling a bit, but we went on with a lot of high-voltage adrenaline.'

In a sharp irony, benefit performances of the show raised thousands of pounds for charities in the kind of 'mob philanthropy' the character of Jimmy so despises. Osborne, however, refused to waive his standard royalty terms – for tax reasons, claimed his agent: the writer intended to donate the money to charity himself later. Renaissance Week in Belfast, during which the entire company donated their fees, included not only £25-per-ticket performances of *Look Back in Anger* but talks, workshops, readings and a preview screening of *Henry V* at the Queen's Film Theatre. 'Our audiences in Belfast, they really hated [Jimmy],' said Emma. 'He was the angry young man, now he's seen as the vicious young man who doesn't know when to stop.' Judi Dench recounted how, after the play's final act when the patrician Helena has been absorbed into Alison's role at the ironing-board, a Belfast woman turned to her neighbour to observe, 'Well, at least that second one was quicker on the ironing than the first.'

They may have hated Jimmy, but they continued to love Ken as one of their own: the £45,000 raised in the course of the week was divided equally between the Northern Ireland Council for Voluntary Action and the Ulster Youth Theatre. For the latter company, a fund was established in order to endow an annual Renaissance Award of £1,000 to a UYT member going on to drama school.

The performance at the Coliseum benefited Friends of the Earth, giving Ken the chance to combine a no-comment on his and Emma's romantic status with an expression of 'green' sentiment: 'Perhaps at some stage I might marry some day,' he said, 'but we are trying to save the Earth first. If there is no planet there is no point.' It was a terrific press-conference quote, although Branagh would be the last person to claim that the ecological battle had been won by the time he and Emma married just four months later during the Lyric run.

The full cinematic release of *Henry V* that autumn (after a royal gala première which raised £150,000 for the Royal College of Physicians' Help Medicine appeal fund and was held in the presence, inevitably, of the Prince of Wales) helped edge out of the schedules a planned tour of Ibsen's tragedy *Hedda Gabler*, to be adapted by a friend of Emma's, novelist Jeanette Winterson. Renaissance said simply that they had not been able to get the actors they wanted for the production. Emma was thus deprived of an opportunity to establish herself as a front-rank theatrical actress. Since *Look Back in Anger* she has been seen on stage only in the 1990 Renaissance tour of *A Midsummer Night's Dream* and *King Lear*. Meanwhile, Ken was being tipped to take over as director of the Chichester Festival Theatre in Sussex, a post which eventually went to Patrick Garland. It would soon become clear that both their futures lay primarily in film. Ken had even mused, 'I can't see myself being onstage for some time now. I really want to disappear and take stock of my life and see what the last seven years has done to me and how it has changed me.' He also considered moving back to Northern Ireland, 'if I can find a way of doing it that isn't the big dramatic homecoming bit.'

Inevitably, all of these vague plans to shift his life down a gear or two after several years of manic hyperactivity were ultimately forgotten

Not the least of his immediate commitments was the delivery of his memoirs. When the publication of Branagh's autobiography *Beginning* was announced, the book was widely decried (before it had been seen) as a *folie de grandeur*. Here was a bloke not yet out of his twenties, who admitted to surprising himself at how conventional he was – 'I don't want to go around as Sir Kevin O'Lovey, young lord of the theatre.' What could he possibly have to write about? The jokes continued for years afterwards: in 1994, firebrand actor Nicol Williamson's return to the West End stage in a one-man show about John Barrymore included the line, 'What kind of asshole does it take to write "My Life In The Theatre" at twenty-eight?' One of the trustees of the play's production company was Kenneth Branagh – it's hard to believe he hadn't given his self-deprecating approval for such a birdbolt.

Why, therefore, did he agree to write the book? 'Money. It's as simple as that. Very vulgar, I'm afraid. Did you expect me to say I wanted to change the world? "Branagh in Art Sham Scandal!"... Renaissance was operating from a tiny room in my flat in Camberwell and was about to tour with three plays. When a publisher put up a handsome advance it allowed me to rent offices for the company.' In fact, seventeen publishers attended the auction for the book, including one who admitted that she had gone along solely to meet Branagh. The offer which was accepted came from Chatto & Windus; the sum was £50,000.

Beginning, published in the autumn of 1989 and serialised in the *Observer* (*The Sunday Times* had made a better offer, but Ken refused to sell the serial rights to a Rupert Murdoch-owned paper), was brightly written and animated in its accounts of Ken's life and work. The occasional lapses into preciousness were regularly deflated by a rich vein of self-deprecating humour. It revealed, however, virtually nothing about the writer.

Almost every project he had ever been involved in was painted as enjoying its success in spite of him – his callowness, tendency to overact and to corpse in fits of giggles – and due to the talent and generosity of those around him. In short, the gentleman did protest too much. The dominant impression was of a man who couldn't quite believe his luck – or, more accurately, one who could believe it but knew it could run out at any time and wanted to seem ready for the eventuality.

Revelations were even fewer and further between where Branagh's personal life was concerned. Few girlfriends were named, and those few either vaguely or pseudonymously; no insights were offered into his own psyche. One critic remarked in the *Daily Express* that 'while it takes you at a breakneck pace through 244 pages of what Kenneth did, it devotes surprisingly little to what Kenneth is.' A man who, according to friends, had a life plan mapped out until his fortieth birthday conveyed little in his autobiography of the determination which had taken him so far so quickly, nor of the sometimes heavy emotional price he found himself paying for it. The only real demonstration of his personal skills was in the style of the book itself, which was easy and relaxed, with an impetus which he hoped would carry the reader along rather than stop to ask some of the many questions which his account begged.

The suspicions of many were summed up by one detractor in particular. 'Who is this little shit? This man who is going around saying he's Laurence Olivier. He's gone too far. He's become vulgar, too conspicuous. I mean, this film might be all right – it's got such a lot of *serious lovies* in it, Derek Jacobi and Ian Holm and darling Dame Judi and all – but writing a book about himself as well? It's just too much. It's sickeningly famous. He's *got* to be a shit, a ruthless git, greedy for money and fame and glory, into tearing the wings off butterflies and beating up his granny.' This sniper was, of course, Ken himself, launching into a mock critique and topping it off with a disarming smile – much the same strategy pursued in print throughout *Beginning*.

The book's publication was the occasion for an altogether less sympathetic reassessment of Branagh by Nicholas de Jongh in the *Guardian*. De Jongh acknowledged, in a back-handed compliment, that 'He has proved himself the most accomplished theatrical entrepreneur and self-publicist of his generation,' before arguing that the foundation of his success – his talents as an actor – remained questionable. 'He is talented, personable and shrewd [but] at best magnificently efficient... There is no blaze, no electricity about Branagh's acting – no tension, no governing excitement. Charisma – that indefinable essence – is missing.' Going on to dismiss much of *Beginning* as an exercise in self-glorification, de Jongh concluded that Branagh 'is an actor overdosing on hubris. Is that nemesis waiting in the wings? We shall see.'

Yet for all his eagerness to overcompensate for imagined failings, Branagh showed the same ease with the written word that he had demonstrated in his play scripts. The book had a strong tone, if not of intimacy then certainly of matiness, and the account of his parents' and grandparents' lives in York Street was obviously written with a deep sense of attachment to his roots. One of the twin epigraphs (the other being from *As You Like It*) was taken from the poem *Saturday Night in York Street* by local poet John Campbell. Ken had never met Campbell, but at a book signing in Belfast the poet joined the queue and introduced himself.

Meanwhile, *Henry V* was on its way to becoming both a critical and commercial success. Branagh made the cover of *Time* magazine in November, and the following month the New York Film Critics' Circle voted him Best New Director of 1989 amid news that American corporation CBS was about to buy a 15 per cent stake in Renaissance Films as part of a three-picture deal. In January, as the deal was confirmed, Branagh also won the *Evening Standard* Award for Best British Film of the Year, and Queen's University of Belfast announced that that summer he would receive an honorary Doctorate of Literature 'for distinction as an actor and services to the theatre'.

When the Oscar nominations were announced the following

year, it was no surprise that the shortlists for Best Actor and Best Director included Kenneth Branagh. When the ceremony rolled around, however, Emma did not accompany him to Los Angeles. 'They were in Japan at the time,' remembered John Sessions, 'doing *King Lear* and the *Dream*, and it meant he had to get an understudy. Emma felt that if they both went it would be letting the show down, so she stayed behind.' Sessions himself was Branagh's guest at the presentations, and Ken remembered 'introducing John to Steve Martin in the lavatory. I was completely star-struck. Nicholson was in the wings and said, "Hi, I'm Jack. I liked your picture." You're tempted to say, "I know you're Jack, the whole world knows you're Jack." I found it a very emotional evening. I was in tears most of the time.' Although he did not win a statuette in his own right (he would be beaten to that honour by his wife), the film did win an Academy Award for Phyllis Dalton's costume designs, which had been influenced by those in Adrian Noble's RSC production (Dalton had already won an Oscar for dressing David Lean's *Doctor Zhivago* in 1965). And the accolades kept coming: awards for technical achievement and best film from the British Film Institute; European Actor of the Year and Young European Film of the Year at the European Film 'Felix' Awards, whose jury included Ingmar Bergman, Deborah Kerr and Jeanne Moreau.

The film's more prominent fans included Gérard Depardieu, who admired it so much that he bought the French rights in order to prevent a clumsily dubbed version going on release. His ex-agent and good friend Jean-Louis Livi became the film's French producer and the translation was supplied by Jean-Michel Déprats, who had performed a similar task on a version of *Measure For Measure* for France's Centre Dramatique National. Depardieu released both subtitled and dubbed versions, for the latter of which he himself provided the voice of King Henry. Depardieu later said that, when he was chairman of the 1992 Cannes Festival jury, he had wanted to award Emma the best actress prize for *Howards End*, but had been out-voted and had sulked for hours. The compliment would be partly returned five years later, when Emma took an uncredited cameo part in his second Hollywood movie *My Father the Hero*. Theories abounded as to what the next Renaissance (Film) project would be: *Much Ado About Nothing*, *Macbeth* or perhaps a musical. Before any of these rumours could be proved or disproved, the company's next stage tour got under way – a global itinerary for *A Midsummer Night's Dream* and then *King Lear*, both directed by Ken. He was to play Peter Quince and Edgar respectively (the former reprising his role in Malcolm McKay's production for RADA), with Emma as Helena and 'by far and away the most fascinating role I've ever played,' the Fool in *Lear*. The tour commitment also led her to turn down the lead role in a television version of David Lodge's novel *Nice Work* – she did not, the series' producer hastened to point out to the press, decline the part because of its sex scenes. Furthermore, as mentioned earlier, the Japanese leg of the tour would keep her away from Ken's side at the Oscars ceremony.

The plays were first seen in the UK in Edinburgh in August 1990 before going on to the 2,000-seat Dominion Theatre on London's Tottenham Court Road, the largest theatre in the West End with the sole exception of the London Palladium. Again reviews were mixed. Although listings magazine *Time Out* called the production 'an excellent introduction' to the plays, highlighting once again the theme of accessibility, others were less convinced that this was a positive point. 'It has become fashionable of late to bash the Branagh,' noted the *Daily Mail*. 'On the evidence of these lightly baked offerings, however, I'm afraid it proves a fashion impossible to fight. In both these totally diverse plays he exposes the common weakness he shares as a stage director and a stage actor. This is to go for the surface effect at the expense of any inner conflict.' *City Limits* magazine allowed that 'There is a quiet intelligence working behind these productions,' but lamented, 'If only it had been worked fully through.' The paradox of the Renaissance aesthetic was pointed up by another reviewer, who also took the opportunity to include a sideswipe at Ken's supposed ingratitude to those who first helped him on his way:

'Here is a company presumably founded to allow Shakespeare a fresh start, freeing the Bard from the whims of the state-subsidised directorial autocrats who in fact launched Branagh's career. But does this actor honestly think that his brand of anaesthetised, non-interpretive [sic] Shakespeare does anyone any favours?'

Emma's role as the Fool in *King Lear* came in for particular scrutiny. Hers was not the tortured old variety queen of so many productions, and the extremity of her portrayal provoked correspondingly extreme verdicts. The critic who felt that 'Thompson's Fool with white skull-like face and twisted body is genuinely sharp, funny and wise, bringing a dark humour to the production's sugar-coating' was in the minority. 'Her choice of comic Cockney made me squirm,' said another, while elder theatre-critic statesman Milton Shulman in the *Evening Standard* noted acerbically that 'A Kenneth Branagh production nearly always includes a perverse idea designed to shock or irritate,' and predicted sardonically that the whey-faced, hunched Fool 'could be cultivating future back trouble'.

The most double-edged compliment paid to the pair of plays was in the *Guardian*: 'What the productions prove,' wrote Michael Billington, 'is that Mr Branagh, both as director and actor, is a comedian by instinct.' The backlash was in full swing. Such reviews no doubt played a part in the future of Renaissance: Ken would co-direct but not appear in its next stage production, its final theatrical fling *Coriolanus* was performed only at the Chichester Festival Theatre in Sussex, and Emma Thompson has not been seen onstage since her Helena/Fool pairing.

Ken had also trodden a stage that July to receive his honorary doctorate at the Queen's University of Belfast. He admitted to feeling 'rather a cheat' compared to the hundreds of students who had worked for three or four years for degrees. It was to be followed four months later by one of the Republic of Ireland's national People of the Year Awards, presented by the Taoíseach (Prime Minister) Charles Haughey. As a result of Dr Russell Jackson's involvement with his Shakespearean projects, Ken has also become the only actor to be given an honorary fellowship of the Shakespeare Institute: where other honorary academic titles may be more general pats on the back, fellowship of so specialised a body indicates a high degree of respect for a specific intelligence and talent beyond simply being one of 'the great and the good'.

The time was ripe for his first non-Renaissance screen venture as a director.

Whatever the ups and downs of the 'special relationship' between the United States and the United Kingdom, Hollywood has always had a soft spot for British actors. Since the heyday of Ronald Coleman and Sir Cedric Hardwicke in the 1930s, an English accent in an American film has been used as easy shorthand to denote a certain kind of 'class', whether romantic, intellectual or villainous. 'Professional Brits' such as David Niven and, in a very different way, Michael Caine had become stars by bringing their own aura into whatever film they happened to be appearing in: there is not, for example, even a passing explanation of what Caine is doing in a New York Jewish family in Woody Allen's *Hannah and Her Sisters*; he is accepted because he is Michael Caine.

Things threatened to get out of hand in the late 1960s and early 1970s, when the American television success of *Upstairs, Downstairs* generated an interest in the English as quaint, olde-worlde accessories. One quite prominent husband-and-wife acting couple, who were not even in the series, received an offer from a Hollywood studio executive to move to California – as his English butler and maid. Their salaries would have been greater than their income from acting at the time, although they were both in steady work; however, they were unable to take the proposition seriously. By the 1980s, matters on-screen were less clear-cut: Julian Sands and Charles Dance have traded on their skill at evoking an air of menace rather than specifically upon their Britishness; likewise Alan Rickman, who first came to Hollywood attention in *Die Hard* behind a *mittel*-European accent. Richard E. Grant and especially Bob Hoskins now play American characters as often as they do English ones. Nonetheless, producers continue to be fond of British actors in the belief that they add a little something extra to a film.

Towards the end of the 1970s, however, another kind of British talent began to make its presence felt in Hollywood. Director Alan Parker, who had made pictures like *Bugsy Malone* and *Midnight Express* in tandem with producer David Puttnam, came to Hollywood to make the movie *Fame*. Although his critical and commercial stock has been variable since (not least due to his outspoken views on the Hollywood system, conveyed for a while through a regular cartoon spot in a trade paper), he constituted the idiosyncratic vanguard of a group of British directors who established reputations for visual flair across a number of genres. Ridley Scott was lauded for his work on the first *Alien* movie in 1979 and *Blade Runner* a few years later; his younger brother Tony directed the modern vampire curio *The Hunger* in 1983 before hitting the jackpot with *Top Gun*. Likewise Adrian Lyne, after journeyman work on *Flashdance* and *9½ Weeks*, became hot property with *Fatal Attraction* in 1987. What these three had in common was an early grounding in the field of television commercials, which informed their approach to framing and juxtaposing images on-screen and imbued them with a readiness to let the visuals do the work (sometimes excessively so – many would argue that *Top Gun*, the favourite film of Alex Lowe's teenage character in *Peter's Friends*, is little more than a 110-minute promotional film extolling the joys of being a combat-jet cowboy).

The growing profile of these émigré Brits, together with other directors such as Hugh Hudson and Roland Joffe making Hollywood-scale movies outside America, caused the major studios to pay attention to British talent for other reasons than simply being able to deliver the Queen's English in front of a camera. For a short period in the mid-1980s, David Puttnam even ran the Columbia studio, but soon resigned due to a mixture of frustration at the monolithic studio structure and a lack of conspicuous success in the job. Kenneth Branagh, a hot young actor who had just made a lauded debut 'art' feature as director and showed strong signs of mainstream cross-over appeal, was a prime candidate to be wooed by Hollywood. After he received a brace of Oscar nominations, the suitors were queuing up.

11

All Friends Together

Ken had always maintained that, if the project were sufficiently attractive to him, he would have no qualms about 'going Hollywood'. The screenplay for *Dead Again* (written by Scott Frank, who also penned Jodie Foster's directorial debut *Little Man Tate*) had been commissioned by producer Lindsay Doran in 1986 when she was at Paramount. It combined a twin-strand detective story and a bizarre romance with the topic of reincarnation. Doran, now working with Sydney Pollack's independent production company Mirage, was looking for a director for the film – which, as a Mirage production, would carry the prestigious name of Pollack as executive producer – 'with a committed visual style [but] who was also a humanist and would not sacrifice the characters for the visual ... and that is a difficult commodity to find'. After seeing *Henry V*, she realised that Ken combined the qualities Mirage were looking for in a director. She immediately sent him the script of what was to be his Hollywood debut proper.

It was, he said, the chance to realise a childhood fantasy. As a young lad waiting for his parents to come home from work to Mountcollyer Street, he would sit in front of the television. 'I saw great films like *Spellbound* and *Dial M For Murder*, and I wanted to make big pictures like them one day. And I longed to play a detective in a trenchcoat and trilby.' It is unlikely that such Hitchcock films would be screened in the afternoon as he

187

remembers; indeed, in another version of events he relocated the scene of his deduction to the cinema. 'I suppose you might say this movie has been made with my mum in mind. She has always been a huge Hitchcock fan, and the earliest pictures I remember were the murder mysteries with outrageous plots I saw from the back stalls of cinemas when I was growing up in Belfast.' Such inconsistencies arise at least partly from Branagh the publicist's keen awareness of what makes the best copy in any given instance. Ken's mother herself, though, confirmed that her son was movie-mad. 'He was always dreaming on the sofa about films . . . or watching old movies on television when he should have been doing his homework.'

One way or another, the dream was obviously close to his heart. Branagh and Thompson were in Los Angeles for a run of *King Lear* and *A Midsummer Night's Dream* at the Mark Taper Forum in February 1990 when the Oscar nominations were announced, including Ken's citations for Best Actor and Best Director for *Henry V*. 'We were living in the Oakwood Apartments in Burbank,' recalled Emma. 'Rain was coming in through the ceiling and we had the four posts of the bed set in water-filled ashtrays to keep the ants out of the sheets. Ken was up all night on the couch waiting for news of the nominations. There was a receiver-shaped dent on the side of his head. It took all morning to get him off the ceiling. After that, the scripts came in by the truckload.'

But the scripts were for the most part tediously unimaginative, according to Ken. 'I was sent 4,000 lives of Shakespeare, several lives of Chekhov, and lots of scripts with battles in them . . . "Yeah, let's get that Branagh kid, he's good with battles!" I wanted to do [Thomas Hardy's novel] *The Return of the Native*, but I don't think most of the studios knew quite how to take me. Then I picked up *Dead Again* off the script pile and literally could not put it down.' He and Emma read the script between matinée and evening performances of Shakespeare at the Taper and were riveted. 'The story is the real star,' he said. Emma agreed: 'This was the first one we picked up that didn't have a battle. We were rather thrilled by that, but even more thrilled when we read to the end and discovered it was intelligent and witty and all tied up. We were sitting on a sofa taking turns reading to each other. We had to read through to the end to find out what happened.' They then took a brief break to watch all of Alfred Hitchcock's classic suspense pictures before embarking on the enterprise.

The film's hook was its reincarnation theme, allowing for twin plot-lines as private detective Mike Church (Ken) simultaneously attempts to discover the identity of an amnesiac woman (Emma) and tries to solve the mystery of the dreams which plague her. They turn out to be past-life memories of a murder involving European émigré composer Roman Strauss and his wife Margaret (Ken and Emma again). Ken described himself as 'sympathetically agnostic' to the idea of reincarnation, but his emotional armour prevented him from volunteering for past-life hypnotic regression himself. 'I met a lot of people when I was researching the film who had been regressed. I can't just write off the accounts of intelligent people as nonsense... I felt like I was witnessing a pretty powerful phenomenon. I absolutely refused point-blank to be regressed myself, though. There was no way they were putting me under. I just don't like the idea of loosening up whatever is in there in my subconscious. I won't have a massage for the same reason – I'm afraid I'd start crying or something.' Emma did volunteer to be regressed, quipping, 'I once went to a psychic and he said that in a past life I had been married to my mother, and that my father and sister were our children. I'm sure Kenneth could have been my son, my servant, my Egyptian toyboy or my pet turtle,' but again Ken vetoed the idea.

He also refused to allow himself to be 'put under' by the Hollywood lifestyle. 'We definitely wouldn't move there. It's such a strange place. It's like being in a movie – everything is so familiar and yet it remains unreal, because it belongs to the screen. The whole time I was there I couldn't quite believe it.' Now that he was being actively courted, he had no desire to 'go Hollywood'. 'What would I do with all that money?' Emma enjoyed herself immensely: 'Every day I drove to work, with the radio on and the breeze blowing in my hair; I thought to myself, "Good Heavens, this is quite thrilling. It's like Ken and Em's Big Adventure."' On the topic of Hollywoodisation, though, she was even more down-to-earth than Ken: 'I'd be so unhappy living over there – anyway, I've just had a new kitchen put in.' She claimed that at one benefit for Martin Scorsese she hid in a corner, and at the end of the evening smuggled the left-over cookies home in her handbag.

Paramount had loaned Ken an appropriately swish automobile for his stay in Los Angeles. 'I felt like a man in a sketch,' he said, 'this British creature driving a Ford Mustang convertible through the gates of Paramount . . . One day someone mentioned we were on the same lot where Orson Welles had filmed parts of *Citizen Kane*. I felt very romantic about that, like here I was, truly in the Land of Movies.' However, eventually he switched the Mustang for a beaten-up Toyota Corolla, with the excuse that 'I'm not mechanically minded.' On another occasion, he was even blunter about his lack of Californianness: 'Do you know, Emma and I are the most fucking boring, boring fucking people in the world. All I ever wanted to do in Hollywood was come home, glass of wine, bowl of something in front of the telly and blank off.' He was so un-Hollywood, he admitted, that during a particularly stressful time in the making of the film, his idea of a comforting treat to buck himself up was to go down to Santa Monica Pier with Emma for some fish and chips. 'Being both director and star can be a strain,' he said. 'So much added responsibility. I'd like to just act in a film, to see another director at work. I may act in a film before the turn of the year, I haven't made up my mind yet.' When he did just act in someone else's film, a year later, he demanded that his name be removed from its credits.

Hollywood was eager to accommodate Ken, even if 'the studio executives used to expect me to walk into their offices wearing a fluffy white shirt and a pair of black tights.' But he went in determined to strike a deal that would take into account his own strengths – and weaknesses. He required, he said, support from the core production team he had worked with on *Henry V*; he also wanted to play both Roman Strauss and Mike Church, with Emma as Margaret and the amnesiac woman, Grace. Scott Frank 'had originally written it for four people, with the idea that there were many more twists to the plot. But Ken said to me, "Let me be your Lon Chaney." I thought of *Dr Strangelove*, and I realised this could work.' Lindsay Doran admitted that 'Ten minutes with Ken, and he can talk you into anything,' and Paramount's motion picture chief David Kirkpatrick simply acknowledged, 'We all knew very well that when you buy Ken Branagh, you buy the whole package.'

Paramount's decision to lavish on Ken the benefit of actors like Andy Garcia (just then on the point of breaking into the big-time), Donald Sutherland and even Robin Williams – in an uncredited supporting role – was due to a combination of generosity to the new boy and a desire to temper the unfamiliar British names on the film with more immediately recognisable talent. The generosity proved limited, too, when it came to megabuck budgets (the picture cost around $14 million), but *Dead Again* wasn't that kind of film anyway. 'The fact that the film was budgeted at the lower end of the scale gave them the leeway to go along with the things that I asked for, which were really all to do with artistic control. It wasn't a question of being very principled on my part, it was just that if you took my legs away or tied my hands behind my back I couldn't make the movie.' Despite his antipathy to the West Coast lifestyle, Emma spoke highly of his innate ability to handle the wheeling and dealing aspect of things: 'He's got an instinctive understanding of the place. He just arrived there and started to work it out, because that's the kind of brain he has.' Lindsay Doran was astonished: 'He is so focused [that] sometimes he only filmed a scene once or twice. Those were the shortest dailies I've ever attended.'

For Mike Church's California accent, Ken worked with three dialect coaches. He then tried his new screen voice out in the real world. 'I screwed my courage to the sticking point once

191

and went to the movies to see how I'd do. I went up to the counter and ordered a Diet Coke and popcorn and prattled on about this and that before I realised the counter person was from Mexico. I think the next person I talked to was Chinese. I soon realised it would be a long time before anyone in this melting-pot woke up in a cold sweat to wonder if Ken Branagh had finally got that accent down.'

An early upset over 'artistic differences' had resulted in Donald Sutherland leaving the film – because his previous picture went over schedule or due to unhappiness with his role and billing, according to differing accounts. Branagh asserted his artistic control by replacing Sutherland with Derek Jacobi, recreating a little bit of Renaissance in Hollywood. 'The execs' eyes flickered a bit,' he said of the studio's response to his request, 'but they knew I would have happily walked away if they'd said no. I told them I didn't know how to direct films in isolation; I needed all these other people to help me.' Ken had also insisted that designer Tim Harvey, costume designer Phyllis Dalton and composer Pat Doyle be brought on to the project. Then, of course, there was Emma, his co-star twice over. 'I thought Ken really wanted, *needed* a star,' she admitted, 'but he said he wanted someone he could do emotional shorthand with. And I think we look right together. I'm sure Michelle Pfeiffer would have been wonderful, but would she have looked right with Ken?' In a further *Henry V* link, particularly eagle-eyed and trivia-minded viewers will spot that in the opening sequence, in which Roman Strauss is pictured on death row on the day of his execution, the number on the prisoner's uniform is 25101415, the date of the Battle of Agincourt – a subtle literary variation on Hitchcock's habit of inserting 'McGuffins' into his films.

It's not the place of a biographer to offer personal opinions, but it must be said that I belong to the group of people who just can't see the film's appeal. It simply tries too hard in every department. The supposed stylistic 'homages' to Hitchcock are so blatant as to seem like the work of a tyro, eager to impress. Those who saw Derek Jacobi in the title role of the television series *I, Claudius* on BBC or PBS in the 1970s and made the connection with a stuttering young boy in the film's 1948 scenes could quickly put two and two together and predict that he and Jacobi's 1980s character would be one and the same, and that Jacobi's luxuriant stammer would return in the final reel. (The portrayal of the character led to complaints to Branagh and Sydney Pollack from the National Stuttering Project in America.) Above all, Branagh's attempts to play the humorous strain of Chandleresque *noir* detective stories are irksome. For someone who once claimed to be 'as camp as a row of tents', he simply couldn't set his camp meter at a low enough level to pull it off. Emma dominates every scene in which they both appear, and does so with her usual much more discreet, seemingly minimal performance.

Audiences at *Dead Again*'s disastrous sneak preview screenings reacted similarly, laughing at inappropriate moments and even walking out. It was, said Ken, 'like having your innards laid out in front of you'. Paramount sent the film for re-editing, but to no avail. The movie was about to be consigned to the shelf when, in desperation, Ken suggested that the 1940s scenes, which had been shot in colour, be reprocessed in black and white. According to one source, there may have been an element of image-consciousness to his suggestion: 'He has lips in black and white which he certainly doesn't have in colour.'

The change in reception at the fourth set of previews was momentous. *Dead Again* was lauded by the *New York Times* as a '*coup de cinéma*', by the *Los Angeles Times* as a 'stylish and witty sonnet to the ghosts of Hollywood past' and succinctly summed up by *Newsweek* as 'highly entertaining claptrap'. For a few weeks the movie even grossed more than what was then the most expensive motion picture of all time, the Arnold Schwarzenegger vehicle *Terminator 2*, raking in $12.6 million in its first two weekends. There were the inevitable hostile reviews (largely in the UK) – 'I'm just glad we weren't sent home in unmarked crates,' said Emma – but also unrestrained praise.

Ken confessed himself 'relieved, completely and utterly

relieved. I'm brilliant at taking bad news and find it very hard to deal with the rest of it. That's a troubled, puritanical, Protestant upbringing for you.' He was presumably speaking of Protestant 1960s Northern Irish culture as a whole, as those adjectives fly in the face of all his other accounts of his childhood; moreover, the impression given by his responses to previous bad news and bad reviews is that his brilliance in dealing with them is largely a matter of finding reasons to discount such negative opinions whilst justifying himself on his own terms. Still, in America at least, there was little call for such defensiveness over *Dead Again*. Ken was forecast to be Hollywood's Golden Boy of the 1990s by *Entertainment Weekly* magazine, but although the American production outfit the Samuel Goldwyn Company largely financed his next two Renaissance pictures it would be three years before he made his next true 'Hollywood' picture, and that would be shot not in California but at Shepperton.

Emma, meanwhile, turned up in the costume comedy-drama *Impromptu*, released in the UK in spring 1991. Directed by James Lapine (better known for writing the books of several Stephen Sondheim musicals) and set in nineteenth-century France, this film may well be destined for rediscovery in years to come, featuring as it does both Emma Thompson and Hugh Grant, who improbably plays the composer Frédéric Chopin being amorously pursued by cross-dressing female novelist George Sand (Judy Davis). The cast is bizarrely eclectic: Sondheim/Lapine musical stalwarts Bernadette Peters and Mandy Patinkin rub shoulders with Brits such as Julian Sands and Anna Massey, while Anton Rodgers turns in one of his sitcom performances as the Duc d'Antan.

Thompson plays the Duc's wife, who invites a salonful of assorted geniuses to her country house without realising what is immediately apparent to the viewer: the chaos that would be caused by gathering so many artistic temperaments under one roof. She herself is roughly seduced by the painter Delacroix. Her part is all giggles, embarrassment and aristocratic twit-dom, and Thompson gets full value out of it, as if playing a slightly less brainless Continental forebear of Miss Money-Sterling from her *Young Ones* appearance. The occasional comparisons to Joyce Grenfell which her early comic work had elicited were dusted off once more.

She was under no illusions about the artistic integrity of the picture or of her character. 'The woman's a complete idiot, but actually very touching. I loved the script, so baroque and unusual, and the language, the full-bloodedness of it. I'd always wanted to work in France, and I wore a lot of very funny dresses. I think sometimes actors get terribly serious because they want to deny the fact that a lot of it involves getting dressed up in exciting clothes that make you feel different. You get to wear them all day and wander around and actually be that person – it's bliss.' She was less happy about the Rubenesque shape of her body while filming: 'During *Look Back in Anger* my metabolism just gave up for a while and everything made its way quietly on to my hips.' But the film's costume designer, who had previously dressed Emma in *Fortunes of War*, was enthusiastic about the extra two stone: 'He got the corsets out and said, "This is the sort of body you can do something with." I was like a tube of toothpaste.'

If Emma's body had more pronounced curves than she would have preferred, *Impromptu*'s script likewise undulated in and out of its intended shape, peppered with anachronisms and uncertain exactly what its emotional register should be (no one actually utters the archetypal crass historical-drama line, 'Hello, Chopin – my, that's a nasty cough,' but Hugh Grant's first and last lines in the film are both composed entirely of 'ahems'). Unsurprisingly, the actors respond with performances of correspondingly variable sizes. The overall effect is unsettlingly like watching *The Draughtsman's Contract* remade by Ivan (*Ghostbusters*) Reitman. *Impromptu* vanished with barely a trace from cinemas, but still lurks around on rental video release, a skeleton wearing a paper party hat in the closets of almost all concerned.

After the fun and frocks of *Impromptu*, late 1991 proved a distressing period in Emma's personal life, as she suffered a

195

series of bereavements in an echo of those during her first year at Cambridge. Her uncle James (Phyllida Law's brother) and her old boyfriend Simon McBurney's father died within a short time of each other; a few months later her godfather, director Ronald Eyre, who had given her away at the Cliveden wedding, also died. 'It was like some mediaeval curse,' said her mother. 'We can't get over the fact that all these divine men managed to drop off the twig with such alarming alacrity. We are bleached of men. Thank God for Ken.'

Ken's compulsion always to be doing several things at once if at all possible (and even if not) continued unabated. One of the many projects in which they were rumoured to have expressed an interest was a film dealing in parallel with the life in captivity in the Lebanon of English hostage John McCarthy and his friend Jill Morrell's campaign to free him: both Paramount (who had made *Dead Again*) and the BBC were apparently working on scripts. A Paramount spokesman said, 'Branagh is big news here at the moment. The McCarthy story is a sure-fire winner and to get the two together is obviously a potentially winning situation.' There had even been talk that Ken would take the title role in the film version of Leslie Charteris's *Saint* stories, following in the footsteps of television Simon Templars Roger Moore and Ian Ogilvy (as he would later be tipped as one of a field of candidates to assume Moore's old mantle as 007). More plausibly, he was said to be planning a version of *Othello* with his French supporter Gérard Depardieu in the title role.

But once *Dead Again* was in the can, it was back to England – after (incredibly for Ken and Emma) an honest-to-goodness holiday, a three-month walking tour of Ireland and Scotland – to the Renaissance Theatre Company for what was to be its last project on the London stage, Chekhov's *Uncle Vanya*, co-directed by Ken and Peter Egan for a nine-venue tour beginning and ending at familiar venues: the Grand Opera House in Belfast and the Lyric, Hammersmith. It was the only one of his Renaissance theatre productions apart from *Twelfth Night* (*The Life of Napoleon* had at root been a John Sessions project which Branagh backed) in which he did not appear. 'I'm not, strictly speaking, right for anything in this play,' he admitted. The two middle-aged main characters, Vanya and Astrov, were played by Egan and Richard Briers, a pairing familiar to television viewers from the sitcom *Ever Decreasing Circles*. (Egan went on the following year to play the fiftysomething Jimmy Porter in *Déjàvu*, John Osborne's belated, horrendously splenetic sequel to *Look Back in Anger*.)

Chekhov had always insisted that his portrayals of melancholy, middle-class Russian country life should be played as comedies; his characters, trapped in little lives of sterility and inertia, were ridiculous rather than tragic. He professed himself mystified, for instance, at the gloomy *longueurs* in the final act of Stanislavski's original production of *The Cherry Orchard*; they had made forty minutes, he said, out of what should have been played in fifteen. Renaissance took the author's intentions on board, without quite going to the lengths suggested by Ken's joky proposal that they should change the title to *Oops, I've Dropped Me Vanyas* in order to pull in the punters.

For Richard Briers the play was an opportunity to reinforce the revelation of Renaissance's *Twelfth Night* and *King Lear* that he was capable of more than a telegenic goofy grin. 'It's not putting too fine a point on it to say that meeting Ken has altered my life,' he said at the time. 'I was knocked back when I was offered [the role of King Lear] – and so were a lot of other people, I expect! Ken had turned me from a comedy man into a character actor.' Yet his Vanya – an accommodating man finally waking up to the realisation that he has wasted twenty-five years of his life managing his posturing brother-in-law's estate – was consistently judged on the terms he strove to escape. Audiences proved over-eager to laugh even at moments of anguish merely because the anguish was being conveyed by Briers, and a few critics sniped that some of the cast had 'apparently taken an Awayday to Ayckbourngrad'. The decline of comedy into final-act pathos is delicate and difficult to achieve, and opinions were often sharply divided as to the production's success in this respect. To some, it was 'exceptionally moving' (the *Daily Telegraph*), anchored by Briers' 'bitterly comic ... unforgettably poignant' Vanya (*The Times*); to others, 'a production which majors in self-pity' (the *Financial Times*) and 'reduces Chekhov's masterpiece to situation-tragedy' (the *Guardian*). Branagh had voiced hopes that the same company might tackle all of Chekhov's major works – yet another idea that vanished on the air. Briers has continued to play a number of character roles – Leonato in Ken's film of *Much Ado About Nothing*, a part opposite John Gielgud in his 1993 short film *Swan Song* (an adaptation of a Chekhov short story), and the 1994 West End and touring production of David Storey's *Home* – but his public image remains frustratingly tied to TV sitcoms.

Three weeks after the London run of *Vanya* ended, Ken returned to another old stamping-ground. When the *King Lear/Midsummer Night's Dream* tour had played in Reading, he had agreed to give a talk to members of his old amateur company, Progress Theatre, about his early days and experiences on his subsequent rise to prominence. 'Then we had a chat privately,' recounts Chris Bertrand, 'about how we were desperate for funds for the new building. He said he'd put his fund-raising hat on and give it some thought. Several weeks later Pauline Gray [Progress's membership secretary, who had helped to coach Ken on his drama school audition speeches a decade earlier] was phoned from Hollywood, where he was doing *Dead Again*. He said he'd already made all the arrangements.' Ken had organised a preview screening of *Dead Again* at the Reading Hexagon to benefit Progress, a month before the film premiered in London. 'He'd done everything that needed to be done, all we had to do was man the event. He came on, introduced the film and did a little spiel about Progress.' Bertrand remembers Branagh as being particularly nervous before making this address. On his return to his seat he whispered, 'Was that all right?' It was all right by Progress: the screening on 22 September made almost £5,000 and helped pay for the theatre's planned extension. The Reading event had not, however, been the first UK preview: that had taken place ten days earlier. Ken had had a clause written into his contract that the film would be screened first in Belfast, again in aid of the Northern Ireland Council for Voluntary Action and the Ulster Youth Theatre. This time £10,000 was raised.

When *Dead Again* was released, Ken had spoken of his enthusiasm for the craft side of film-making. 'Apart from my basic disposition to enjoy a good story, I particularly enjoy the possibility that I might be allowed to make other films. So I now get a real kick out of watching technical stuff in other films and saying, "Oh yes, I did that in one of my many two films."' He seemed already to know that the stage side of Renaissance activity was destined to lie dormant. When it was suggested that one use for his fees from Hollywood pictures might be Renaissance, he had replied with a noncommittal 'Mmm, yeah.'

All the remaining major appearances by the Renaissance Theatre Company would in fact be radio productions of Shakespeare plays, jointly financed by the BBC and Random Century Audiobooks. The first of these was *Hamlet*, broadcast on Radio 3 on 26 April 1992. Sir John Gielgud, who had made his own radio debut as Hamlet sixty years earlier and who had advised Ken on his first attempt at the role at RADA, played the Ghost; Derek Jacobi was Claudius, Judi Dench appeared as Gertrude and Richard Briers as Polonius. Once again Sophie Thompson played Ophelia, with Emma as the Player Queen. The melancholy Prince was, of course, Ken, who professed to preferring the medium of radio for the play because it avoided the possibility of off-putting audience participation. 'It is a real joy to deliver the soliloquy "To be or not to be . . ." in the studio. I would be terrified of doing it in the theatre. If you turned the lights up you would find that the front two rows of the audience would be mouthing along to the play.' An unlikely opinion to come from someone who had already played the part twice on stage, and must have known at that point that he would do so again before the year was out.

His next film project was announced as a Shakespearean

comedy – 'I haven't decided yet which one; I haven't read every play Will ever wrote. I didn't become aware of Shakespeare until I was sixteen. Now I'm making up for lost time.' He was determined to put together 'a big international cast, black and white', to reinforce his view of Shakespeare as a writer of popular and accessible drama.

In fact, before that film got underway, the couple managed to slot in a project which was thoroughly English – indeed, thoroughly Cambridge. *Peter's Friends* concerns the reunion of a Cambridge student revue group ten years later at the country house of one of the group. It starred Ken, Emma, her mother Phyllida Law (Phyllida Mother-in-Law, as she was unkindly dubbed in some quarters), Imelda Staunton, Tony Slattery, Stephen Fry, Hugh Laurie and Rita Rudner, and was written by Rudner and her husband Martin Bergman, thus reuniting five of the Footlights *Cellar Tapes* company. In fact, the opening revue song of the film – an excruciating litany of London Underground stations sung to the 'can-can' tune of Offenbach's *Orpheus in the Underworld* – was first heard in the 1977 Footlights revue.

These figures from Emma's history created something of an extended-family aura around on-screen events; in addition, Branagh contacts were in evidence both on and off the screen. Alex Lowe (whose first stage appearance at the age of fourteen was as Ken's public-school fag in *Another Country*) played the housekeeper's sixteen-year-old son Paul, with whom Emma appeared momentarily in another parodic sex scene; Ken's younger sister Joyce acted as unit runner on the film. Roger Lanser, whom Ken had met eight years before as the cameraman on *The Boy in the Bush*, had been engaged as director of photography after visiting him in Hollywood during the making of *Dead Again*. The conversation then, said Lanser later, had been 'like one of those California things... sitting in the jacuzzi, saying, "We must do a picture together," and you think, "Yes, in my dreams."' But, as with his undertaking to help Progress in their fund-raising activities, Branagh had been as good as his word, and Lanser found himself in the

English country house which doubled as principal location and the film's production nerve-centre (an organisational stroke repeated with the Tuscan villa of *Much Ado About Nothing*). The film was emphatically rooted in thirtysomething territory, as a group of people who had met first when they were teenagers grappled with the vicissitudes of adulthood: incompatibility in marriage, infidelity, cot death, personal insecurity and AIDS, to name a few of the topics which crop up in the picture. The soundtrack was tailored to this generational feel, consisting as it did of a selection of evocative early-1980s 'adult-orientated rock' such as Tears For Fears' 'Everybody Wants to Rule the World' and Queen's 'You're My Best Friend'. Bizarrely, Branagh remarked that 'The exciting thing about directing was that I could choose the songs. We had to write snivelling letters to "Sir" Bruce Springsteen and co. for them because they were so integral to this film. A lot of the artists were fans of *Dead Again*, so that helped.' It was claimed that the appearance of Springsteen's 'Hungry Heart' marked the first time 'The Boss' had allowed one of his compositions to be used in a film.

Peter's Friends was a low-budget, character-driven film. 'We used a tenth of the budget of *Dead Again*,' said Ken, 'so I felt I had more control. People don't kick up so much fuss when there's less money to waste. To that extent, it was a much more personal film to make.' A couple of years later he revealed that the figure of one-tenth was a slight exaggeration, but even the (relatively) minuscule real figure for a picture like this had been enough to frighten off Paramount. '*Peter's Friends* cost $3 million; I'd just made *Dead Again* which cost $15 million and made about $40 million in America, so they said, "We'll do anything you want." I told them about *Peter's Friends*, [and] they said, "Fine, we'll read it over the weekend and ring you on Monday." They never do, of course, because they can't stand to give you bad news ... They finally said, "We don't know how to make a film like this." You'd think they'd say, "Give him *Flintstones 2*, that'll make lots of money, and then let him do his funny little English film."'

Once again, Ken was feeling wistful about the effects upon

his life of his compulsively intense working habits, and the story of *Peter's Friends* was an opportunity to reassess personal priorities. 'I've certainly reached a point in my life where I'm very interested in maintaining friends and valuing friendship in the face of a difficult world.' But as an English version of *The Big Chill* it's lacking – Cambridge isn't Berkeley, and even the final revelation of the reason for the reunion (that host Peter has contracted a certain virus) is both predictable and mawkishly handled. The class parody was too rarefied for much of the audience to appreciate, and their winces at the ludicrous behaviour of these stereotypes were unmodulated by laughter. Imelda Staunton had said, 'We want the audience to care about the characters. We don't want them to see us as a group of rather uppity people on a posh weekend and say, "So what?"', but inevitably there was more than a little of such response. The navel-gazing aspect was sometimes uncomfortably pronounced: with the landed gentry exception of Peter, for instance, every member of the revue company was given a profession in the media world.

Emma came off tolerably as a dowdy, scatty spinster and editor of a series of self-help books. Her first scene – as Maggie strews her flat with pictures of herself so that her cat doesn't miss her while she's away – is a deliberate parody of Emma's own fondness for Post-It notes. (Robbie Coltrane once found his house papered with the things after the couple had been to stay: on a painting, 'This is dreadful'; on the stairs, 'Black banisters went out of style twenty years ago'; on the dog-basket, 'This animal is a health hazard.') The irony of her line 'Fill me with your little babies!' wasn't lost on an audience which knew Stephen Fry to be, like the character of Peter, a celibate gay man. But, like the role of the Duchesse d'Antan in *Impromptu*, it wasn't terribly demanding; in a film which hinges on the seductive believability of the characters for its appeal, she and Rita Rudner seemed to be stereotypes rather than individuals. More subtle and comically richer was her guest appearance as children's entertainer Nanny Gee in the acclaimed American sitcom *Cheers* (a series in which Roger

Rees, who played Hamlet in the 1984 RSC production opposite Ken's Laertes, guested several times), in an episode entitled 'One Hugs, the Other Doesn't'. 'I only got the part because Glenn Close had to drop out,' she said, but the final version of Nanny, bopping around in an outsize mauve jumpsuit singing kiddies' songs, is distinctly un-Close-like. The sting in the tail, that Nanny Gee was the first wife of the bar's psychiatrist regular Frazier, added a further dimension to one of Emma's finest screen comedy performances, with little of the humour of embarrassment which characterised the part of Maggie.

Ken's role in *Peter's Friends* was that of a screenwriter now living in Hollywood, with an obscene amount of wealth and a fashionably unstable marriage to the star of his TV series, played by Rudner. (The title of the fictional series, *Who's in the Kitchen?*, recalls a joke of the time about the perceived 'luvvie' nepotism surrounding him: 'I'm in the kitchen, darling' – 'Ooh, can I be in it too?') It was an unsympathetic part which included more than a little self-exorcism. Ken's own near-breakdown at the time of *Henry V* had shown him how inconsiderate he was capable of being to others and, although since his early days with Progress Theatre he has been reluctant to bare any part of his own soul through acting, it's hard to doubt that the role of Andrew was to some extent informed by that experience. But, at his moment of maximum drunken obnoxiousness, Andrew is pulled up short by the realisation of the value of his friendships, confesses to having been 'an absolute dribbling arsehole' and shows every sign of redemption – again, it would seem, a mirror of Ken's own attitudes (not to mention his own vocabulary in moments of passion – 'the most fucking boring, boring fucking people in the world'). He's effectively admitting: I can be a consummate bastard at times, but for some reason you put up with it all, with that undercurrent of insecurity, 'Please like me.'

Yet simultaneous with this uncharacteristic breast-beating came another stage in his self-reinvention: the lad from York Street had become indistinguishable from the old Footies crowd. Press interest in the film centred not on its content, but on the personal and professional bonds which linked so many of the actors. The *Sunday Telegraph* ran a collective profile on them which, in a telling testimony to the degree of Ken's assimilation by the group, was headed 'The Branagh Pack'. At the end of the film's premiere at the London Film Festival, the audience were told to stay in their seats while the Branagh party left, an act of *hauteur* which angered many – 'That is a courtesy reserved only for royalty,' fumed one provincial paper.

Peter's Friends was a diversion from the main thrust of planned Renaissance activity: an opportunity to squeeze in a project which combined fun with (it was hoped) a little more serious content, and which was not a huge financial risk if it were not to come off that well. And at any rate, by the time the film was released, shooting on *Much Ado About Nothing* had already been completed and Ken was in rehearsal for *Hamlet* with the Royal Shakespeare Company. There really was no slowing him down.

12

Tower of Ivory

Although the rumours years earlier about Ken's appointment to the artistic directorship of Chichester Festival Theatre were untrue, he did appear at the theatre in 1992, in the title role of Shakespeare's Roman tragedy of public life, *Coriolanus*. The last Renaissance stage production of all – with Judi Dench as Coriolanus's mother Volumnia, Richard Briers as his devoted friend Menenius and company stalwarts Gerard Horan and Jimmy Yuill as the people's tribunes – was directed by Tim Supple specifically for Chichester. No tour followed the summer run in the Festival Theatre's repertory, there being no time for one before Ken geared up for his return to the RSC that winter.

As usual, he went at the play with a will – so much so that, at a charity gala attended by the Prince of Wales, he did himself a mischief. 'He had to fight with Iain Glen with a fairly hefty sword in the first act,' recounted David Parfitt, 'and unfortunately things got rather out of hand. Ken fractured the end of his finger and was in agony, but went on for the entire three-and-a-quarter-hour drama. He was covered in stage make-up blood, and the poor first aid woman nearly fainted – she thought he'd been run through!'

If Iain Glen failed to draw real blood, some critics came close to doing so. Much of the problem seemed to lie with

Supple's direction; his treatment of the play, in line with the now-familiar Renaissance rallying cry of 'accessibility', may have rendered it linguistically and narratively clear but it also robbed it of much of its power at opposite ends of its spectrum of action. Ken's sneering Coriolanus, utterly failing to conceal the contempt he feels for the people to whom he must sue for the civic office he seeks, proved unable to change gear when it came to the human foundations of his fiery public rhetoric – his relationship with his mother. Likewise, when the stage action erupts into battles, Supple had drilled and choreographed more than fifty local people to act as mobs and armies, but while the spectacle was visually impressive it carried little of the emotional undertow of violence which must pervade the play.

In the title role, Ken himself was variously described as 'a rather petulant young upstart whose spoiled-brat behaviour smacks more of John McEnroe-like tantrums than someone whose "nature is too noble for this world"', 'essentially a natural, reasonable, democratic sort of chap' (much more of an insult than it sounds, given that these qualities are everything that Coriolanus isn't) and, by Jack Tinker of the *Daily Mail*, most influential of the tabloid reviewers, 'a strutting bantam cock, no more terrifying to the state than ...a particularly obnoxious public school senior prefect'. This, in spades, seemed to be the fall that had been awaited, appropriately enough in the role of a man whose pride was his undoing. The few voices raised in admiration were drowned by a chorus of disappointment, and occasionally a murmur of glee that the golden boy's reputation had at last been tarnished. Renaissance's critical reputation over its five-year period of stage productions had begun moderately well, climbed to a peak with *Twelfth Night* and the triple-Shakespeare tour, then fallen into decline; with *Coriolanus* the company's stock seemed to be reaching the bottom of the hill. As the summer wore on, the play's limited run may have become a source of relief.

The autumn brought the release of *Peter's Friends*. Ken

followed the now established pattern by giving it a gala preview in Belfast in aid of the Northern Ireland Council for Voluntary Action and the Ulster Youth Theatre, on 28 October. Critically and commercially it got a lukewarm reception, but given its low budget and the Branagh-Thompson-etc. names, it more than broke even both in Britain and America; besides, it was after all a digression before the next screen Shakespeare.

Also opening that autumn was *Howards End*, starring Emma. The latest of the Merchant Ivory team's sequence of E.M. Forster adaptations showed a sureness of touch and register which had never fully coalesced in their previous projects. The delicacy of Forster's dissection of English class conventions was palpable without tipping over into deliberate ridicule as in *A Room With a View*, and the poignancy of Thompson's portrayal of Margaret Schlegel fully merited recognition. Casting agent Celestia Fox thought, 'It was the perfect role for her to play. Margaret Schlegel is an intellectual, and Emma has a genuine, believable intellect, which is rare in actors. Emma's very real. You think that she's really like the person she's playing, because she's not technical and you can't see her acting. You forget how much of an actress she really is. She's quite tough, but she's tremendous fun and terribly kind to people.'

Margaret Schlegel is the quintessence of intelligent middle-class decency: she mediates in disputes between family members and entire families, and possesses great sensitivity to beliefs and principles which differ from her own while attempting, increasingly vainly, to awaken in others the values of tolerance and responsibility which she feels so keenly herself. She is the moral and, in an everyday sense, spiritual centre of the story without being an ethereal paragon of virtue; an exemplar, within the stifling confines of class and period, of the aspiration to 'lead a good life'. Emma's own deep humanity and sense of social responsibility afforded her an innate affinity with Margaret, a character she could have been born to play. Indeed, just as

Margaret's closest – though never explicitly articulated – temperamental bond is with Mrs Ruth Wilcox (who bequeaths her the house from which Forster's novel takes its title), Emma's relationship with Vanessa Redgrave, who played Mrs Wilcox, was more than a mere matter of words. Producer Ismail Merchant watched as 'Emma went and kissed Vanessa for giving her the opportunity to work with her, whom she had admired for so long. Vanessa hugged Emma and said it was such a pleasure to work with her. It was a unique and touching moment.' One journalist, probably over-indulging in symbolism, suggested also that when Mrs Wilcox secures a sprig in Margaret's hair the moment can also be interpreted as Redgrave handing on a laurel to Thompson as her dramatic heir – a more than magnanimous gesture, if true, given the tempestuous relationship a few years earlier of Emma's husband and Redgrave's daughter Joely Richardson.

Howards End featured many of the usual Merchant Ivory suspects: James Wilby, Prunella Scales, Helena Bonham Carter, and from a generation of rising actors, Scales' son Samuel West and Redgrave's niece Jemma. But it was with Anthony Hopkins that Emma struck up a lasting rapport: Hopkins, on the crest of his theatrical and cinematic rehabilitation after years of alcoholic mediocrity, had followed his Oscar-winning performance as Hannibal Lecter in *Silence of the Lambs* with this more substantial film, guaranteeing box-office and critical appeal alike in the role of Henry Wilcox, who, after being widowed, marries Margaret but proves unable to transcend the strictures of social convention from which his second wife hopes and labours to free his spirit. Hopkins and Thompson shared not only a propensity for underplaying before the camera – making Henry and Margaret's relationship one of significant absences and subtle nuances, precisely as the material demanded – but a sense of humour to lighten the time between takes and the numerous little tediums of a film shoot.

In contrast to such welcome humour, the satirical puppet

television show *Spitting Image* broadcast a wicked Ken and Em sketch during the shooting of *Howards End*, in which the couple were depicted trying to make love, and eventually realising that they could only get it on when a camera crew was present. This was at the height of the media backlash against the couple's perceived 'luvvie' tendencies, and flew in the face of Emma's bouts of body-image insecurity. The rather tasteless double-entendre punchline – Emma sighing, 'Sorry, darling; I've dried' – provoked a number of sniggers behind her back on location the following morning, but her own response is not recorded.

The gala premiere of *Howards End* was the occasion of a protocol gaffe by Emma: she dared to speak to Princess Margaret before being spoken to. The offending remark was 'You're looking gorgeous, as usual.' Emma later explained, perhaps unwisely, that she was used to talking to Prince Charles, who did not stand on such formalities: 'If I did offend then that's tough. But I'm sure not. Princess Margaret has a far greater sense of humour than that.' Whether or not Her Royal Highness took umbrage, the film itself was fêted as Merchant Ivory's finest two hours and sixteen minutes. Thompson's first major role in a serious film, and her first serious cinematic part away from Branagh, was lavishly praised and inevitably tipped for a shoal of awards.

Sure enough, in January 1993 Ken and Emma dominated the *Evening Standard* British Film Awards: he won the Peter Sellers Award for Comedy for his performance in *Peter's Friends* and she the Best Actress Award, while *Howards End* was named best film. In March the British Academy of Film and Television Arts also gave Emma its Best Actress Award, and Ken picked up the prestigious Michael Balcon award for his contribution to cinema... at the age of thirty-two.

Howards End had garnered nine Oscar nominations, including one for Emma as Best Actress. She had already won five American awards for her role including a Golden Globe, and the aforementioned Best Actress awards as well as one from the London Film Critics' Circle. (At the *Standard* awards she had remembered her Footlights character Juliana Talent, and realised, 'It's awful to discover that you have become the subject of your own early satire.' Unlike Juliana, she began her own Golden Globe speech, 'Oh, crumbs,' and protested that she had had to borrow her clothes because 'we're not used to this sort of thing in England.')

However, by the time the last of the American awards (from the National Board of Review) was announced, Emma was in a health farm in Surrey, with a chest infection and a rash. 'I think I might be allergic to too much of that kind of attention,' she said, elsewhere describing the effect of nomination as a sensation 'like having a very severe virus and getting married.' Illnesses (including a sudden attack of eczema earlier in the year) apart, she seemed in public to be taking the plaudits in her stride, but admitted, 'I probably don't quite realise how nervous I will be at the Oscars. I'm probably going to have some sort of frothing fit before it and be flown home to England in a wooden crate.' Richard Briers had joked with her that she would no longer want to talk to the likes of him. With typical tart self-parody, Emma replied, 'No, I won't. Bugger off.' In fact, she realised perfectly well how nerve-racking the whole Oscar business was; during this period she took herbal tranquillisers.

Her one-liners belied a very serious attitude towards the award: Hollywood sources reported that she had flown back and forth for several weeks in support of her chances. When she discovered that an English Sunday newspaper supplement had interviewed a studio executive who had worked on several of the couple's films, she faxed him a demand for full details of his comments. In an attempt to get away from the 'hulking great bluestocking' image, she was even photographed nude by Lord Snowdon in a pastiche of Velázquez's 'Rokeby Venus' – although, after winning the Oscar, she pulled out at the last minute from a similar shoot for the British edition of *Esquire* magazine, in which she was to have appeared naked and sprayed gold.

In all the ballyhoo, little attention was paid to the fact that Ken's *Swan Song* – a thirty-minute film based on a Chekhov short story set the night after a provincial actor's final performance, and featuring John Gielgud and Richard Briers – had also been nominated in the short film category. Much more comment was excited by his non-attendance at the ceremony; as they had done three years earlier with Ken's nominations for *Henry V*, work schedules prevented both from going to Hollywood. Emma was accompanied by her mother, and the accounts of both women suggest that they were at their most star-struck and kittenish in the exalted company, comparing the class of megastar at their respective tables, and the like.

The Oscar for Best Actress was presented by Anthony Hopkins, her screen husband in *Howards End*. The two had agreed that if Hopkins saw her name on opening the envelope, he would simply say, 'Oh, fuck,' and walk off the stage. He welshed (no pun intended) on the deal. 'All I could think was, oh no, your hems are going to get caught,' said Emma. 'And I could see my mum sitting forward in her seat with the sort of expression on her face she used to have when I was in school assembly.' Having long argued that women should be given more fulfilling cinematic roles in their own right rather than simply as adjuncts to men – a quality shared by *Howards End* and the screenplay on which she had herself been working, of Jane Austen's *Sense and Sensibility* – she ended her acceptance speech with an echo of Colin Welland's less than prophetic declaration at the 1982 ceremony: instead of 'The British are coming,' Emma's cry was, 'The women are coming.'

When the presentations themselves were over (she had been stunned to find herself at the same table as Clint Eastwood – the two compared their statuettes), Emma spoke of her immediate plans to go home to Ardentinny and celebrate with the entire village: significantly, she called the Scottish village 'home' rather than West Hampstead. At a party after the ceremony, an English journalist chanced upon Emma in 'celebratory' mood, and asked her if she had had a chance to ring Ken with the news. Yes, she said. What had his response been? '"I'm asleep, don't bother me now."' (She was in similarly mickey-taking mood after the 1994 ceremony: spotting a 'tired and emotional' Barry Norman interviewing the glitterati for BBC Television's *Film '94* at one of the night's parties, she bore down on him and before he could open his mouth asked with gleeful mock solicitude, 'How are you – are you all right?')

Brian Blessed had maintained before the ceremony that winning the award would not turn Emma's head. 'She will take it with a pinch of salt. She'll probably give it to her mum for a bookend.' In fact, she went one better, and installed the Oscar in a place of honour in the couple's West Hampstead home – the loo, where they had previously hung a framed blow-up of *Dead Again*'s first weekend American box-office take of $6.5 million. 'It sits on the cistern. Friends who drop in at our house will make an excuse and say they have to answer the call of nature as soon as they arrive. What they really want to do is pick up the Oscar and make their own little acceptance speeches to the mirror.' Ken added, 'We like to give our friends a little privacy with their Oscar fantasies behind a locked door.'

Emma's Oscar may have disrupted the balance of power and fame within the relationship. Suddenly, Thompson was a name: the screenplay of *Sense and Sensibility*, on which she had been working for some time, was the subject of active discussions with Sydney Pollack's production company, Mirage. Emma had characteristically put a great deal of thought into even minor details of the adaptation. Her old director of studies, Dr Jean Gooder, remembers that 'Right in the middle of the exam-marking season I got a postcard from Emma starting with the usual "Dearest Jean" – high-flown actress! – and asking what I thought was *the* poem that Marianne and Willoughby shared in the book as the ultimate experience when discussing each other's tastes. This card arrived just before the Part II examiners' meeting, so over the lunch break I amused the combined examiners by asking them, and some wonderful speculative literary arguments arose from this. Emma and I agreed that although chronologically impossible, it would have to be Byron – the likelier candidates really wouldn't have had the same impact – and we decided that we could go from the publication date of *Sense and Sensibility* rather than the writing date.' Such a minor anachronism would cause few screenwriters to pause for an instant, but Emma felt compelled to justify even this slight departure from a true chronology in terms of the book's own history. (Later, in December 1993, a reading of the script at Kenwood House on Hampstead Heath featured Ken's former girlfriend Amanda Root as one of the Dashwood sisters, as well as Robert Hardy – who had a part in *Mary Shelley's Frankenstein* – Francesca Annis, Stephen Fry, Hugh Laurie and Geraldine McEwan.)

The Oscar also meant that Emma's next 'solo' picture was eagerly awaited. *The Remains of the Day*, on a budget which had been cut from $26 million to $11.5 million (further testimony to producer Ismail Merchant's talent for making one dollar look like several on screen), is quite as fine a piece of work. Even hardened Merchant Ivory-haters have been touched by the beautifully understated tale of a butler in an aristocrat's country house in the 1930s (his lordship was played by James Fox, elder brother of *Another Country*'s producer Robert and brother-in-law of casting agent Celestia) who refuses to allow love into his life. Kazuo Ishiguro's novel derives its power from an elegant first-person narrative by the butler, Stevens, the carefully crafted banality of which allows the reader to glimpse the core of emotion which Stevens has suppressed even from himself over the decades.

In the film Thompson's goodhearted but spurned housekeeper, Miss Kenton, and Anthony Hopkins' Stevens convey the unsaid magnificently as they portray a love story that never was, and share several of the most affecting non-kiss scenes in cinema for many years. For once in a straight dramatic work, however, Emma contravened the succinct judgement by a Cambridge acquaintance of Ken's and her respective dramatic styles, that 'he "does acting", she just acts.' Her efforts to portray Miss Kenton's nervousness and uncertainty are easily misinterpreted as an ill-judged attempt to insert too many 'grace notes' into her performance. This may partly be a matter of class; Thompson, described by the same Cambridge source as 'irredeemably middle-class', was playing a character at the genteel end of the below-stairs social bracket. She could afford neither to coast in her usual style of acting nor to veer into a broad portrayal, and seemed not quite at home with the minor tics that she used to establish Miss Kenton. Notwithstanding this discomfort, she never unbalanced the delicate equilibrium of a story which is constructed around the un-acted-upon aspects of Stevens' and Miss Kenton's relationship. *Howards End* and *The Remains of the Day* together had confirmed Emma Thompson as a screen actress of the first calibre: she had graduated with honours from the years of misinformed perception as a mere adjunct to her husband.

The reason for Branagh's inability to travel to Los Angeles was that he was in Stratford-upon-Avon, finally playing *Hamlet* for the RSC, the company whose gargantuan clumsy corporate structure he had so disliked. Probably only that part could have lured him back. He felt that his sympathy with the role had increased as he ceased to be a *wunderkind* and attained an age where the Prince's preoccupations become more universal: 'In your early thirties your parents start to go and you start to think more about death... Hamlet is a part which obsesses me, and I find death a subject of constant fascination and curiosity. The whole notion of mortality is what we are all obsessed with from the moment we arrive here. My intense enthusiasm for the play springs out of what light it sheds on all of that.'

To those who turned up to the theatre knowing him as a

phenomenon rather than a stage actor, his performance was a revelation. The experiences of the two previous runs at the part had paid off; here was a Prince who blended thought and deed, action and paralysis with dazzling clarity – even his madness was crystalline. Branagh onstage had finally delivered himself of what he was good for.

The critical consensus was that the promise displayed in his Renaissance production had now come good. 'The muffin face of his youth now has a commanding gravitas,' said Jack Tinker of the *Daily Mail*. 'The voice can soar the verse to the heavens or draw us into his innermost thoughts by its quiet confiding.' Tinker averred that 'both emotionally and physically he is undoubtedly the great Hamlet of our time. I have seen none to match him in many a season.' London's arts listings magazines were equally fulsome: 'Kenneth Branagh owes me £3.40 – I paid good money to see *Dead Again*,' began the *City Limits* review acidly, before continuing, 'But he's more than forgiven after creating a magnificently classic Prince Hamlet. Branagh presents the indecisions, vacillations and tergiversations of Hamlet without selling short the bursts of dynamism, the fury and passion. He reclaims the soliloquies as the clear, comprehensible and illuminating passages they should be, rather than the ring of cordoned-off cultural megaliths they've become; in fact, throughout he restores one's faith in the ability of contemporary actors to speak verse without awkward Peter Hall-ese end-stopping... The Branagh backlash stops here.'

The plaudits were deserved. Minimal cuts in the unwieldy hybrid script of *Hamlet* that survives had left the running time at around four hours, but director Adrian Noble (with whom Ken had worked on the RSC's *Henry V* eight years earlier, and who was now the company's artistic director) had drawn a batch of performances which not only clarified the often dizzyingly opaque language, but presented real relationships between characters. The family aspect was particularly strong, not only between Hamlet and his mother Gertrude

(Jane Lapotaire) but also between courtier Polonius and his children Laertes and Ophelia. As the maddened Ophelia, Joanne Pearce (Noble's wife) was almost impossibly moving in a scene which daunts every actress who attempts it. But the play belonged to Branagh – almost literally, after so many excursions in the role. This was the triumphant Hamlet he had always wanted to embody. If he was indeed taking the adulation of Emma badly (his mock truculent remarks to the press about playing second fiddle to her sounded worryingly like double-bluffs, even to those outside the media who didn't make a living by seeing smoke where there was no fire), the finest reviews of his stage career and a pair of sell-out runs at London and Stratford would give him some comfort before he embarked on the Shakespearean comedy film enterprise he had already announced.

Before that, however, his next big-screen appearance (filmed before *Hamlet*) sneaked by virtually unnoticed, largely because he had his name removed from the credits. *Swing Kids*, aimed at the teenage market, was based on the real-life existence of a group of fanatical followers of American jazz music in Hamburg in the late 1930s, during the rise of that other fanaticism, National Socialism. The Nazis disapproved of 'degenerate Negroid syncopation' and slapped a blanket ban on swing parties, making outlaws of the sharp-suited, jitter-bugging youngsters. The story follows two boys in particular as the persecution increases: Thomas (played by Christian Bale, who had been the dead boy carried across the field of Agincourt by the King in *Henry V*'s climactic sequence) succumbs to the twin seductions of power and belonging, joins the Hitler Youth and becomes a 'poacher turned game-keeper', whilst Peter (Robert Sean Leonard) resists both the pressure and, in particular, the blandishments of Herr Knoepp, a Gestapo officer wooing his widowed mother. That officer, brooding in shadows and speaking in a low-key Anglo-German-American accent (one respect in which his talents unarguably surpass Olivier's), was played by Kenneth Branagh.

216

It's an adept performance, combining the granite core of King Henry with a strong, but not excessive, vein of oleaginous smiling villainy as Knoepp attempts to insinuate himself as, er, Peter's friend. The movie as a whole, too, is surprisingly successful, concentrating on the personal aspect of the narrative without taking the opportunity to go in for black and white moral sermonising until a wildly over-indulgent closing sequence which plays the martyrdom card far too heavily (and at the final stroke of which Ken, to do him credit, looks perceptibly pained). As Branagh's first unremitting bad-guy film appearance, *Swing Kids* is a long way from being an embarrassment. Quite the reverse: it demonstrated that he wasn't worried about any possible effect the role might have upon his image.

Yet when the film came out his name was nowhere to be seen on it. The official line held by Disney, who (through their subsidiary Hollywood Pictures) made the movie, was that he didn't want to overshadow the young stars of the film (a scruple which didn't seem to bother Barbara Hershey, playing Peter's mother). More likely is the fact that, after directing and starring in three films of his own, Ken's Hollywood agents were concerned that minor billing would not adequately reflect his status in the movie world – the all-too-frequent argument over billing, in short, and not the sort of thing likely to occur to Ken himself: after all, he had directed an uncredited Robin Williams in *Dead Again* without any such palaver. Nonetheless, his contract had contained a clause permitting removal of his name, so removed it was. Branagh, however, continues to acknowledge it in his own filmographies, lending weight to the belief that agents' paranoia lay behind the decision to keep him out of the credits. Furthermore, the film had introduced Ken to another actor with whom he would work again almost immediately. Robert Sean Leonard subsequently appeared in the next Renaissance project, playing Claudio in *Much Ado About Nothing*.

Much Ado was, Ken told the *Belfast Telegraph*, conceived in Mountcollyer Street, when he used to stretch out on the settee and read Shakespeare plays. 'I could visualise his characters acting out the story on a stage or in a film. I was only nine, but I was fascinated by ideas like that.' Journalist Eddie McIlwaine failed to challenge Ken with the fact that he had told him exactly the same story about Hitchcock movies at the time of *Dead Again*'s release, or that he had admitted to the same writer less than a year earlier that 'I didn't become aware of Shakespeare until I was sixteen': once again, the Branagh charm carried all before it, including quibbles about his consistency.

He confessed that his first filmic vision of *Much Ado* came in a moment when his attention wandered during Judi Dench's stage production of the play. He imagined what was to become one of the movie's opening images – the visitors to Messina riding back from war, their horses materialising out of the heat-haze and looking for all the world like a Bardic Magnificent Seven. (In much the same way his King Henry, for one insane moment during the siege of Harfleur, conjures up the Lone Ranger on his rearing steed: a cloud of smoke, a flash of flame and a hearty 'Once more unto the breach, dear friends'.) But when the *Much Ado* image first occurred to him, he had not even begun to shoot his first film.

Ken spoke after a 1994 screening of the film of his attitude towards the play: 'I regard *Much Ado* as truly one of the sunnier plays; it doesn't sit as strongly on the melancholy side as some of the others.' Nevertheless, whereas plays like *As You Like It* and *A Midsummer Night's Dream* – the so-called 'festive comedies' – have plots driven by periods of licensed misrule after which there is little doubt that normal service will be resumed, *Much Ado About Nothing*, despite its throwaway title and primarily romantic content, does contain elements of greater darkness. The malcontent figure of Don John, the bastard brother of Don Pedro, maliciously sets about upsetting the course of true love by imputing faithlessness to the young and innocent Hero. Her betrothed Claudio's repudiation of her at the altar is genuinely troubling, and only a chance discovery by the low-comic characters of the Watch

218

restores order before a possibly fatal duel can be fought. The play contains real dramatic meat as well as both broad and refined humour and its dominant theme of romance; of all Shakespeare's comedies it lends itself most readily to the sensibilities of a modern cinema audience.

As a result of the commercial success of *Dead Again*, Branagh was in a position to recruit transatlantic as well as domestic talent for Renaissance projects. The cast of *Much Ado* included not only Renaissance stalwarts – Phyllida Law, Brian Blessed and Richard Briers, along with Ken's older mates Gerard Horan and Jimmy Yuill and Emma's former colleagues Ben Elton from *Alfresco* and Imelda Staunton, her right-hand woman on *Thompson*; even long-time Renaissance composer Patrick Doyle (having played Court, one of the English soldiers, in the film of *Henry V*) was given the opportunity to combine his acting and musical skills as the minstrel Balthasar – but the 'big international cast, black and white' which he had mentioned when announcing his intention to film a (then unspecified) Shakespeare comedy.

Robert Sean Leonard (whose first major film role had been in *Dead Poets Society*) followed Ken from *Swing Kids* to play Claudio, Denzel Washington signed up for his first film after Spike Lee's *Malcolm X* as the nobleman Don Pedro, and Keanu Reeves (who had in fact approached Branagh) played his wicked illegitimate brother, Don John, wisely eschewing the constricted English accent he used in *Bram Stoker's Dracula*. None of the Americans attempted strangled 'proper' Shakespearan voices, in line with Renaissance's aim of repudiating what Emma Thompson called the 'attractive and dangerous myth that the British do Shakespeare best'. Ken explained that he had 'always admired American film acting for its emotional recklessness ... and I think that's how you should do Shakespeare.'

However, Dogberry, the constable in charge of the Watch and a character almost solely dedicated to churning out Shakespeare's now tiresome comic malapropisms, was played by Michael Keaton, now a major screen force in the wake of the

Batman movies. Keaton played Dogberry as a lurching, growling but hopefully humorous psychopath, a kind of Bardic Beetlejuice with a strange guttural 'Oirish' accent, over the top and into the stratosphere (if asked which part of Ireland his character came from, one would have to reply most of it, judging by the accent). His performance is the weakest link in the film. The thirty-minute television programme made to promote the picture similarly revealed Keaton to be less than fully integrated into the company on location, arriving later than the others to shoot his scenes – perfectly reasonable in respect of scheduling, but diluting the degree of bonding with the rest of the cast. Whilst Denzel Washington and Robert Sean Leonard 'goofed off' in costume with Richard Briers and Brian Blessed for the cameras, Keaton (in baseball cap and shades) spoke less than eloquently about his relief in such a set-up from the strain of having to be the Star of the Film.

Once again, Ken scheduled a rehearsal period before shooting began, 'to build up a rapport between the actors and to talk to people who could provide them with some kind of system' for working with Shakespearean language. The American actors, he said, were more preoccupied with 'technical details' – line readings, scansion, the significance of repeated words and so forth – whilst, in a reversal of dramatic stereotype, it was the Brits who were asking, 'Well, what am I thinking here?' His rehearsal system, a mixture of read-throughs, blocking and games, bore useful fruit in both general and particular respects: 'We had this disparate group of people and yet were portraying a community. For instance, why do Don Pedro and Don John, who are brothers, have that sort of strained relationship? So we had a sort of confession about family relationships, and one of the actors had fallen out with his brother over something that objectively was quite trivial but meant a great deal to them, and Denzel Washington took that idea up and got a great deal from it.'

As a whole, *Much Ado* was the epitome of what Malcolm McKay describes as Ken's great ability to 'make it clear', in terms of both language and characterisation. In the King's wooing of Katherine in *Henry V*, and in the Renaissance Shakespeare productions, the actors' clarity of sense and naturalness of delivery had drawn accusations from viewers that they had made up the lines themselves – people didn't expect things to be so comprehensible. The published version of the film script demonstrated the same openness and accessibility. It was not by any means a shooting script; Branagh had obviously rewritten the directions to convey a sense, not of how the film was made, but of the tone of the finished work. The script plainly came from the same wry, mordant pen as *Beginning*, which likewise delved only as deeply into the original matter as the author wanted to, hoping to make up in readability and entertainment value what it lacked in insight.

The picture itself also carried a suspicion of Ken's tendency to want to enlist the complicity of a knowing audience; it worked magnificently as a movie in terms of narrative development, character and sumptuous visual imagination, but the more cynical English viewer might fancy he detected a whisper of, 'Psst – you're educated folk, you know as well as we do that we're taking a few liberties with Shakespeare, but we're not doing anything crass, just tweaking it here and there to make a bloody good film. And it works, too, doesn't it? And you can forgive us the occasional bit of cheek (ssshh, don't mention Dogberry), can't you?'

And one could. A sensitivity and awareness underpinned the whole enterprise, a commitment to the play's world of protocol and honour, and above all of love. *Much Ado* is a pair of intertwined love stories: as Claudio and Hero (Kate Beckinsale, daughter of the late television comedy actor Richard Beckinsale, making her feature film debut) fall in love almost at first sight, are sundered by groundless calumnies and finally reunited in Act 5, so much of the high comedy comes from the 'merry war' between Benedick and Beatrice, two magnificent wits formerly in love and now dedicated to besting each other in verbal duels until they are tricked by the others into acknowledging the depth of their true feelings for each other. These two sparring partners were, of course, played by Ken and Emma. She called the characters 'an archetypally perfect blueprint for a relationship. Total equals. We made, I suppose, as feminist a reading of it as possible, without changing the meaning of it altogether. It's a remarkable part, for me anyway, because she's so angry, she's so fucking angry! They went off to learn how to ride and joust and things and she wasn't allowed to go because she was a girl, and I think the anger and confusion and bewilderment started then, and I think it's still very much with us.'

In the context both of their body of work and their personal lives, it was hard to watch Ken and Emma's performances without succumbing to the temptation to search for insights into their relationship as a whole: two powerful and articulate equals, including one who consistently kicks against the prejudice suffered because of her sex – a couple almost too evenly matched to fit comfortably into a relationship. Moreover, once again Emma's performance showed the greater range and depth of nuance, with subtle allusions to Beatrice's past betrayal by Benedick – the very circumstances in which Ken allegedly proposed to her. He acknowledged that 'Emma and I are not a thousand miles away from the characters of Beatrice and Benedick. We had both experienced long-term relationships before. You sort of dance around a bit' – or clash claws.

The six-week shoot in Tuscany was in some ways more of a romp than the finished picture. Emma, along with Phyllida Law, once again indulged her fondness for cooking for the cast, and was the first on hand with water for gasping actors after long, hot, dusty takes – and occasionally in other situations. The promotional programme is interspersed with Briers and Blessed improvising an involved mock *South Bank Show* discussion in the personae of a couple of ageing English drama queens, which culminated in Blessed deadpanning, 'What I really hate about Kenneth Branagh is that he's young. And talented...' As the speech progressed, their subject's wife decided that this time a comically curt 'Bugger off' wasn't enough, and topped off the scene by spraying them liberally with water. The camaraderie masked the ever-present conventional pressures of film-making: 'For all the glory of making such things, there are people with chequebooks and stopwatches, and people with artistic temperaments,' said Ken, 'so you try and create the conditions for people to enjoy it. I feel rather guilty saying it, but everybody had a good time.'

Chasing the Light, the 'film about the film', also laid bare the planning and execution difficulties which can lie behind a single shot, albeit an audacious one. Ken's habit of thinking in images and then setting out doggedly to realise them (which he said, once again, had been born of growing up watching movies on television) had led him to conceive a grand and elaborate final shot for *Much Ado.* The camera was to pan around from the final wedding in front of the villa's private chapel, mingle with the entire company dancing merrily, reel in and out of them through the villa itself and into the gardens on the other side, before mounting a crane and rising ninety feet into the air for a final vista of the gardens, villa and the Tuscan hills. He explained, 'I felt that the last part [of the film] should wrap up the "fairy tale" and have a flourish; I also suspected there might be an element as people watched it of "Christd, he hasn't cut yet!", and that might be fun ... Those all-in-one things create a kind of theatricality on the set, which is very bonding. We had this mad Scottish composer Pat Doyle teaching 300 Italian people how to sing "Sigh no more, ladies", which in itself was very entertaining!'

That final image was marvellously lyrical and celebratory, but hell to achieve. Orson Welles had pulled off an astounding four-minute tracking crane shot for the opening scene of his 1958 film *Touch of Evil,* but had not tried to move the camera on or off the crane itself. Recent years had seen the development of the Steadicam, an enormous and cumbersome apparatus resembling a mediaeval instrument of torture which is strapped to a cameraman to enable him to follow shots on foot (rather than on the usual 'dolly', a firm podium running on rails) without jiggling the filmed image in the annoying way typical of hand-held camerawork. Consequently, the picture itself would be smooth throughout the shot. Branagh has demonstrated a great (some might say excessive) fondness for the use of Steadicams in his films, so the choice on this occasion was clear.

Choreographing the scene was another matter – a question of sending couples and lines of dancers off in the right direction at the right instant in perfect synchronisation with the travels of the camera (not to mention hoping that the cameraman actually found the crane platform as he backed towards it). Moreover, only a limited time was available before the sun moved directly into the line of the final crane sequence, with the risk of 'whiting out' the filmed images. The three-minute continuous shot required fifteen takes in heat which peaked at 106 degrees Fahrenheit before all concerned were satisfied. Its visual poetry rounds the film off beautifully without betraying the anguish necessary to achieve it – and Branagh had the satisfaction of having gone one better than Orson Welles into the bargain.

One of the most intriguing credits on the film attributes 'Trumpet Effects' to Ken's RADA contemporary Mark Hadfield. Hadfield does not appear in the film – certainly not in a named role; he may be in a crowd scene or two – and the music as a whole was by Pat Doyle as usual. The credit may simply be a private joke; perhaps Hadfield, visiting the location, made the offscreen farting noise in the first Dogberry scene or some such contribution. It's a point for trivia buffs rather than a full-blown mystery.

This time Ken's Shakespeare film was allowed to be shown in competition at Cannes, there being no bicentennial politicking in the air as with *Henry V* in 1989. Its full cinematic release occurred in America before Britain – it was, said Ken, 'too risky to open first' in a country 'which loves to just take the piss.' (An American promotional visit by Emma was placed in jeopardy when her baggage, including her passport and wedding ring, was stolen the night before she flew out. Equipped only with a birth certificate, she was waved through by New York's hard-headed immigration officials with the words, 'Fine, an Oscar-winner. Go through.') The strategy paid off, and once again Branagh outgrossed Schwarzenegger (this time in *Last Action Hero*). British industry recognition for his success and influence came with his appointment in August to the board of the British Film Institute.

13

Bringing a Classic to Life

As always, projects overlapped so that, by the first preview of *Much Ado* in August—again in Belfast, again in aid of NICVA and UYT, but with some money also going to the Fold Housing Trust in one of whose properties Ken's grandmother Elizabeth Branagh lives—pre-production had already begun on *Mary Shelley's Frankenstein,* his £28 million second Hollywood movie, which he was to direct as well as playing the Baron, with Robert De Niro as the monster.

Although *The Godfather Part III,* released in 1990, had not signalled the Hollywood rehabilitation which director Francis Coppola had hoped for, the commercial success of *Bram Stoker's Dracula* had once again given him room to work. *Frankenstein* was conceived as a follow-up to *Dracula,* with a degree of faithfulness to the original story signalled by the inclusion of the author's name in the title, and with similarly extravagant make-up effects. Coppola was to produce a joint venture between his own Zoetrope company and Columbia's sister outfit TriStar, which had bought an option on a script by Steph Lady in 1991. (Later reports would credit the script to Lady and Frank Darabont, from a story by Lady and Jim V. Hart, the screenwriter of *Dracula* and Steven Spielberg's failed Peter Pan movie *Hook.*)

A number of competing Frankenstein projects were in development by major studios at the time: producer Jon Peters was working on a contemporary version for Columbia, Warner Brothers were courting *Batman* director Tim Burton and Arnold Schwarzenegger for a movie of their own, and Anne Rice (whose novel *Interview with the Vampire* was being filmed by Neil Jordan at around the same time as Branagh's picture) was said to be writing a remake of *The Bride of Frankenstein* for Universal. However, TriStar was first off the starting blocks, approaching Coppola in late 1992. Film industry newspaper *Screen International* reported that October that self-imposed Hollywood exile Roman Polanski had been approached to direct Willem Dafoe (star of *Mississippi Burning* and *The Last Temptation of Christ*) to star. A month later Ken had been signed instead of Polanski, with De Niro committing himself to the project in April 1993; Coppola predicted that with these two names, the picture would equal *Dracula*'s worldwide gross take of $200 million. Among the "talent" signing up for the film in the following months, one unusual name stood out: John Cleese. Sean Connery had reportedly declined the role as Victor Frankenstein's mentor Doctor Waldman, leading to the former Python's involvement in what—not counting his own latter-day Ealing project *A Fish Called Wanda*—was only his second "American" movie (he had played an eccentric English sheriff in Lawrence Kasdan's 1985 western *Silverado*.)

Ken spoke after shooting had been completed of mulling the *Frankenstein* project over in his mind even during rehearsals and performances of *Hamlet* at the RSC: "The themes are very similar: birth, life and death, and the meaning of all three. Victor Frankenstein is a man obsessed with death, obsessed with resisting it, and acting on his preoccupation . . . and the creature faces Victor with the spectacle of what he has done. The explicit connection of father and son has given me much more than I shall ever give it."

He insisted that the film be largely shot at Shepperton (with some location work in the Swiss Alps); "Ninety percent of it is on the backlot," he declared. "It's a big, old-fashioned studio picture. When I say that, of course, I don't know what I'm talking about, but I imagine it. What a big, old-fashioned studio picture would be." On the crucial question of what the monster would look like, he would say only, "We're going for a look very far removed from the Boris Karloff, bolts-in-the-neck, square-head thing." He decided not to offer Emma a part in the film; there was no obvious role for her, and "There's never been any agenda to just work together. There's a certain scrupulousness that says, 'This is not appropriate' "—not to mention the consideration, remarked upon only half in jest, that after the Oscar "we'd be lucky to get her." She visited the set only once, as she was working on her *Sense and Sensibility* script at the time before embarking on three films virtually back to back in 1994.

Ken admitted to a certain amount of awe in meeting both Coppola and De Niro: "The Godfather was on one side and Raging Bull on the other and the two of them talking across me. I felt like a man from Surbiton in a sketch, saying 'So glad you're interested in being in my film, Robert' . . . I think [De Niro] is a genius. He's very thorough, he checked me out left, right and centre." At the film's Belfast premiere in November 1994, he offered a more oblique account of gaining the superstar's trust: "De Niro was quite worried about me; I think he suspected that I would turn up in a fluffy white shirt and a pair of black tights with a skull under my arm. [This is obviously one of Branagh's routine self-deprecating "luvvy" jokes.] But Liam Neeson is a great friend of his, so this film benefits from the working of the Northern Ireland Mafia: Liam did the great favour of sitting Robert De Niro's mother up on his knee on her 80th birthday and singing *Danny Boy* to her, which was enough to make Robert think that anybody from this part of the world was OK."

Once aboard the project, Ken was determined to bring out more than simple violence and explore the metaphorical elements of Mary Shelley's story—"It's much more than schlock-horror, it's about a father and son, parenting"—whilst refusing in public to speculate on a career in directing Hollywood films which would be largely dependent on the whims of studio executives: "Their attitude to what's bankable changes on a daily basis. I don't think I've ever got a script that wasn't covered in fingerprints. I just know that if this is a blood disaster, they won't be offering me other $45 million movies. It's very cruel and ruthless." Despite his growing international reputation, he stated baldly that "My future is absolutely tied up with making movies in this country."

Rehearsals had begun in September 1993, in accordance with Ken's belief that character difficulties can most profitably be sorted out before the cameras roll, which they did in late October. The director was more and more conscious of the numerous metaphors to be brought out of the script: shortly after principal photography ended, he opined that "The themes in the book are more relevant today than ever. The advances in genetic science become more extraordinary with each passing week." Earlier, he had offered what was virtually a poster blurb for the film: "A passionate romantic love story of epic proportions in which a man's desire to know the unknowable sweeps him into a living nightmare"—it's fairly safe to assume that his tongue was probably in his cheek on this occasion . . .

Secrecy on the *Frankenstein* set was aggressive, and largely explained in terms of suppressing leaks about Robert De Niro's prosthetic make-up as the monster. Interest was fierce as to how the Baron's creation would look on screen, with unauthorised photographers constantly being found on the set. "It was a ludicrous situation," said David Parfitt; "we had a helicopter overhead, we were chasing two blokes through the woods—we were under siege." Production company Shelley Films was granted an interim injunction against one photo agency, pending a full trial (not yet held at the time of writing) which could have farreaching legal effects if it decides that copyright can protect not only finished films but also design aspects which form an integral part of the completed work. Parfitt, speaking of the legal definition of works in which copyright subsists, thinks "It would be hard to argue that costumes, make-up and sets aren't 'works of artistic craftsmanship'." If the court finds in *Frankenstein*'s favour, Kenneth Branagh could well end up in the legal as well as the artistic history books.

Certainly every effort was made to keep secret the nature of the monster's make-up—efforts which chimed with Robert De Niro's exceedingly shy character offscreen. When Ken conducted a party of youngsters from Belfast around the set, they were left wondering about the identity of the man sitting off at one side with a bag over his head; not even they were allowed to glimpse the prosthetics, whether on De Niro or his stand-in. (Renaissance regular Shaun Prendergast also tells the story of how, searching the studio set-up for his friend Aidan Quinn, he saw the back of someone's head in make-up with what he thought were the familiar long dark locks of Quinn's character Captain Walton; bearing down with a friendly Geordie cry of "How are you, ya old cunt?", Prendergast was rewarded with one of De Niro's finest Max Cady narrow-eyed glares.)

Inevitably, though, the secrecy also fuelled speculation about the director, whom De Niro jokingly called "Fat Boy". It was widely rumoured, to the extent of being held as "common knowledge", that Ken was having an affair with his co-star Helena Bonham Carter. These rumours followed a rash of unfounded allegations on the set of *Much Ado* about Emma and Denzel Washington, then about Emma and Keanu Reeves (who had actually spent the shoot in vain pursuit of Kate Beckinsale), and *Ken* and Washington. According to Bonham Carter, "It got so bad that he joked about going out to dinner with Robert De Niro: "Well, we'd better not go out together or people will say he and I are having an affair next.' The rumours about Ken and me started even before I had met him. They are embarrassing and completely fictional. Everybody immediately thinks that if you are playing lovers, then you must be lovers, that it can't be just acting. But when it comes to doing it on screen it's so bloody technical you just get on with it."

Gossip columnist Nigel Dempster (who had previously run a misleading item suggesting that Ken was considering filming *Twelfth Night,* with Richard Briers returning to his stage triumph as Malvolio) went so far as to write a "non-story story" denouncing all the rumours of affairs as "groundless tittle-tattle"; the satirical magazine *Private Eye* went one further and printed a parodic item in "Nigel Dumpster's Hollywood Diary" about Ken and Emma, "who I can exclusively reveal are married, despite having different surnames," and repudiating supposed allegations about Emma and Al Pacino, and Ken and Australian soap actress-turned-pop singer Kylie Minogue (the mind boggles . . .).

Meanwhile, Emma was discovering that after the Merchant-Ivory feast came the reckoning. According to the venerable tradition of the British media, it was now time to snipe at her. The supporter of so many worthy causes was more than happy to take a part in *In the Name of the Father,* the Universal film based on the autobiography of Gerry Conlon, one of the Guildford Four. The early 1900s had seen the long overdue release of the Four, the Birmingham Six and the Maguire Seven (Annie Maguire, Conlon's aunt, was accused of running a bomb-making factory), similarly framed for their alleged parts in Provisional IRA pub-bombings in England almost 20 years earlier—the victims of police with a witch-hunting mentality and of a judiciary system which seemed at the time to believe that those accused of terrorist offenses were innocent until proven Irish. No amount of apology or compensation could give sufficient recompense for years behind bars, and the law gave only grudging redress: no police officer has ever been convicted of falsifying evidence or using violence to extract confessions in these cases. Nor is it even true to say that all the innocents were released. Conlon's father Guiseppe, convicted in the Maguire case, died in prison.

In the Name of the Father is both a cry of anger at a terrible and blatant injustice, and a moving story of reconciliation between an estranged father and son under the most trying circumstances. Daniel Day-Lewis is frighteningly intense as Gerry Conlon, the young no-hoper and petty criminal who happened to be in the wrong place, at the wrong time, with the wrong accent; he is matched pound for pound by the Oscar-nominated performance of his Bristol Old Vic theatre school contemporary, stage actor Pete Postlethwaite, as Guiseppe. Thompson played Gerry Conlon's lawyer Gareth Peirce, a part unfortunately written as the kind of offbeat but essentially English decent type she can play in her sleep—arriving soaking wet out of a rainshower at a police records office, discovering falsified interview records by chance and smuggling them out, while behaving rather like Joyce Grenfell adrift in an episode of *L.A. Law.*

However, although undeniably a fine movie and a great story, director and co-writer Jim Sheridan (who had first worked with Day-Lewis on *My Left Foot*) took numerous liberties with the facts. Even Annie Maguire objected to some of the narrative nips and tucks which had been made, and which on occasion *increased* the potential incrimination (in particular, Conlon and Paul Hill never even set foot in Maguire's house, the alleged bomb factory, yet the film shows them visiting her at home). The film's climactic scene, in which the Four are freed on appeal, is a travesty of reality. It shows Thompson as Peirce, representing all four of the appellants (as she did not), in a Court of Appeal (where Peirce, as a solicitor, had no right of audience under English law), cross-examining a police officer (as if at a trial of first instance, rather than simply presenting evidence to the judges— in any case, the policeman was a fictional composite character) about Conlon's and Hill's alibi (which had also been embroidered), and at one point requesting to approach the bench (in best American style, but unheard of in a British court) . . . to be greeted with the classic courtroom-drama line, "This is most irregular"! Jim Sheridan stated in an interview that he had originally shot the appeal as it happened, but decided that it needed to be made more cinematic; one waspish critic noted, "So he's saying he refused to let the facts get in the way of a good story—isn't that what the Surrey police did in the first place?" Murmurs on the streets of West Belfast even intimated that one of the two central premises of both book and film was not entirely true, and that Guiseppe Conlon went to his grave still blaming his son Gerry for his unjust imprisonment; there is no evidence at all for such an allegation, but in a climate in which events were seen to be "tightened up" for cinematic purposes, such grapevine talk did no-one any favours.

The English liberal press, conscious of the outrage that had been perpetrated but keen to find an excuse to cavil about the other side of the story, seized on the film's factual infidelities and reacted with ostentatious sniffiness, fulminating that it

233

could create sympathy for real terrorists—especially amongst Irish Americans who might as a result be more inclined to make donations to IRA fund-raising organisation Noraid—and pondering patronisingly on the damage that involvement in such a film might do to the credibility of its stars. Of course, it did none whatever: Day-Lewis, Thompson and Postlethwaite all picked up Oscar nominations for their performances, although none won an award—in the year of *Schindler's List* and *Philadelphia* the Academy of Motion Picture Arts and Sciences was practising its own form of political correctness. More importantly still in the real world, the republican and loyalist ceasefires a few months later vitiated the arguments about giving the oxygen of publicity to the "armed struggle". In a year or two it may be possible to judge *In the Name of the Father* dispassionately according to cinematic and factual, rather than implicitly political, standards.

In March 1994 Ken hosted the BAFTA Production Awards, staged at Belfast's Grand Opera House. One of his other local engagements, opening the Royal Victoria Hospital's Regional Neonatal Intensive Care Unit, gave the press another chance to ask him about starting a family; "Well, you never know, you'll just have to wait and see!" On this occasion even Ken's mother chimed in: "I wonder when they are going to present me with a grandchild. They spend so much time apart because of their work, you see."

The couple were now deemed so newsworthy that even the unsurprising story that they would be attending the 1994 Oscars together was given column inches. More noteworthy was the announcement, which had been expected for some time, that Renaissance activities were to be wound down. There were, it was said, no plans for any more plays, films or radio productions under the banner. In a 1988 television interview Ken had mused that "Companies have finite lives . . . say three, four, five years, however long it continued to do good work," so he clearly had never envisaged Renaissance as being a permanent enterprise. As the set-up diversified into films, less time and effort became available for the original stage activities; more cynically, as Branagh accrued a reputation as a director, he not only had less time but less need for an ongoing company of his own; in an industry where many films' administration is channeled through one-off companies in order to protect subsequent projects from liability, he had simply outgrown the constrictions of Renaissance.

Many were surprised to read at that time that *Henry V* was still £1.5 million short of recouping its original budget (now set at £5 million compared to the £4.5 million figure in common currency at the time of its production; interest accrued on five years of debts accounted for the half-million-pound discrepancy). The shortfall was due to creative accounting, said some; according to one industry source, "Eddie Murphy's film *Coming to America* took $120 million and still hasn't broken even on paper." On a more tightly budgeted production like *Henry V* where even some craft workers agreed to defer their payment until the money had come in, more people are hit if break-even is not achieved. However, Renaissance Films had managed to attract so many small investors at an early stage by means of Stephen Evans' carefully assembled programme under the government-backed Business Expansion Scheme. Explained one newspaper's financial pages, "Unfortunately, the investors are discovering that the neat five-year framework of a BES scheme is rather unsuited to the film industry, in which producers only learn the financial position from the film's distributors a couple of years after the film is launched—and actually get the cash even later. The £1.5 million shortfall in fact applied to Renaissance Films' income over the three films for the last year for which accounts were available, the twelve months to 30 September 1992. The lack of tangible profits was due not to the company's having handled its books imaginatively, but simply to the manner and speed at which the industry moves.

Of the company's demise, David Parfitt commented, "We have talked about various ways of continuing, even about Renaissance becoming a charitable trust, but nothing seemed to come together. So in the end we decided to shelve the theatre company

235

and keep the name in case we want to resurrect it. The film company has to stay in existence for the moment to process income from *Much Ado* and *Peter's Friends,* which we hope will pay off the debts on *Henry V.* But it will not be producing anything else. Renaissance was never permanent. When we started, we only planned for an 18-month season."

Renaissance was mourned more as a concept than a set of major achievements. "[It] established no individual style or ethic, and it did disappointingly little to bring on young actors," said one critic, "but it did do something equally important: it recharged the batteries of older ones, encouraging Judi Dench and Geraldine McEwan to try their hands at directing and establishing Richard Briers as a major classical performer."

The final Renaissance production was to be a radio version of *King Lear* with Sir John Gielgud, broadcast in April 1994 to celebrate the knight's 90th birthday. This time around Emma was cast in the more predictable role of Cordelia, and Ken played Edgar's wicked bastard half-brother Edmond. The all-star cast included not only the usual Renaissance suspects but Eileen Atkins, Bob Hoskins, Keith Michell, Denis Quilley and, in a remarkable tribute, the minor part of the Herald was taken by the former artistic director of the RSC and the National Theatre, Sir Peter Hall. Gielgud himself, in a display of his renowned and endearing tactlessness, said of Ken at the time that "You can't call him great. In a way he's a better organiser and director than actor. It's a danger today that actors become famous too soon. It's so wicked the way the press tries to make Kenneth and Emma into the new Burton and Taylor." (A couple of years earlier, when Emma had rubbished all Olivier/Leigh and Burton/Taylor comparisons in a newspaper interview, the journalist had riposted by suggesting homey veteran actors Michael Denison and Dulcie Gray as the template for the couple—the suggestion was greeted with warm laughter.)

Emma had also made a brief and uncredited appearance in the film *My Father the Hero.* Hollywood was in the grip of the French-remake fever which had begun several years earlier with *Three Men and a Baby* (from *Trois Hommes et un Couffin*), continued with *The Assassin (Nikita)* and has more recently even embraced Arnold Schwarzenegger (whose 1994 *True Lies* recycled *La Totale*). Legend has it that, before the vogue had fully taken off, Gérard Depardieu had been on the receiving end of movie-biz myopia when an unnamed studio executive praised his *Cyrano de Bergerac* as "a really neat remake of Steve Martin's *Roxanne*" (ooops . . .). But Depardieu himself was now crossing over from French-language films to becoming a Hollywood property. *Green Card* had been a success, commercially if not critically, and someone had the bright idea that he should reprise his role in *Mon Père Le Héros* for the global market. The original film had been amusing but hardly great, and *My Father the Hero* fell several notches short even of that modest standard. The plot is flimsy, to say the least: Depardieu's character takes his 14-year-old Franco-American daughter by a former marriage on a Caribbean holiday; in order to appear older and cooler, she pretends that he is in fact her lover, and complications arise with—as the saying goes—hilarious consequences. Or not, in this case.

A subplot concerns the daughter's jealousy of Depardieu's new girlfriend, who for the bulk of the picture is heard only as a voice on a telephone line or an answerphone (and who although living in Paris has an English accent), with an occasional tantalising shot of a woman's hand replacing a receiver. In the final minute of the film, as Papa calls to propose marriage to this mysterious woman, the camera tracks up a reclining female body to reveal that Depardieu's beloved is in fact played by Emma Thompson. The role is a friendly, joky manifestation of the continuing Branagh-Thompson-Depardieu association begun when the *"acteur-vigneron"* (as his passport proclaims) acquired the French rights to *Henry V* to forestall a shoddy dubbing job on its release in that country. The friendship has yet to bear full cinematic fruit, however, and *My Father the Hero* will not be remembered as a major link-up; the final "phoning home to E.T." scene, relying as it does on the humour of audience recognition rather than any inherent amusement in the script, is one of the film's comic highlights. Enough said.

After this mild diversion, Emma's 1994 schedule proved to be even more bruising than that of her manic husband: she took leading roles in three films within six months. February saw her in Scotland for the BBC/WGBH Boston co-production *The Blue Boy,* a ghost story written and directed by Paul Murton; the childhood friendship from Ardentinny, which Emma honoured by starring in Murton's graduation film *Tin Fish,* continued with her lead role opposite Northern Irish actor Adrian Dunbar, seen most recently in *Hear My Song* and *The Crying Game* and looking in *The Blue Boy*'s publicity shot uncomfortably like a surrogate Branagh. Thompson and Dunbar play Marie and Joe Bonar, thirtysomething Glaswegians who after many attempts succeed in conceiving a child; Joe accedes to Marie's requests to take her on a break to the Highlands, where they become supernaturally embroiled in the local legend which gives the film its title. After being previewed at the Edinburgh Film Festival, *The Blue Boy* was screened on BBC over New Year 1995.

From Scotland she went to Hollywood for *Junior,* which on paper looked to be Thompson's most bizarre project yet: an Ivan *(Ghostbusters)* Reitman-directed comedy co-starring Arnold Schwarzenegger and Danny De Vito, reuniting the stars and director of *Twins.* Arnie and Danny played doctors who discover a miracle fertility drug; when refused an F.D.A. licence, the pair take desperate measures to prove the drug's efficacy—in other words, Arnie gets pregnant. Emma was to play Arnie's love interest, the scatty, clumsy English scientist in whose lab the increasingly bulbous Teuton continues to work.

The box-office disaster of *Last Action Hero,* a film which overestimated the readiness of Schwarzenegger's audience to accept clever self-parody from him (and was outgrossed at one point by *Much Ado About Nothing*), left the Austrian-born hulk in dire need of a comeback. The answer was intended to be twofold: the special-effects bonanza *True Lies,* re-uniting him with *Terminator* director James Cameron for what is apparently the most expensive movie ever made (with costs in the region of $120 million), and *Junior* (also known during shooting as *Oh Baby*). If proof were needed that Emma Thompson was now a hot property, the fact of her being drafted apparently to revive the flagging career of Arnold Schwarzenegger provided conclusive evidence.

Scarcely drawing breath after these obstetric frolics, she returned home before flying to Venice for the shoot of *Carrington,* the story of early 20th-century Bloomsburyites, painter Dora Carrington and biographer Lytton Strachey; Strachey was played by Jonathan Pryce, the man who once throttled Ken's friend John Sessions for not shutting up during an improvised comedy sketch on *Whose Line Is It Anyway?* The film (not yet screened at the time of writing) marks the directorial début of writer Christopher Hampton, who was responsible for both the hit play *Les Liaisons Dangereuses* and the screenplay for Stephen Frears' film version *Dangerous Liaisons.* Playwright and director John McGrath, who is producing *Carrington,* confirmed that despite her punishing work schedule Emma was keen to honour her long-standing commitment to the project, and received nothing but support and encouragement from Ken in her efforts to fit the picture in.

Ken spent the autumn gearing up for the release of *Mary Shelley's Frankenstein.* The movie was set to première in the United States on Wednesday November 2nd, followed by a screening as the opening film of the 1994 London Film Festival on November 3rd and a general release the following day—a state of affairs not calculated to endear Branagh to the LFF's administration, given the drain which a major cinematic release might exert on the Festival's own box-office takings during the crucial first week. His native town, too, had its usual charity screening in the presence of the director, although this time studio politicking had dictated that rather than a preview, Belfast should receive a simultaneous première on Friday 4th.

The initially mixed previews of the picture in the United States had not dissuaded Columbia/TriStar from believing that they had a hit on their hands. TriStar's chairman when the deal was signed (Mike Medavoy) was unseated in January 1994, and the nature of Hollywood studios is such that new régimes often give less than wholehearted support to their predecessors' projects in favour of their own "babies"; however, Branagh's champion at the studio, Marc Platt, was still in place, and TriStar were said to be predicting a box-office take of as much as $100 million from *Frankenstein*—half what Francis Coppola anticipated, but still very healthy indeed.

It was intriguing to note that even in the "teaser" cinema trailers for *Frankenstein* aimed at the American market, Helena Bonham Carter's name had migrated from its place on the initial billing to a position in the coveted space "above the title" along with De Niro and Branagh, while such Hollywood assets as Aidan Quinn and John Cleese remained below. It was arguable whether, solely on the strength of *A Room With a View* and *Howard's End,* Bonham Carter possessed the mainstream transatlantic box-office clout to warrant such a position; it appeared that she had a champion on the production who was keen to raise her profile. Once again, however, the explanation turned out to be more prosaic; the initial below-the-title billing was a mistake, and Bonham Carter's agent quickly arranged for the restoration of her name to the originally agreed position. The lesson for media speculators is simple: never make presumptions about on-set developments when the all-pervasive machinations of contractual politicking can more readily explain any irregularity.

Professional movie-watchers had been put on their guard by *Frankenstein*'s trailer, full of vertiginous camera shots none of which seemed to last more than half a second, and by leaked information about preview response. One audience opinion card from a sneak US screening read, "I got dizzy watching this film"; Branagh recounted the fact with what turned out to be misplaced pride. When the picture was finally unveiled in London press screenings in late October, the critical apprehension proved all too well founded.

It seemed as if the scale of the production had turned Branagh's head. As he had unwisely determined to show his ability to pastiche Hitchcock in his first Hollywood production *Dead Again,* so *Mary Shelley's Frankenstein* set out to bring modern cinematic sensibilities to the Gothic genre, incorporating the elements both of torrid romance and of eldritch horror. It was a noble intention, but the arsenal of film techniques which he used to try to achieve it were akin to using a steamhammer to crack a nut. The entire film, for instance, was drowned in Patrick Doyle's most pervasive and obtrusive score to date, which rather than underlining dramatic and narrative points rammed them down viewers' throats.

Ken's taste for filming with a Steadicam, and for throwing in the occasional crane shot, was another major annoyance factor. Some of the sets, such as the lecture theatre at Ingolstadt University, seemed to have been designed with no other consideration than to provide extreme camera angles; walking and running were almost ridiculously preponderant. Furthermore, vast swatches of the film were edited almost as jerkily as the trailer had been, which added to the disorientation. Such camerawork may well look agreeably flash when *Frankenstein* is subsequently released on video: on the big screen it is simply dizzying in a not at all uncomplimentary sense.

The sense of a studio-centered picture was fully realised, but where Coppola's own *Dracula* had made a virtue of such a budget-related necessity, *Frankenstein* managed to spend more and achieve less. Some interiors of the Frankenstein house were recognisable even in medium shots as painted flats, and in what seemed to be a disastrous oversight, at one point when Victor's beloved Elizabeth stomped off up the house's sweeping staircase in high dudgeon, suitably solid staircase sound had not been dubbed on, so that Bonham Carter was audibly tramping up a set of plywood steps.

Such a ubiquitous feeling of artifice detracted from the real drama rather than complementing it. Instead of being filled with apprehension that Victor's young brother William will inevitably become one of the monster's victims in a couple of reels' time, the audience might wonder distractedly why his doting father never thought to install any kind of banister on the staircase; when they should have been subliminally appreciating the huskier, more De Nironian quality acquired by John Cleese's

241

speech at pregnant moments (as a hint that Cleese's character, Waldman, will later provide the brain for De Niro's monster), they just furrowed their brows as to why Cleese's speech was so obviously pitch-shifted down half an octave.

The original novel skirts hazily around the actual process of assembly and revivification of the monster, a fact which has given generations of film-makers enormous scope for constructing Gothic Heath-Robinson laboratories in which the scene can take place. However, Branagh's ideas about the theme of birth and parenting led to a "resuscitation" scene which teetered on the fine line between impressiveness and absurdity, as creator and creature slithered crazily in what was meant to be a couple of hundred gallons of amniotic fluid. Harder still to take seriously was the alternative to the time-honoured "bolt of lightning on a dark and stormy night" as a source of electrical current to jolt the monster's heart back into motion. De Niro's creature was jolted into "life" by a charge derived from a large sac filled with electric eels!

Branagh's custom of using actors he had previously worked with was taxed almost to the limit on *Frankenstein*. Accommodating old friends like Gerard Horan and Mark Hadfield was easy enough (they played, respectively, a family retainer and one of the family near whose cabin the monster hides); regular second-string players such as Shaun Prendergast and Alex Lowe, too, could be found roles as mariners on the polar expedition to whose captain the dying Victor tells his grim tale in flashback. Victor's father was played by Ian Holm, and the blind old man in the woods by Richard Briers (whose unknowing line to the melancholy monster, "It can't be as bad as all that," generally elicited hoots of derision eclipsed only by De Niro's monsyllabic response—after much tortuous thought—"Worse"). But why, for instance, are Victor and his new friend Henry (Tom Hulce) elbowed rudely aside on their first meeting by a young boor who utters a single line and is never seen again? The oafish Schiller appears nowhere in Shelley's story, but a place, however fleeting, had to be found for Richard Bonneville, who had been Laertes to Branagh's Hamlet in the 1992–3 RSC production. The aura of "jobs for the boys" grew more palpable.

Amid all the mistakes and indulgences, it is easy to overlook the film's strengths. The monster's prosthetic make-up lived up to the expectations which had been generated by the secrecy surrounding the design. De Niro's face, resembling a railway map in the network of sutures which traversed it, left him little scope for registering his emotions. Yet by using the limited facial movement afforded him, and most of all through a virtuoso range of eye acting, he succeeded in imbuing the "daemon" with a range of feelings and passions which, distorted as they were by the nature of his existence, were recognisably human.

Paradoxically, too, one of the most affecting scenes in Helena Bonham Carter's screen career to date was played under similar prosthetics. Probably the most palpable liberty taken with Shelley's story was the decision to have Victor Frankenstein resurrect his newly-wed bride Elizabeth after her murder by his first creation. It was a blatant nod to the wholly inauthentic "Bride of Frankenstein" notion, but the resulting scene transcended its tacky origins. As Victor and the monster vie for Elizabeth's affections, the realisation slowly seeps across her scarred face that her own existence is now artificial and, rather than accept such a mockery of life, she immolates herself. The rich filmic resonances of this final sequence (invoking as it does a clutch of earlier screen moments including Miss Havisham in David Lean's film of *Great Expectations,* Schwarzenegger in *Terminator 2* and Ripley in *Alien*[3] could not overshadow the profound pathos of what had gone before it.

British reviewers were for the most part equivocal about the film, whose release was attended by a blaze of media hype. From virtual invisibility a few short weeks earlier, Branagh was suddenly ubiquitous: denying to Barry Norman that Coppola had "interfered" in any way—"What do you say? 'Buzz off, Francis . . . what was that film you made, anyway, *The Fairy Godmother* or something?' "; being hailed on *The South Bank Show* as the creator of the latest in a series of classic Frankenstein films; in the ultimate mutual media back-scratch, he even interviewed De Niro for BBC TV. But the publicity wasn't enough to give the movie "legs"; its business tailed off, so that by mid-January 1995 it had barely scraped £6 million in UK gross takings. In the much larger American market it fared even more disappointingly; far from advance predictions of $100–200 million, its first ten weeks pulled in a paltry $22 million, a figure which represents only around half of the film's production budget, let alone publicity and distribution costs.

After a brief period of being highly visible (if not inescapable) to publicise the film's release, Ken was suddenly out of sight again once the lie of the commercial land became apparent. The suggestions were that he was taking the film's relative failure badly: a New York paper reported that he had been so panicked by the film's reception that he had taken a cab to his London agent Patricia Marmont's office, fired her, gone on to the London hotel of his American agent and done the same, only to apologise the following morning and re-hire both.

Filmgoers had made up their minds about *Mary Shelley's Frankenstein* despite what had largely been critical politeness and even generosity; the poster slogan "Be Warned" took on an ironic significance. But neither audiences nor reviewers could really come to any strong conclusions about *Junior* on its release (later in November in the US, the following month in Britain).

In terms of plot, the film turned out to be very much what had been expected: trading largely on the comedy that arose from the notion of America's favourite macho man joining the pudding club. However, the diametrical personality changes undergone by Schwarzenegger's character as a supposed result of the increased level of female hormones in his body proved too much to swallow; the script relied too heavily on old-hat stereotypes of women as creatures of whim, flighty things who care more about whether they have anything to wear for that special occasion or how they are perceived by others than about matters of real importance. The alleged womanly traits of Arnie's character constituted the kind of antiquated claptrap at which Emma Thompson could normally be relied upon to unleash a broadside.

Emma's own character was scarcely better written. From her first entrance—careening on an out-of-control furniture cart into Schwarzenegger—it was clear that this was Joyce Grenfell territory again: comedy bereft of the spikiness which Emma can bring to a performance, comedy which wants an easy time of it. In the second half of the film, as Schwarzenegger approaches full term and the stakes rise, she is allowed a serious side to her personality. In both modes, Thompson did everything asked of her, but little more. *Junior,* after all, was a screwball comedy— what Hollywood-watchers have been known to call a "nobrainer".

This description, though, denies the most central problem that faced the film, a problem which only one British reviewer managed to pinpoint. Put simply: how do you succeed in making a comedy on such a subject in the middle of an abortion war? With both "pro-life" and "pro-choice" lobbies in America keeping a high, vocal and sometimes homicidal profile, the team behind *Junior* realised that they would have to tread with extreme caution. In the end, both camps were appeased: the pro-lifers by mother-to-be Arnie's determination to ignore the terms of the experiment and go to term, the right-to-choose side by his bellowed "My body! My choice!" as he scrambles to void abduction by the authorities. But comedy relies on upset, whether it's an upset of expectations or an upset of sensibilities, and a film which is so compelled not to upset anybody can only hope to be a mediocre comedy.

And so it proved. Despite the names of Schwarzenegger (now once again riding high after the commercial comeback of *True Lies*) and De Vito, *Junior* could only make number four in the American box-office charts in its opening week, and its theatrical life was as short as that of *Frankenstein.* Ken's film at least had positive ambitions to create a contemporary distillation of the spirit of a great Gothic tale, and featured in Robert De Niro a player who, whilst undeniably a great star, has never been a solid box-office draw; *Junior* had at least one such name (arguably two, if one counts De Vito), but its ambitions seemed primarily to be negative—not to tread on anyone's ideological toes. *Frankenstein*'s flaws can be pinpointed and discussed, as above; the consistent mediocrity of *Junior* is in many ways more depressing.

In Britain at least, the New Year television screening of *The Blue Boy* was a timely reminder that—when given the chance—Emma Thompson was a powerful, unshowy actor. Paul Murton's 63-minute film had none of the overblown suspense or *Grand Guignol* shivers normally associated with ghost stories on the screen; it took place in a world where ghostly influences were experienced in a disquieting but above all matter-of-fact way. As Marie Bonnar, realising whilst on a short holiday that her husband has been having an affair, Emma utterly eschewed melodrama. Nervously pushing her hair out of her face and briefly hitting herself for being so possessive as to go through Joe's pockets for evidence, it was a wonderfully naturalistic performance which caught in wordless camera shots a quite different pensive quality from the Merchant Ivory "English rose" films. It was also a double chance to acknowledge the Thompson/Law family's Glaswegian roots; Marie's mother was played by Emma's own mother. (Phyllida Law had also made a blink-and-you'll-miss-it appearance in *Junior,* as the midwife of a natural childbirth haven.)

Despite the setbacks of *Mary Shelley's Frankenstein* and, to a lesser extent, *Junior,* Branagh and Thompson remain hot properties. In little more than a decade they have built up remarkable bodies of work in a number of differing areas, and acquired fame, fortune (despite their modest protestations to the contrary) and an enormous standing in their fields. Ken's apprehension about his prospects for future big-budget projects should *Frankenstein* flop has yet to be proven or disproven. At the moment the mere mention of either's name gives a project prestige and increased viability, and of course causes the press and media to salivate at the whiff of another story. They have now even received the perhaps unquestionable accolade of a joint biography before they even hit middle age. The inevitable question is: what now?

14

They Might be Giants

One of the most familiar sounds in the film world is the fervent protestation of an actor that they want their private life to remain separate from their professional career, and be left to live privately. All too often, of course, it's yet another device in the arsenal of public image: trotting out such lines makes it easier for journalists to speak of so-and-so as being a plain and simple man or woman, or as wrapping around them a Garboesque air of mystery.

In Ken and Emma's case, though, the absence of grandeur seems genuine. They could by now afford to live in their own high-security compound, but they hang on to their West Hampstead semi. Although both are consummate players of the publicity game when it is necessary, they no longer court attention for its own sake; likewise, when unwelcome notice is paid to them, their irritation isn't so much the tantrum of stars who have begun to believe their PR handouts, but simple vexation at not being allowed to get on inconspicuously with what they want to do in terms of actual living. Not that their working habits often leave much chance for the latter. Branagh in particular has mused that he's been too workaholic to do much proper living; friends testify that this is truer than he'd like it to be, and it accounts in part for his uncertain self-image.

Insecurity is also demonstrated (not always intentionally) by Emma. She, too, can double-bluff: "Ken's too hard-working for sex . . . well, most of the time" cannot conceal the feeling at the heart of the flip remark. As early as 1988 she had remarked, "One is aware of time progressing and I do feel an inkling to have a child. My mother thinks I'm coming up for it now." Such half-asides were sprinkled through her interviews until in 1993 she mentioned that she and Ken were actively talking of starting a family that year: "I can hear my biological clock ticking away. I don't want to leave it too long. Of course, I don't take it for granted that I am able to conceive—or that Ken can be a father, for that matter."

Within a month, however, she was singing a more fatalistic tune: "I think conception at the moment would be tricky; Ken is so tired at the moment, doing so many jobs." Or, put more bluntly, "I should think all of his sperms are on crutches." Ken's own attitudes to children had been tempered by a gruelling weekend babysitting, and frequently changing, a friend's child— "the night of the long nappies," as Emma called it. By 1994, in a magazine article she wrote herself, she seemed to have gone off the idea entirely: "Yes thank you, we're very happy, but I don't want to have children right now. I'm not broody at all: lots of my friends have had children recently, and they don't get any sleep, which I think would be ghastly. We'll see. The point is that I'm not feeling any pressure." Either the ticking of the biological clock has grown less insistent, or developments in the couple's lives (whether personal or professional) have super-vened to change her mind. It should not be forgotten either that when she wrote the article in question she had just finished the back-to-back shoots of two "obstetric" projects, *The Blue Boy* and *Junior,* and that she might well have had quite enough of ab-dominal bumps for the time being.

Emma has, though, continued to advocate amorous adventures before marriage. She told *U.S.* magazine, "[Marriage is] an ex-tremely dangerous step. I mean, how stupid can you get? You put all your eggs in one basket and say you're going to stay with this person for the rest of your life. Talk about taking a risk! It's the most frightening thing I've ever done, but that's because I took it seriously. If you feel in your heart that you're a monogamist and not a polygamist—which I think a lot of people are—you are prepared to take that risk." Elsewhere, she had expanded: "Making room for another person's soul in your life is a Herculean labour. The feelings that follow the honeymoon euphoria are very complex. I would never be able to handle sexual infidelity, for instance"—as evidenced by her alleged response to Ken's alleged affair early in their relationship.

Marriage to a woman of such thoughtfully and passionately held convictions has unquestionably wrought an effect upon Branagh. Before Emma, his only ideologically-slanted statements had been to speak of his hatred for the institutionalised repression of all forms of organised religion (the legacy of his Belfast upbringing) and to repudiate any notion that Renaissance might be cited as an example of the virtues of Thatcherite "individual enterprise" in the arts (making it quite clear that he had "got on his bike" only because the government had siphoned off all the petrol, so to speak). After their meeting came the charity benefits for Friends of the Earth, Northern Irish charities and the like, along with a greater inclination to ponder on Issues with a capital I. Emma has noted with a smirk that we are now a little more likely to hear Ken saying things which mightn't have occurred to him before he met her; he does indeed seem to have become more conscious of the wider responsibilities that come with prominent status, although not to the extent to which Thompson herself feels them.

After their respective and wildly differing rises to prominence and their period of ostentatious togetherness, a new phase has settled in, which may indicate either a relationship being sustained across independent high-profile careers in the same business, or that cracks are beginning to show. Rumours of imminent separation were flying early in 1994 and again just after New Year 1995, but no substantive evidence has yet come to light.

Kenneth Branagh—attaining a seat on the board of governors of the British Film Institute when he was 31—is on his way to becoming a front-rank Power in the movie world, one of the prime movers whose projects are green-lighted because they *are* their projects; despite having claimed, "I'm not sufficiently hard-nosed to be some titanic showbiz mogul", he has amply demonstrated both the charm and the influence to be just that.

Like Richard Attenborough, he also has the reputation to attract international talent and finance for projects which either could not be supported by the British film industry or, if they did get completed, would emerge on a much lesser scale than necessary to be successful either on their own terms or at the box-office. *Much Ado About Nothing* heralded a shift in perception of Ken, which *Mary's Shelley's Frankenstein*—for all its critical and commercial disappointment—has now completed: he is no longer looked upon as a British director, but as an international one. Few British figures can pull off such transitions: the Scott brothers, directors Ridley and Tony, have been based in the United States until their 1994 purchase of Shepperton studios, and even David Puttnam's coin has looked rather tarnished since the débacles of the Bill Forsyth film *Being Human* (which Putnam left midway through its production) and his troubled period at the helm of Columbia.

Furthermore, Branagh has created what so far seems to be a critic-proof aura; even *Dead Again,* savaged by British reviewers, did healthy business—and, as an industry figure noted, "Everyone said it was a piece of pulp, but they didn't say it was a piece of shit." At the risk of repetition, *Frankenstein* went into a rapid tailspin despite, not because of, its notices. The experience of that picture's reception will no doubt teach him to show some restraint for a while in terms of the genres he tackles, though without letting himself get painted back into the Shakespeare-and-battles corner. He may go through a period of having to settle for smaller budgets. Yet it's not immutably true that in Hollywood you're only as good as your last film: James Cameron, Ridley Scott and even Martin Scorsese have all made weak films at some point in the last decade, but each was nevertheless supported on subsequent projects which re-established their stock. Moreover, Tinseltown is still in one of its periodic hot flushes of Anglophilia in the wake of *Four Weddings and a Funeral.* Though some doors may be harder for Branagh to push open in the short term, few will remain locked to him.

At the time of *Much Ado*'s release, Ken was thinking aloud about filming a comedy set in Belfast. "We couldn't ignore the Troubles, but people do get on with their lives in the province and that could be the theme." Undoubtedly the ceasefires would make it easier to consider genuine location work for such a picture—a different and much more welcome kind of shooting in the streets of Belfast; in what was obviously more than just blarney, Branagh himself volunteered at the Belfast première of *Frankenstein* that "I feel a bloody sight more comfortable here than in Los Angeles, I can tell you." Longtime Renaissance associate Gerard Horan, who had himself been filming in Belfast at that time, commented on the vast difference in atmosphere after only a few weeks of the ceasefire: "Yesterday we were up around [strongly Republican areas] Clonard and the Falls Road, and there were some kids actually playing with a policeman, hanging off his shoulders, which you wouldn't have seen before; and the squaddies had got their glengarries on instead of helmets and were actually smiling and waving at people as they went past in cars. The geography of central Belfast could be Leeds or Manchester, with that big confident Victorian architecture and everything; the first time you came here during the Troubles it was extremely disconcerting to see people pointing guns at you in uniform out the back of tanks, and now it's the other way round. I hope and pray that it continues." It's a racing certainty that Ken will have been making inquiries as to how he can both utilise and contribute to this change.

The Return of the Native also cropped up once again as a project he remained keen to realise, and he and Emma were being mistakenly mentioned in connection with the £4 million BBC television adaptation of *Pride and Prejudice* in production at the time of writing, no doubt as a result of crossed wires regarding the *Sense and Sensibility* project. In addition, his name has been linked with a long-standing project on Hollywood's back burner, *Shakespeare in Love* (on which Universal were ready to begin shooting in 1992 with Daniel Day-Lewis and Julia Roberts, but left their formal offer too late to secure Day-Lewis and as a result of his non-participation also lost Roberts); the film was set for

251

an early 1995 start under the direction of Ed Zwick (one of the creators of *thirtysomething* and director of the movie *Glory*), but once again this was simply a case of the rumour-mill's eagerness to link Branagh with any Shakespearean project in the vicinity, as a name with international "Bard credibility".

Emma spent a brief period after New Year 1995 on a health farm—unsurprisingly, given the frentic year she had just experienced. Hers had also become a name to conjure with in Hollywood; she was tipped (along with Geena Davis and Robin Wright) to replace Jodie Foster in the Ridley Scott-directed *Crisis in the Hot Zone* (based on the true story of a virus outbreak in an American research facility) after Foster's withdrawal, because "the script wasn't ready" or on being told that the part would be rewritten as a supporting role to Robert Redford, according to differing reports. However, such decisions were forestalled by the Twentieth Century-Fox project's collapse in the face of Redford's insistence on a script acceptable to him, and the conspicuous presence on rival production and release schedules of Warner Brothers' virus picture *Outbreak,* starring Dustin Hoffman and directed by Wolfgang Petersen. (Another possible Thompson/Redford vehicle bruited about in late 1994 was Rob Reiner's *The American President*).

Merchant Ivory were reported to have brought the rights to her *Sense and Sensibility* screenplay in January 1994 (she had said before embarking on the task that she planned to consult with that team's regular scriptwriter Ruth Prawer Jhabvala), and in June Columbia Pictues green-lighted the project, with Ken to direct and Emma to star; that autumn, however, the news broke that Ken had left the picture. *Sense and Sensibility* is currently set to be the first film on which Emma is the only one of the couple with a non-performing creative input.

Emma is plainly also on her way to the front rank, in her case of film stardom. (Ken noted incredulously that when the bookmakers' odds on the new James Bond were announced, "I was 15-1 and *my wife* was 30-1!") Although she has said that she prefers the satisfaction of creation on paper to that of representation on the screen—"Writing is something I can carry on with till I die. It gives me far more pleasure than being a famous movie star"—projects such as *Junior* and even *My Father the Hero* are evidence that she is already hot property, and feels quite able to alternate "fun" projects with her more serious roles. One can even see her directing occasionally in the future, if a project sufficiently close to her heart should present itself.

She has been succinctly described as "our generation's Katharine Hepburn" by her old Footlights mentor Martin Bergman: "the poise, the professionalism, the ability to perform comedy or drama with equal skill, the ability to create female characters we know and recognize, and whose personalities begin with their minds rather than their cleavage." It's too early to have any real notion, but in terms of career longevity she shows every sign of being able to equal Hepburn, and in terms of bankability to outstrip her. She certainly plans to be around that long: on my initial approach to her concerning this book, she replied, "Should you fancy writing [in] about 25 years, then let's boogie . . . there's a lot left to do and I've only just begun!" The type of performance which is her particular strength may go out of fashion, but will never go out of style.

Kenneth Branagh, meanwhile, is likely to move increasingly towards direction rather than acting, as being the activity in which he can most fully control the finished form of a work. In film terms, at least, he seems to be becoming a more accomplished director than actor, certainly in terms of his own projects (when Branagh is directed by other people his performance shows a different calibre of discipline from his self-directed appearances; even with Hugh Cruttwell on hand, he sometimes lets himself get away with too much). When asked in mid-1994 of the prospects for a return to the stage, he said, "I'm not sure when, but I want to and will do, I hope. Rather than run a company I'd like to see what happens, just be an actor on the stage." He admitted that directing and acting in the same film was sometimes too much: "Maybe I won't have to do it in future, because I've got a bit more confidence about directing. But I enjoy acting, and it's a bloody sight more fun than directing, which is completely and pottily mad."

However, even Emma, in a telling aside in the recent magazine article which she wrote herself, described her husband as "director Kenneth Branagh" without mentioning his acting; the magazine confirmed that this was the description in Thompson's own copy rather than the interpolation of a sub-editor. If the person closest to Ken writes of him in these terms, it gives strong corroboration to predictions that the acting side of Branagh's screen career seems set to diminish in importance. As for theatrical ventures, in 1993 film industry newspaper *Screen International,* predicting that Ken will shortly be one of the one hundred most powerful "players" in the business, described him as a "former stage actor" only a few months after *Hamlet* had ended its Stratford season. To outside observers at least, Branagh's future path seems relatively clear.

Speculation is continually rife about their future. They will undoubtedly receive their "gongs"—Sir Ken and Dame Emma— just as soon as the government thinks they are old enough to bear the titles with dignity. As for the undercurrent of the question—what of their future together?—on such a point, biographical scrupulousness will always take a back seat to idle musings. Both in professional and personal terms, they seem to stimulate and support each other with enviable consistency and solidity. If their paths continue to diverge, their differing foci—not to mention work schedules—may make such mutual support more difficult to sustain. The number of successful long-term director/ actor marriages can be counted on the fingers of one mutilated hand.

Nevertheless, Emma, in her 1994 magazine article praising feminist pioneers, took the opportunity to digress briefly in order to try and scotch allegations elsewhere of personal and professional tensions within the marriage: "It's important to both Ken and myself that our marriage be a partnership. That means that I don't feel in the least bit competitive with him in our work; that I feel as much satisfaction and pride in what I've achieved in my life as he does in his. I don't think of myself as less than him, or consider myself to be in his shadow. What we are is friends—and that's how we intend to keep it." Shortly after she won her Oscar, Ken likewise said that one shares in one's partner's achievements rather than being envious of them.

It is not the place of a book like this to speculate on such matters, nor is such speculation rightly any of our business. What can be said with certainty is that, in terms of the careers of Kenneth Branagh and Emma Thompson, the last word will not be written for many years to come.